Evolutionary Economics and Social Complexity Science

Volume 3

The Japanese Association for Evolutionary Economics (JAFEE) always has adhered to its original aim of taking an explicit "integrated" approach. This path has been followed steadfastly since the Association's establishment in 1997 and, as well, since the inauguration of our international journal in 2004. We have deployed an agenda encompassing a contemporary array of subjects including but not limited to: foundations of institutional and evolutionary economics, criticism of mainstream views in the social sciences, knowledge and learning in socio-economic life, development and innovation of technologies, transformation of industrial organizations and economic systems, experimental studies in economics, agent-based modeling of socio-economic systems, evolution of the governance structure of firms and other organizations, comparison of dynamically changing institutions of the world, and policy proposals in the transformational process of economic life. In short, our starting point is an "integrative science" of evolutionary and institutional views. Furthermore,we always endeavor to stay abreast of newly established methods such as agent-based modeling, socio/econo-physics, and network analysis as part of our integrative links.

More fundamentally, "evolution" in social science is interpreted as an essential key word, i.e., an integrative and/or communicative link to understand and re-domain various preceding dichotomies in the sciences: ontological or epistemological, subjective or objective, homogeneous or heterogeneous, natural or artificial, selfish or altruistic, individualistic or collective, rational or irrational, axiomatic or psychological-based, causal nexus or cyclic networked, optimal or adaptive, microor macroscopic, deterministic or stochastic, historical or theoretical, mathematical or computational, experimental or empirical, agent-based or socio/econo-physical, institutional or evolutionary, regional or global, and so on. The conventional meanings adhering to various traditional dichotomies may be more or less obsolete, to be replaced with more current ones vis-à-vis contemporary academic trends. Thus we are strongly encouraged to integrate some of the conventional dichotomies.

These attempts are not limited to the field of economic sciences, including management sciences, but also include social science in general. In that way, understanding the social profiles of complex science may then be within our reach. In the meantime, contemporary society appears to be evolving into a newly emerging phase, chiefly characterized by an information and communication technology (ICT) mode of production and a service network system replacing the earlier established factory system with a new one that is suited to actual observations. In the face of these changes we are urgently compelled to explore a set of new properties for a new socio/economic system by implementing new ideas. We thus are keen to look for "integrated principles" common to the above-mentioned dichotomies throughout our serial compilation of publications. We are also encouraged to create a new, broader spectrum for establishing a specific method positively integrated in our own original way.

More information about this series at http://www.springer.com/series/11930

Natsuka Tokumaru

Social Preference, Institution, and Distribution

An Experimental and Philosophical Approach

Springer

Natsuka Tokumaru
Graduate School of Economics
Kyoto University
Kyoto, Japan

ISSN 2198-4204 ISSN 2198-4212 (electronic)
Evolutionary Economics and Social Complexity Science
ISBN 978-981-10-0136-9 ISBN 978-981-10-0137-6 (eBook)
DOI 10.1007/978-981-10-0137-6

Library of Congress Control Number: 2015959925

Springer Singapore Heidelberg New York Dordrecht London

Printed on acid-free paper

Springer Science+Business Media Singapore Pte Ltd. is part of Springer Science+Business Media (www.springer.com)

Preface

The main purpose of this book is to provide behavioral theories of economic agents involved in distribution processes under various institutional conditions by using economic experiments. The emergence of experimental methods in economics over the last two decades seems to have radically changed basic behavioral assumptions of standard economics, namely, rationality and selfishness. However, experimental methods have not been satisfactorily applied to theories of institutional or evolutionary economics, despite the presupposition of such theories that individuals have not only utilitarian incentives but also social preferences that depend on social institutions and vary with changes in those institutions. The application of experimental methods to reexamine and enrich behavioral theories related to institutional theories is required to develop such theories. Additionally, income distribution has been regarded as a major problem in economics and one about which economists have failed to reach a consensus. Consensus is lacking because the problem of income distribution involves various factors, such as distribution justice, economic policy, market mechanisms, and social institutions. Thus, related empirical studies are lacking. Conversely, distribution experiments have been typical in experimental economics since its beginnings, yet few studies have interpreted experimental results from an institutional perspective.

In this book I have performed four distribution experiments that presuppose different institutional conditions and economic agents (workers, investors, companies, citizens) and examined the results from an institutional perspective. The experiments performed in this book are basically modified versions of the dictator game and public goods game that are popular in experimental economics, but are designed to derive institutional implications for the actual political economy. Through these experiments I have examined the institutional conditions under which individuals' social preferences, such as opportunism, egalitarianism, performance-based remuneration, or labor-value radicalism, are enhanced or refrained, together with the associated social or economic consequences. Further, I have provided implications for the actual economy and have reexamined the validities of historical theories of distribution.

This book also provides philosophical discussions on how experimental methods should be applied and extended for application to economic theories intended to explain institutional evolutions. Most of the results of experiments presented in this book, as well as past experimental studies, show that *social preference matters* when people act, which contradicts the neoclassical assumptions of *homo economicus.* Assuming these results are correct, how can they help in the development of social knowledge and contribute to public policy for designing appropriate institutions? If people are motivated by both utilitarian concerns and social preferences, what kinds of social institutions are preferable for enhancing their motivations, productivity, freedom, and social welfare? How can inspiring results proposed by experimental economics, such as inequality aversion, the endowment effect, or risk aversion, be applied to explain actual social economy or propose economic policy? To direct these questions, I have introduced historical discussions on human behaviors in the social sciences, examining the meanings of experimental methods in the history of economic thought. The final goal of this book is to demonstrate a way to apply experimental methods to institutional evolution.

I believe that economics should return to its origins, as a *moral science*, in the sense that it should examine how to achieve a balance among several social values. When I was an undergraduate student of economics, I was impressed by the sophisticated theoretical system of microeconomics that strictly predicts the optimum allocation of goods to a person with certain preferences and budget constraints. Simultaneously, a question arose in my mind—why does economics not consider the optimal allocation of resources to achieve different social values among individuals with different abilities and motivations? Economists seem to regard most social values as involving trade-offs, such as productivity versus equality or personal freedom versus social welfare, where social policy can prioritize either side of these trade-offs. However, we could ask whether this is really the case and whether we should seek a way to satisfy both values to realize the sustainable development of human society. I hope this book can contribute to answering these questions.

Kyoto, Japan Natsuka Tokumaru

Acknowledgments

There is a large number of people I have to acknowledge for their help in writing this book. I first wish to thank Professor Hiroyuki Uni of Kyoto University, who acted as joint researcher on Chaps. 3 and 4 and had the patience to read and criticize the entire manuscript. I also appreciate the help of Professor Kiichiro Yagi, my supervisor at the Graduate School of Economics, Kyoto University, who introduced me to interdisciplinary research. At the University of Vienna, I was inspired and learned a great deal from discussions on the philosophy of social science with Professor Karl Milford, my supervisor. Professor Sobei H. Oda of Kyoto Sangyo University introduced me to a whole new world of experimental economics. I also wish to thank Professor David Harper, Professor Takanori Ida, Dr. Tetsuya Kawamura, Professor Makoto Kogawara, Dr. Jun Matsuyama, Professor Kazuhito Ogawa, Professor Rebecca Schmidt, Professor Hiroyuki Takezawa, Professor Kazuhisa Taniguchi, Professor Hiroyasu Uemura, and Professor Naoki Watanabe for providing beneficial and productive comments and criticism on my research. Experiments performed in this research owe much to the superb laboratory environment at Kyoto Sangyo University and Kyoto University, as well as to numerous student participants and laboratory assistants. I would also like to express my gratitude to Dr. Kenju Akai, Dr. Tetz Hakoda, Mr. Koji Kato, Mr. Taro Koda, Dr. Takanori Kudo, Ms. Tse Tsz Kwan, and Dr. Yan Zhou for their outstanding support. Additionally, I am appreciative of Dr. John Lambino and Edanz Group Ltd. for their superb English editing services. This research was financially supported by a Japan Society for the Promotion of Science (JSPS) Grant-in-Aid for Scientific Research (KAKENHI) for JSPS fellows (Chaps. 2 and 6), Ministry of Education, Culture, Sports, Science and Technology Grant-in-Aid for Scientific Research (KAKENHI) (B) 26285048 (Chaps. 1 and 7), the Graduate School of Economics, Kyoto University (Chaps. 3 and 4), and the Kikawada Foundation (Chap. 5). I thank *Political Economy Quarterly* for granting reprint permission for Chaps. 3 and 4, as well as Cambridge University Press for granting reprint permission for Chap. 6. Finally, I wish to express my gratitude to Professor Yuji Aruka, editor of the series, and Mr. Yutaka Hirachi, the publisher at Springer. I could not have written this book without everyone's support and encouragement.

October 26, 2015 Natsuka Tokumaru

Contents

Chapter 1
Introduction: Applying the Experimental Method to Economic Thought: From Adam Smith to Vernon Smith

Abstract This paper aims to identify the significance of the emergence of experimental methods in economics, by reviewing behavioral theory in the history of economic thought. Economists have adopted numerous approaches in their attempts to resolve what is called *das Adam Smith Probleme* (the Adam Smith problem)—how to theoretically explain human behaviors driven by social and selfish incentives. For example, Menger separated economic aspects from social aspects, Mises or Weber established a comprehensive concept of purposive behavior, and Keynes strategically avoided micro-foundations for macroanalysis. Moreover, Popper attempted to solve the problem by introducing situational logic that understands human behaviors as appropriate responses to given social conditions. Meanwhile, institutional economists such as Commons attempted to understand humans as acting according to rules in given social institutions. Based on these historical discussions, this paper proposes three meanings of experimental methods: (1) such methods enrich micro-foundations of economics, by enabling the testing of behavioral hypotheses regarding human action under social institutions; (2) such methods serve to create micro-foundations for macro-theory, based on assumptions regarding a "behavioral trend"; and (3) such methods enable the reexamination of the behavioral assumptions of past theories.

Keywords The Adam Smith problem • Behavioral assumptions • Economic experiment • Situational logic • Institutional theory

1.1 The Emergence of the Experimental Method in Economics

The emergence of the experimental method in economics seems to have strongly impacted standard economic theories by challenging the central behavioral concept of *homo economicus*, which identifies humans as seeking to maximize their utility in a given condition under perfect rationality[1] and by enriching behavioral assumptions

[1]The behavioral assumptions associated with *homo economicus*, according to standard economic theories, can be summarized as follows: "Economic agents are rational"; "Economic agents are

N. Tokumaru, *Social Preference, Institution, and Distribution*, Evolutionary Economics and Social Complexity Science 3, DOI 10.1007/978-981-10-0137-6_1

using the newly introduced empirical method. This is symbolized by Vernon Smith, the most representative experimental economist and winner of the Nobel Prize in 2002. Behavioral or experimental economists have performed various kinds of experiments or empirical investigations examining individuals' behaviors or incentives in given situations. For instance, the dictator game, one of the most popular experiments, involves a participant (a dictator) sharing a pie of money (e.g., $10) with another anonymous participant (a recipient). Despite the expectations of standard economic theory, according to which the dictator would distribute the entire pie to himself and leaves nothing to his partner, most participants do not behave in this way. Many experimental results imply that individuals are not only motivated by selfishness but also by reciprocity, fairness, and social norms.

Although methods introduced to economics by experimental economics appear "revolutionary" compared with standard economic theories, the empirical results they have brought so far have not been novel but rather belong to knowledge that already exists. Through our daily experiences, we know human beings are often selfish, though not always, and that our actions are motivated partly by concepts such as care for others, morality, reputation, and social norms. We know that while we behave rationally in most cases, sometimes our behavior is wrong or even stupid, and this also applies to the behaviors of others. Putting it differently, the concept of *homo economicus* itself is a theoretical artifact, which presupposes strong assumptions of selfishness and rationality to construct a coherent system of the discipline, and thus it is no more surprising if experiments "empirically" falsify such an artificial concept. Even if one admits the "usefulness" of neoclassical models as a tool to give a framework for providing predictions or falsifications of empirical assumptions,[2] questions remain regarding how the "new" empirical results of experiments change economics.

The human behavior that underlies most social facts has been a central theme of economics since its beginnings. If one opens a book from the Age of Enlightenment, one will find plenty of discussion on the "nature," "sense," "customs," or "actions" of humans, together with the analysis of their relevance to the social sciences[3] (cf. Locke 1689; Smith 1759). After the marginal revolutions by Jevons, Walras, and Menger in the nineteenth century, mainstream economics has elaborated models based on both mathematical settings and the idea of human actions being motivated by complete selfishness and rationality under perfect information. Those artificial premises enable economists to establish coherent logical models,

motivated by expected utility maximization"; "An agent's utility is governed by purely selfish concerns, in the narrow sense that it does not take into consideration the utility of others"; "Agents are Bayesian probability operators"; "Agents have consistent time preferences according to the discounted utility model"; "All income and assets are completely fungible" (Wilkinson 2008, p. 5).

[2]Camerer and Loenstein (2004) states, "The neoclassical approach is useful because it provides economists with a theoretical framework that can be applied to almost any form of economic (and even noneconomic) behavior, and it makes refutable predictions" (p. 3).

[3]For instance, Locke (1689) states, "Custom settles habits of thinking in the understanding, as well as of determining in the will, and of motions in the body; all which seem to be but trains of motion in the animal spirits" (p. 529).

explaining economic phenomena such as market prices being in "equilibrium" as a consequence of human rationality and existing conditions. The sophisticated logical models of economics give the discipline the status of "a queen of the social sciences," yet were also criticized as "unrealistic" until the discipline was given the disgraceful nickname of the "dismal science." Simultaneously, economists outside the mainstream developed different assumptions regarding human behaviors that were directed at more realistic explanations of economic phenomena, such as work on entrepreneurship by Schumpeter (1934), on partial knowledge by F. A. Hayek (1945), and on opportunistic behavior by Williamson (1985). One may say that although the concept of *homo economicus* may be theoretically elaborated and broadly prevalent, it is merely a point on one among numerous branches of economics and has been reached only through a long historical process.

If experimental results are already known and have already been discussed by previous economists, what is the place of economic experiments, as a new method of the social sciences, in the history of economics? In this chapter, I try to scrutinize this question by seeking an overview of human behavior in the history of economics and by identifying the meanings of an emergence of the experimental method. The chapter has the following structure. In Sect. 1.2, I present a brief overview of how human behavior has been treated in the history of economics, focusing on behavioral theories. In this section, I first describe what is called *das Adam Smith Probleme* (the Adam Smith problem), i.e., the contradictory behavioral characteristics described in Smith's two works. Then, I discuss Carl Menger's attempt to resolve this problem in a famous methodological debate with the German historicists. Next, I describe L. v. Mises' attempts to overcome the problem by identifying the social sciences as comprising purposive behaviors. After that, I discuss J. M. Keynes' strategic methodology to avoid micro-behavioral foundations. In Sect. 1.3, I explain situational logic proposed by Popper that regards human actions as activated by certain social conditions. Then, I describe J. R. Commons' institutional economics, which is understood as a concrete version of situational logic. Based on discussions of the methodology of situational logic, I consider the roles and meanings of experimental methods in the history of economic thought. In the final section (Sect. 1.4), I explain the scope and methods of this book, i.e., distribution experiments set in institutional and historical perspectives, and give a brief overview of the book's content.

1.2 "*Das Adam Smith Probleme*": Human Behaviors in the History of Economic Thought

1.2.1 From A. Smith to Methodenstreit *Between Menger and the German Historicists*

Notably, Adam Smith, known as the "father of economics" based on his work *An Inquiry into the Nature and Causes of the Wealth of Nations* (Smith 1776) in which he described a market mechanism driven by selfish human behavior, was also a professor of Moral Science at Glasgow University. Seventeen years before the publication of *The Wealth of Nations*, Smith published *The Theory of Moral Sentiments* (Smith 1759) in which he explained social order based on the "sympathy" that individuals feel with others. Although the objects of these two books were quite different, they employed similar structures and methods; both books derived explanations of macro-level social facts from certain micro-level human behavior and other transcendental factors such as the "invisible hand of god" or an "impartial spectator." In Smith's view, appropriate social allocation of resources can be achieved through a market process where individuals pursue their interests via the "invisible hands of god" that coordinate supply and demand. Similarly, social norms are explained in terms of individuals, who feel various kinds of sympathies with others. According to Smith, by feeling sympathies with others, individuals develop an "impartial spectator" in their own minds who judges the appropriateness of their behaviors, and these judgments constitute the basis for social norms.

Regarding Smith's two representative works, the questions that may arise are why the concepts of human behaviors Smith employed in the two books are so different from each other and how one should regard these seemingly opposite concepts and theoretical systems coming from a single author. Similar questions were discussed among German economists in the nineteenth century as "*Das Adam Smith Probleme*," in a context of criticizing excessive market fundamentalism and laissez-faire policy (cf. Viner 1927). Smith, an original ideologue of the laissez-faire economy consisting of individuals who purse self-interest, also described a moralistic society comprising individuals having sympathy. Is this not a great contradiction? Human beings not only pursue their self-interest but are also social beings with other motivations—thus, a market may not fully function if left to function without constraints. Naturally, it could be said that such a problem, proposed in an oversimplified form that ignores the historical context, is a pseudo problem. Raphael (2007) claims that Smith's view of humans evolved between the moral sentiments and the wealth of nations, and thus *das Adam Smith Probleme* may not exist at all. However, controversies related to *das Adam Smith Probleme* have continued because they involve fundamental questions about how economics should treat human behaviors that are sometimes selfish and sometimes altruistic and questions regarding the kind of science economics should be (e.g., a moral science or one more analogous to the natural sciences).[4] As Young (1997) states, "unlike old soldiers, old Adam Smith problems neither die nor fade away." Here I refer to the problem as having *symbolic* connotations in relation to human behaviors and the social sciences and ignore the issue of historical context.

One can see a version of *das Adam Smith Probleme* in a famous methodological debate (*Methodenstreit*) between German historicists and Carl Menger, who is regarded as having participated in the marginal revolution with Jevons and Walras

[4]For recent discussions of the Adam Smith problem, see (Paganelli 2008; Lundestad 2014).

and built the foundation of modern economics. The dispute concerned the main purposes of economics and the methodologies it should follow: on the one hand the German historicists believed that economists should derive historical laws by observing entire national economies; on the other hand Menger claimed that economists should derive strictly universal laws by analyzing each component of the economy, including humans seeking self-interest. The methodological issues in the debate closely concerned how economists should treat human behavior.

German historicists like Roscher and Schmoller believed the national economy is a "diversified and comprehensive phenomena" like an organization and thus should be investigated by collectivistic observations and examinations from various aspects of society, including both selfish and unselfish human behaviors. For them, each element of the national economy, such as laws, customs, and politics, is closely connected, and the various elements interact with one another. Thus, to understand the national economy requires that one know "all the aspects" of it. Based on this principle of investigating "all the aspects" of social phenomena, Roscher started his analysis of human beings as being motivated by both a public spirit and selfish incentives (Roscher 1843).

Menger believed the method of German historicists, which involves the investigation of every aspect of a society and of humans, does not maintain strict universality of economics. He further tried to reform Roscher's methodology, by detaching the "economic aspect" from other aspects of society and analyzing each component, including selfish human behavior. The theory of political economy "has only the task of affording us *the understanding of a special side of human life, to be sure, the most important, the economic*" (Menger 1883, p. 87). Schmoller criticized Menger's methodology, which breaks social phenomena into individual elements such as goods and humans before identifying humans as selfish beings (i.e., the concept promoted by Smith), as a naïve work by an immature author (Schmoller 1883). Menger responded to this criticism by claiming that the aim of economics is to identify the laws that govern the "economic aspect" of society, laws that can be identified by breaking and analyzing fundamental elements of an economy, including the selfish behavior of human beings. Specifically, Menger stated:

> ...humans truly are guided in their economic activity exclusively by consideration of their individual interests. ...Only when we think of man as always being guided by the same motive, e.g., self-interest, in his economic actions, ... only then does each action appear to be strictly determined. Only with the above presupposition are laws of economy conceivable. (Menger 1883, p. 83)

For Menger, the abstraction of human behavior according to the motivation of self-interest was necessary to derive universal economic laws (Fig. 1.1).

Most modern economists seem to have followed Menger's justification when they establish micro-models involving humans that maximize their self-interest or utility under given conditions. However, questions remain regarding whether a man can strictly "separate" economic aspects from all other social activities as Menger

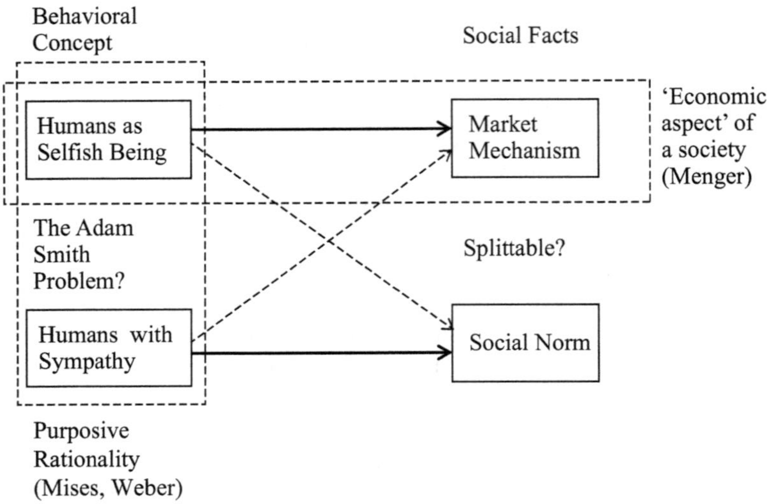

Fig. 1.1 Theoretical structures of behavioral concept and social facts

claimed and whether the concept of humans as selfish beings is always valid in relation to economic activities. Logically, Menger tried to justify his theoretical method to focus on the selfish aspect of human behavior, by saying that his claim is not that "all humans pursue their self-interests" $(\forall x)\ (H_x \rightarrow S_x)$ (*Ha*, *a* is a human being; *Sa*, *a* pursues self-interests), but that if humans act in the economic world (or the economic aspects of a society) they always pursue their individual self-interests: $(\forall x)\ (\exists W_E)\ (H_x \wedge x \in W_E) \rightarrow S_x$. From such selfish behaviors and given certain conditions, one can derive an economic law that explains an economic fact according to Menger: $(S_x \wedge C_1) \rightarrow F_1$. However, this thesis does not retain logical universality because even if such an economic world exists in relation to the selfish behaviors of humans, it does so only as an existential statement. Consequently, the latter thesis does not exclude $(\exists x)\ (\exists W_E)\ \left(H_x \wedge x \in \overline{W_E}\right) \rightarrow \sim S_x$, and thus can be rewritten as $(\exists x)\ (H_x \rightarrow S_x)$. Accordingly, the law derived remains as the following existential statement: $(\exists x)\ (S_x \wedge C_1) \rightarrow F_1$. This statement is not strictly universal, as attempted by Menger, and does not exclude that the economic law is derived from other types of human behavior: $(\exists x)\ (\sim S_x \wedge C_1) \rightarrow F_1$.

Empirically, we can easily find evidence to counter Menger's idea of strict universal laws of economics in our daily lives and in our observations. As Schmoller maintained, our economic activities are undertaken under certain social conditions such as local laws, transaction customs, and social norms and cannot be strictly separated from them. An unselfish and honest merchant may succeed because his positive personal characteristics led to him being trusted by his customers. Similarly, managers who earn profits through extreme greed cannot survive in the long run, as is shown through numerous examples involving recent corrupt activities by enterprises.

1.2.2 L. v. Mises' Human Action and Praxeology as an Original Discipline

L. v. Mises, who was a spectator to the methodological debate, tried to solve the problem concerning human behavior and the social sciences by establishing a comprehensive concept of human behavior. In *Human Action* (Mises 1949) as well as *The Ultimate Foundations of Economic Science* (Mises 1962), Mises tried to establish his view of the comprehensive theoretical social sciences, which he calls "praxeology." According to him, all propositions of praxeology can be a priori derived from an "ultimate category of action," which asserts that man acts rationally to achieve ends. "Praxeology is a priori. All its theorems are products of deductive reasoning that starts from the category of action. ... What praxeology asserts with regard to human action in general is strictly valid without any exception for every action" (Mises 1962, p. 44). It is interesting to note that Max Weber, who was also deeply affected by *Methodenstreit*, also attempted to establish a comprehensive social science based on a central concept of human behavior as purposive rationality (Weber 1904, 1913).

What Mises intended by praxeology was to satisfy empirical validity of human behavior and strict universality of theories simultaneously by building up a comprehensive concept of human behavior that covers all possible behaviors. According to him, the ultimate category of action is a "final cause" (Mises 1949, p. 23) for all social causation, and all social laws can be derived from that category. However, on the one hand, Mises claims empirical validity of praxeology, saying "praxeology conveys exact and precise knowledge of real things" (Mises 1949, p. 39); meanwhile, on the other hand, he does not conceal that the category of action, the final cause of praxeology, is a theoretical tool introduced for instrumentalist reasons: "Action is, *by definition*, always rational" (Mises 1933/1960, p. 3).

However, the ambition to establish an independent discipline based on purposive rationality of humans was less successful and accepted by both economists and social scientists. Perhaps this is because the concept of purposive rationality is too general and contains many (seemingly incoherent) behaviors, and thus one does not need behavioral concepts to explain social facts. If one infers that a social fact X is triggered by human selfish behavior B_X, while social fact Y is triggered by human unselfish behavior B_Y, and simultaneously one cannot theoretically distinguish behavior B_X from B_Y because both are "purposive rational," then a question exists of why one needs to explain different social facts by human behavior (Fig. 1.1). As a logical inference, if a purposive human behavior simultaneously involves opposite behaviors, it can be expressed as a statement "if human a displays behavior B or human a does not display behavior B, then F' $(Ba\text{V} \sim Ba) \rightarrow F$, which contains a tautological premise and may be regarded as always true when F is true".[5]

[5]Regarding the tautological problem of a conceptualization of human action by Mises, see Tokumaru (2009).

1.2.3 Keynes' Strategic Avoidance of a Micro-foundation for Macroanalysis

Instead of building up and scrutinizing a behavioral concept, other economists such as Keynes strategically avoided those discussions and developed comprehensive analysis of the macro-economy. Keynes' theoretical system on effective demand, unemployment, or interests is not based on behavioral analysis. Keynes might have thought that deliberate microanalysis is not necessary to understand macro-level economics that should be directed to policy-making.

Although Keynes' theoretical system lacks behavioral analysis at the micro-level, his theory presupposes a certain type of human behavior. For instance, his main theorem of multiplier effects presupposes that individuals increase their consumption in response to increased income triggered by public investments. This presupposition differs from behavioral assumptions based on rational expectations theory, which presumes individuals do not respond to their short-term increase in income triggered by public investment, because they also expect increased tax in the future and hence refrain from consumption. Keynes (1936) also introduces his behavioral assumption when he explains a mechanism of market fluctuation. According to Keynes, the stock market resembles a "beauty contest" that sees participants select six photos of women from a total of 100, with prizes available to those who picked the most popular: the results of such a competition depend not on one's own judgment but rather on the judgments of others (pp. 153–158). In giving this example, he described a decision-making process involving investors in a stock market that considers how people identify the most valuable stocks and responds to such identification by others. Through this analysis of people's expectations of others, he explained the cause of market fluctuations or bubbles. Keynes' theory contains considerable behavioral assumptions, but perhaps for strategic reasons, he neither explicitly discussed nor gave detailed analysis of human behaviors.

Interestingly, Keynes avoided strict micro-level analysis for macro-level economics, but the premises of his theory were based on certain human behavioral trends. Perhaps his theoretical pragmatism would have prevented him from being drawn into fruitless discussions on behavioral concepts and focus on macroanalysis. However, that does not mean he regarded behavioral analysis as meaningless; rather, his theories are based on behavioral presuppositions, as discussed.

From discussions of human behavior that developed in the history above, we can see that concepts of human behaviors in economics were developed for practical use in a certain theoretical system or were strategically avoided for the same reason. These instrumentalist attitudes may come from the difficulties of identifying human behaviors, which differ from situation to situation, to fit a coherent theoretical system.

1.3 Meanings of Experimental Methods in Economics: Human Behaviors in Situational Logic and Empirical Tests

1.3.1 Popper's Situational Logic for Objective Understanding of Human Behaviors

Instead of identifying behavioral concepts of humans or strategically avoiding the behavioral foundations of macroanalysis, Popper proposes *situational logic* to facilitate objective understandings of human behaviors in the social sciences. According to Popper (1994), objective understandings of human behaviors in the social sciences should not be based on psychological analysis of those behaviors but on "realizing that the action was objectively *appropriate to the situation*" (p. 79). This maintains that humans act rationally according to the social situations they encounter. By introducing this rationality principle combined with social conditions, Popper attempted to direct the social sciences away from unproductive psychological analysis of humans and to redefine human behaviors as social factors. He explains this using the example of competitions. Competitions can be explained using a psychological perspective, such as causing stresses or mental tensions. However, competitions can also be explained as objective social processes, by regarding individual responses appropriate to given competitive situations. For example, a social institution such as a cartel can be explained as a behavioral consequence of humans appropriately responding to given situations involving harsh competition: individuals organize a cartel to maintain competitive advantage.

Thus, in other words, situational logic is not directed at analyzing humans in itself but rather social conditions that trigger certain behaviors. Put differently, situational logic can express the conditions under which all humans act as B. $(\forall x)\,(H_x \wedge C_1 \wedge C_2 \wedge \cdots \wedge C_n) \rightarrow B_x$. Situational logic presupposes human rationality in a broad sense but not as something rigid and perfect. Avoiding persistent debates on behavioral concepts, Popper converted such concepts for application to problems involving social conditions. Because the task of economics for Popper is explaining unintended consequences of human actions, those processes are well explained not by psychological explanations of behaviors but by a complete situational analysis of human behaviors. As described by Mises, human behavior thus resembles "a category of human action" that is purposive, as discussed in the previous section. However, Popper's situational logic differs from that of Mises in that it is not an empirically valid conceptualization of humans but a theoretical reconstruction of human behaviors for explaining social institutions. Thus, Popper converted a problem of the conceptualization of human behavior to a situational logic for explaining social institutions, saying "We might construct a theory of intended and unintended institutional consequences of purposive action" (p. 80).

By introducing situational logic, Popper seems to have successfully avoided unproductive conceptualization and subjective understandings of behaviors. However, he did not give any actual theory involving situational logic. This is because his discussions are mainly focused on an epistemological problem of how objective knowledge is possible in the social sciences and not on concrete explanations of social facts.

1.3.2 Human Behaviors in Social Institutions

Whereas Popper focuses on epistemological discussions on situational logic and social institution, institutional economists such as W. C. Mitchell and J. R. Commons developed original theories that explain human behaviors in social institutions. Unlike neoclassical economists, these institutional economists regard humans as existing in an environment they construct themselves via social institutions. Institutions contain formal rules such as laws, as well as informal rules, such as transaction customs, and organizational rules that are socially accepted and prevalent. They regard humans as those who play a game according to a given set of social rules and conditions. Thus, humans are described not as having a fixed response pattern but as potentially acting in one or more of several possible ways, where institutional conditions activate certain patterns of human behavior.

J. R. Commons, one of the founders of institutional economics, described human activities as regulated by social conditions, using his original term of "going concern." In his view, individuals are under the collective control of the "going concern" to which they belong and try to adapt themselves to the conditions of going concerns. Commons (1934) identified "going concern" in a very general sense as including families, enterprise, labor unions, and nations. According to him, every going concern has "working rules" that regulate the behaviors of members. He distinguished three types of transactions among individuals, namely, bargaining transactions, managerial transactions, and rationing transactions. According to Commons, bargaining transactions are typical market transactions between buyers and sellers; managerial transactions concern transactions occurring in hierarchical relationships between superiors and subordinates within a going concern like an enterprise; and rationing transactions concern setting up working rules in a going concern or deciding distributions among members. By describing human behaviors as they are regulated in going concerns and distinguishing three dimensions of transactions, he explained human behaviors as being activated under certain social conditions. Commons calls those social conditions "institutions," saying "an institution is defined as collective action in control, liberation and expansion of individual action" (Commons 1931, p. 651).

Commons' ideas of human behaviors, influenced as they are by institutional theories, have considerable empirical content but are less elaborated in a theoretical sense. His idea of "going concerns" seems compatible with our experiences in that most of us behave in ways that do not deviate from expectations in social organizations. Actually, Commons developed institutional theories based on his experiences in his public work for the state of Wisconsin. However, those observations are given in a mixed form and cannot control many possible factors that might affect individuals. Because "going concern" is identified in a broad sense and designates only an aggregate version of social conditions, it does not specify special social conditions that activate certain human behaviors.

1.3.3 Experimental Methods for Testing Behaviors and Preferences Under Social Conditions

In this subsection, based on the discussion above, I would like to propose three meanings of experimental methods in economics for empirically testing hypotheses.

As we have seen, Popper introduced situational logic to avoid psychological understandings of human behaviors and direct them to objective social knowledge. Situational logic understands human behaviors as responses that are "objectively *appropriate to the situation*." By introducing situational logic, Popper succeeded in converting unproductive discussions on behaviors into social theories related to social conditions (that activate certain actions) and their consequences. However, his situational logic was limited in epistemological discussion and lacked concrete hypotheses on humans and social facts.

We also have seen that Commons' idea of a "going concern" has rich empirical content but connotations that are too broad to specify a certain social situation that activates human behavior. He maintained that human actions follow different rules under different social organizations, and he did not strictly identify that individuals engage in behavior B_x under condition C_x, with the consequence of social fact F_x ($C_x \wedge B_x \rightarrow F_x$). Because Commons derived his ideas on institutional economics based on his experiences of policy-making processes, this way of theorizing situational logic may be quite natural based on his observations, yet it is theoretically obscure.

From the limitations of the situational logic used by Popper and the institutional economics used by Commons, we could derive the following first thesis on the meanings of experimental methods.

Thesis 1: The experimental method enables economists to test a behavioral hypothesis that refers to a certain set of social institutions to activate a certain human behavior.

Because experiments enable experimenters to observe how subjects respond under given experimental settings and controlled social conditions, they enable the identification of a specific behavior as a response to a specific social institution. As is shown in Fig. 1.2, lab experiments enable the construction of an artificial institutional environment by asking participants to learn a certain set of rules and play a game using those rules. A participant is financially motivated to earn

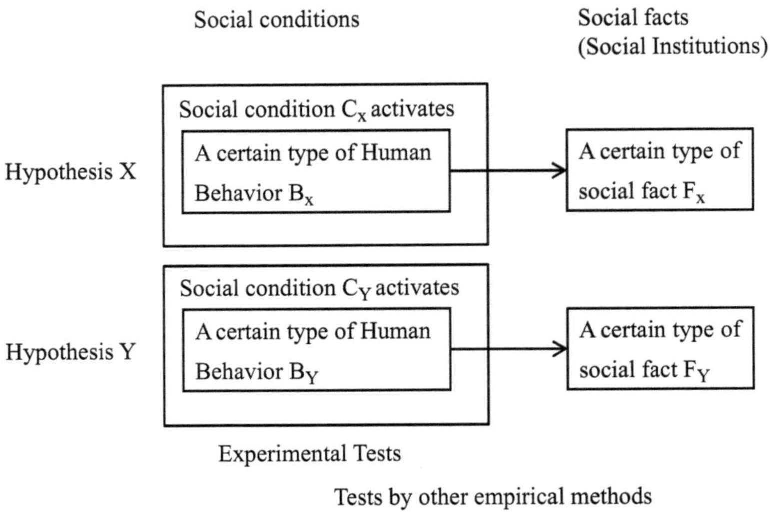

Fig. 1.2 Institutional explanations of human behaviors and social facts

money in the game but also restricted by a given set of rules and interactions with other participants. By analyzing the concrete responses of participants under given experimental settings as a set of data, a researcher can test a hypothesis regarding a human behavior that can be activated by an institutional condition ($C_x \rightarrow B_x$). This method can enrich theories of social institutions.

The second meaning of the experimental method in economics seems to be that it serves to explain macro-level social phenomena, based on a micro-level behavioral foundation through the "theory of behavioral trend." In the discussion above, one may question the optimal method of treating the diversity of individuals' preferences and behaviors related to the same social institutions, as identified by experimental tests. Because if an experimental test shows that some individuals acted selfishly and others acted unselfishly under identical experimental settings, the problem of tautology, as discussed by Mises, may reoccur. Restated, if we admit different individuals respond to the same social institutions, what kinds of theories can we derive from the facts without falling into relativism? In relation to this problem, we may be able to learn the strategy of Keynes, namely, to understand human behaviors as a dominant *trend* for explaining macro-level theories. To explain a macro-social phenomenon as a consequence of human behaviors, we do not need to know precisely how each person acted, and instead a behavioral assumption such as "most people under this social condition act in this way" would be sufficient. Behavioral assumptions of multiple effects would be enough if most people increase their consumption in response to a short-term increase in income. Thus, we can summarize the second meaning of the experimental method as follows:

Thesis 2: Experimental method is important because it provides micro-level behavioral assumptions for explaining macro-level social phenomena. The assumption is expressed in the form of a "behavioral trend"; that is, most people act in a certain way under a certain social condition. This assumption enriches macro-level social theories and subjects them to further examination by empirical tests.

The third meaning of the experimental method concerns reexaminations of historical economic theories. Such reexaminations can examine the reasons why Keynes strategically avoided micro-foundations, why Popper introduced assumptions of general behaviors, and why Commons comprehensively identified social conditions and behaviors. These issues largely stem from historical limitations in the use of experimental methods. Because experimental methods enable scientists to examine behaviors under controlled social conditions, they strategically avoided micro-behavioral assumptions with empirical content. Thus, we can summarize the last meaning of the experimental method as follows:

Thesis 3: Economists can revive a past theory involving behavioral assumptions by experimentally testing its validity, something impossible when the theory was proposed, and behavioral assumptions in themselves may be enriched by results not expected by a theory.

An introduction of a new method into a discipline has always been a possibility, not only to examine the latest theories but also historical theories that remain to be tested. Einstein's theory of general relativity was not examined until Hubbell's astronomical work on redshift based on a telescope survey conducted 12 years later. Similarly, we may be able to examine past economic theories, such as Keynes' "beauty contest" assumption, by performing a market experiment and analyzing results related to how participants modify their expectations of other participants. Restated, all past and present theories should be tested using experimental methods to develop new economic theories, including micro-assumptions that hold more realistic and empirical contents.

1.4 The Scope, Method, and Aim of This Book: Distribution Experiments from Institutional and Historical Perspectives

As we have seen, the emergence of experimental methods in economics is significant to the history of economic thought, which has seen a struggle over how to treat human behaviors with seemingly contradictory incentives. Experimental methods provide micro-level tests of human behaviors triggered by certain social conditions and enrich macro-level theories, by providing an empirical behavioral foundation. Additionally, the possibility also exists of reexamining past theories by testing their behavioral assumptions. Given discussions of historical and institutional meanings of experimental methods, I shall explain the scope and methods of this book, which specifically involve distribution experiments from an institutional and historical perspective.

1.4.1 Distribution in Economic Experiments

Distribution experiments have been the most popular type of experiment since the beginnings of experimental economics and have yielded many inspiring results. Such experiments seem to have achieved successes in observing individuals who make decisions motivated by their self-interest and by the norms they hold in different given situations. The most popular simple distribution experiment is the dictator game (Kahneman et al. 1986), which requires participants to allocate a certain amount of money (e.g., $10) among themselves and other participants. The other type of distribution experiment is the ultimatum game (Güth et al. 1982), which has basically the same design as the dictator game, but the recipients can decide whether to accept or reject a proposal. One rule of the ultimatum game is that both proposer and recipient receive nothing in the case of rejection by the latter. The results of those experiments were intrinsic and informative: many participants did not follow the expectations of standard economic theories, and either separated the available pie 50:50 with others or at least gave their partners amounts that exceeded the theoretically expected minimum.

Regarding the interpretation of those distribution experiments, many inspiring discussions and theories exist on human behaviors. Fehr and Schmidt (1999) explain the results by introducing the concept of "inequality aversion," which implies that individuals tend to avoid unequal distributions with others. Cherry et al. (2002) maintain that self-effort to earn personal property and sufficient anonymity overwhelm other individual behaviors. Frohlich et al. (2004) discuss the intensity of subject "doubt" regarding experimenter honesty and experimental settings (e.g. whether another pair-matched subject "truly" exists) is important in decision-making. Bolton and Ockenfels (2000) tried to construct models that consider individuals' social preferences regarding self-interest, equity, reciprocity, and competition and provide comprehensive explanations of different experimental results.

Given those intriguing results, one may ask how we can apply or interpret those behavioral mechanisms in a context of understanding social phenomena. As I discussed in the previous section, "competition" in itself can be understood from the perspectives of both psychology and social sciences. If a goal of the social sciences is to explain social facts as results of interactions arising from human actions, behavioral tests should be combined with analysis of social conditions that trigger actions and how those actions result in macro-level social phenomena. Camerer and Loewenstein (2004) state, "Behavioral economics increases the explanatory power of economics by providing it with more realistic psychological foundations" (p. 3). However, if "realistic" here is only used in a psychological sense, it would not contribute to better the understanding of social phenomena. Even if we successfully develop a theory of a person's mind under competition, it would not in itself bring further explanations of social facts. We may be able to observe that John becomes aggressive because of the excessive competitive pressures that accompany a promotion. Here the focus of social scientists should be not on John's psychology under competition but on the social facts that result from the actions of individuals under competition. A possible hypothesis may be that excessive competition in a company may decrease corporate productivity owing to decreased cooperation among employees. We should set experimental results in the context of social conditions that trigger behaviors and ask how we can extend given experimental results to understandings of social phenomena.

1.4.2 Distribution in the History of Economic Thought

Besides distribution experiments and their results, distribution has been an area in which many theories or controversies remain untested due to methodological limitations, despite the area being regarded as one of the most important topics that economics should explore. For instance, Recardo (1817) states that "to determine the laws which regulate this distribution, is the principal problem in Political Economy" (p. 5). A. Smith believed economic value originates from labor,[6] and Locke refers to property rights as deriving from labor. Developing Smith's labor value theory and analysis of capital, Marx (1867) maintained that a corollary consequence of a capitalist system is *unfair* distribution, that is, exploitation of workers who own only their labor by capitalists who own means of production. In contrast with Smith or Marx, a market liberalist such as Friedman believes that property should be distributed to people not according to labor, but according to the principle that each individuals should receive income according to their contributions to production by production measurement, they own such as labor, capital, land, machine, and so on (Friedman 1962).

Although distribution remains the most important area in economics, economists appear not to have reached any consensus about this area because of the intrinsic difficulty associated with distribution problems: such problems involve two areas, human self-interest concerns and concerns involving social norms or fairness. As is well known, Max Weber maintained that social scientists should distinguish the problem of *sein* (be) from that of *sollen* (should) and moreover should refrain from making value judgments when investigating social issues (Weber 1904). However, when it comes to distribution, these two problems seem to overlap. With respect to individual decision-making, individuals may wish to disproportionately increase their share based on self-preservation instinct (the problem of *sein*) while simultaneously considering whether their share is compatible with distributive justice or prevalent social norms (the problem of *sollen*). This property of the distribution problem makes its social investigation more difficult and complex.

At the macro-level, different combinations of norms and distribution efficiency seem to be associated with different positions on economic policies. On the one

[6] Smith states that every man "... must be rich or poor according to the quantity of that labour which he can command, or which he can afford to purchase" (Smith 1776, p. 47).

hand, market liberalists claim that wage levels should be decided via market mechanisms and that redistribution via progressive taxation and social welfare decreases economic efficiency because it mutes the incentives of the rich to invest and of the poor to work without depending on public assistance (e.g., Friedman 1962). Basically, their theories expect that optimal distributions of resources can be achieved given market mechanisms that function satisfactorily with minimum government intervention. On the other hand, Keynesians maintain that higher levels of wages and social welfare with progressive taxation often contribute to economic efficiency and stability because of increased effective demand that has multiple effects for the entire economy. Here we find the potential combination of recognition of a fact (*sein*) and value judgment (*sollen*): the central thesis of the former, namely, that the "market contributes economic efficiency," may imply that "property *should* be distributed according to market mechanisms"; moreover, the thesis of the latter that "social equality contributes economic efficiency" may imply that "property *should* be distributed or redistributed to maintain a certain level of equality."

1.4.3 Aim, Scope, and Contents of This Book

Based on the discussions above, in this book I perform four distribution experiments that presuppose different social institutions and attempt to apply the experimental results to help understand actual social institutions. The distribution experiments performed in this book are basically revised versions of the typical dictator game or public goods game. However, in interpreting the results, I attempted to analyze the behaviors of the observed individuals in the contexts of given institutional settings. By revealing the institutional conditions that bring certain actions, I also attempted to show the implications of given experimental results and related situational analysis in actual social situations. As proposed in theses 1 and 2, we can interpret given experimental results in the context of social conditions and apply them to macroanalysis as micro-foundations based on empirical tests.

To interpret the experimental results, I introduce several historical theories from past economists such as O. Williamson, Webbs, Marx, Hodgeskin, M. Friedman, and Barlie. Although these theories naturally suffer from historical limitations, adding them to the discussion is nevertheless fruitful because they are often referenced in radical proposals regarding social economy. For instance, even though labor value theory is regarded as "out of date" for explaining price, the results of distribution experiments reveal that a version of labor value theory remains alive in individuals as a social norm. Thus, as I proposed in thesis 3, past theories should be reexamined using experimental methods to enrich the latest theories.

The content and structure of this book is as follows. In Chap. 1, I discuss the meanings of an emergence of experimental methods by reviewing the history of economic thought to present an overview of behavioral theories. Here I described how social scientists have at different times in the history of economic thought developed seemingly contradictory theories regarding human behaviors. Examples include the theories of the German historicists, C. Menger, L. v. Mises, J. M. Keynes, K. Popper, and J. S. Commons. The conclusion of this chapter is that experimental methods enable us to test hypotheses that refer to human behaviors activated by certain social institutions. Those empirically tested hypothesis provide micro-foundations for macro-theories, in a form of "behavioral trend" under given social institutions. Additionally, experimental methods let us reexamine historical behavioral theories that were tested empirically for their methodological limitations.

In Chap. 2, I examine opportunistic behaviors defined as "self-interested behavior with guile" by Williamson, by performing a distribution experiment involving production that largely depends on participants' luck. According to this chapter, a fairness ideal that individuals potentially hold is not only invoked by experimental institutions as presupposed by previous models but is also invoked in opportunities that individuals occasionally have. The experimental results of this chapter showed that subjects tend to adhere to fairness ideals that benefit their profits. That is, subjects whose relative earnings are higher than their partner's tend to prefer a libertarian distribution, based on the logic of the strong. However, subjects whose relative earnings are lower tend to prefer an egalitarian distribution, based on the logic of the weak. This chapter concludes that individuals can satisfy both social and utilitarian preferences, without exposing their selfishness by engaging in opportunistic behaviors.

In Chap. 3, I examine whether differences in production process—collaborative or independent styles of working and whether individuals' performance information is revealed—affect the fairness ideals of individuals as revealed in a distribution experiment. In this chapter, I examined hypotheses related to both labor dependency and the exposure of individual's performance information as important factors that influence the distribution justice exhibited by individuals. According to the results of the experiments, half of all subjects who were working collaboratively without performance information adhered to an egalitarian distribution, whereas half of all subjects who were working independently and who had performance information preferred performance-based pay. Because the former approximates the current workplace environment, where the labor of different individuals is closely connected and individual performance becomes obscured, this experiment partly explains the observed failures of performance-based payments, a phenomenon that contradicts the ideal of worker fairness. This chapter is a result of joint studies conducted with Professor Hiroyuki Uni.

In Chap. 4, I focus on functional income distribution, which was discussed in the context of macroanalysis by post-Keynesians, and perform distribution experiments involving workers and investors. In these experiments, each subject is assigned the role of a worker or an investor and engages in production with a team member who is assigned to a different role. That is, each subject is pair matched and forms one member of a two-player team comprising an investor and a worker: the investor contributes to production by deciding whether to purchase a calculator, whereas the worker contributes to production by performing calculation tasks. Each subject is then required to distribute team earnings between themselves and their partner. According to this chapter, in the case where investors must work to earn their investment funds, they tend to be more unselfish because they evaluate worker efforts more highly, whereas investors given investment funds as endowments without any labor tend to be more selfish. This tendency may partly explain recent declines in labor wage rates that have accompanied globalization and financialization, trends that make it harder for investors to recognize labor. This chapter is a result of joint studies with Professor Hiroyuki Uni.

In Chap. 5, I ask whether socially responsible investment can be an institution used to govern corporate social activities. I do this by performing experiments involving interactions between investors and companies. The experiments were designed such that corporate activities yield profits as well as positive or negative externalities (a possible real-world example would involve environmental protection or pollution), and investors select the corporations in which they invest. This experiment can be considered a kind of distribution experiment because it simulates how profits are distributed among enterprises, investors, and societies under different institutional situations. According to this chapter, disclosure of information on corporate externalities to the public influences some investors to invest in "good" companies that generate positive externalities; however, total externalities by all enterprises remain negative because some investors and companies adopted free-riding strategies. A combination of information disclosure and the punishment of the company that generated the highest negative externalities was more effective in reducing total harmful corporate activities than was a reward-based rule.

In Chap. 6, I focus on F. v. Wieser's methodology that derives social theories based on piecemeal analysis, from micro-level behavioral assumptions, examined by *Gedankenexperiment*, to macro-level theories of social economy, examined by observation. The aim of this chapter is to present implications for how behavioral or institutional assumptions at the micro-level can be extended to macro-level social theories based on Wieser's methodology. According to this chapter, Wieser starts his economic investigation with linguistic analysis of relationships for each economic element and micro-level analysis of subjective human evaluations. He develops the analysis on how economic institutions emerge from human behaviors and other conditions by introducing introspections and thought experiments as empirical tests of the derived theories. Finally, he tries to develop economic theories into social theories, introducing social conditions under which economic activities are held. Although Wieser's methodology had the limitation of being psychological, this chapter concludes that we could learn from his method by applying the experimental method to theories of social economy in four ways: understanding human behaviors from the perspective of subjective rationality; situational analysis of social institutions that activate certain human behaviors; empirical tests of theories from the micro-level to the macro-level; and methodological motivationalism, where economic agents are understood in terms of whether they exert motivating forces on society.

In Chap. 7, I attempt to show how human behaviors interact with social institutions and how the results of experiments can contribute theories for institutional evolution. According to this chapter, humans both exist in an institutionalized context and through their existence constitute institutions. Additionally, both sides of this interaction should be considered in relation to institutional evolution. The conclusion here is that economic experiments can contribute to a piecemeal process of social policy development by identifying institutional factors that activate certain human behaviors.

In this book, I have generally attempted to show a way to extend new behavioral theories proposed by experimental methods to theories of social economy that contribute to institutional evolutions. Naturally, conditions differ between an experimental design and a real society, and one should be careful when applying observed results from the laboratory to a real economy. One should also consider historical contexts and past theories in attempting to interpret experimental results. In other words, the empirical facts given by economic experiments may not be facts in vivo but rather facts in vitro. Thus, it is important to refrain from over generalizing results obtained only from experimental work and applying them to the actual social economy. However, if new empirical facts become available, even if they are based on experimental work, social scientists should consider how to interpret them and apply them to understand the actual social economy. I hope that this book shows those trials and enriches the micro-behavioral foundations by introducing experimental method and applying it to understand concrete social facts concerning distributions among individuals with different social preferences. Additionally, I wish those derived social hypothesis would contribute to give political implications for designing appropriate institutions that enhance individuals' motivations and productivity as well as social welfares for sustainable economic development.

References

Bolton GE, Ockenfels A (2000) ERC: a theory of equity, reciprocity, and competition. Am Econ Rev 90(1):166–193

Camerer CF, Loewenstein G (2004) Behavioral economics: past, present, future. In: Camerer CF, Loewenstein G, Rabin M (eds) Advances in behavioral economics. Princeton University Press, New York, pp 3–51

Cherry TL, Frykblom P, Shogren JF (2002) Hardnose the dictator. Am Econ Rev 92(4):1218–1221

Commons JR (1931) Institutional economics. Am Econ Rev 21:648–657

Commons JR (1934) Institutional economics: its place in political economy. Macmillan, New York

Fehr E, Schmidt KM (1999) Theory of fairness, competition, and cooperation. Q J Econ 114(3):817–868

Friedman M (1962) Capitalism and freedom. The University of Chicago, Chicago

Frohlich N, Oppenheimer J, Kurki A (2004) Modeling other-regarding preferences and an experimental test. Public Choice 119:91–117

Güth W, Rolf S, Bernd S (1982) An experimental analysis of ultimatum bargaining. J Econ Behav Organ 3:367–388

Hayek FV (1945) The use of knowledge in society. Am Econ Rev 35(4):519–530

Kahneman D, Knetsch JL, Thaler RH (1986) Fairness as a constraint on profit seeking: entitlements in the market. Am Econ Rev 76(4):728–741

Keynes JM (1936/1961) The general theory of employment, interest and money. Macmillan/Maruzen, London/Tokyo

Locke J (1689) An essay concerning human understanding (1894). Clarendon Press, Oxford

Lundestad E (2014) The Adam Smith problem: a reinterpretation. J Scott Philos 12(2):181–197
Marx K (1867/1962) Das Capital. Buch I, Marx-Engels Werke, Band 23. Institut für Marxismus-Leninismus beim ZK der SED. Diertz Verlag, Berlin
Menger C (1883/1985) Investigations into the method of the social science with special reference to economics (Untersuchungen über die Methode der Socialwissenschaften, und der Politischen Oekonomie insbesondere. Verlag von Duncker & Humblot, Leibzig) (trans: Nock JF). New York University Press, New York
Mises L (1949) Human action: a treaties on economics. Yale University Press, New Haven
Mises Lv (1933/1960) Grundprobleme der Nationalökonomie: Untersuchungen über Verfahren, Aufgaben und Inhalt der Wirtschafts und Gesellschaftslehre. Epistemological problems of economics (trans: Reisman G). Van Nostrand, Princeton
Mises L (1962) The ultimate foundation of economic science: an essay on method. D. Van Nostrand, Princeton
Paganelli MP (2008) The Adam Smith problem in reverse: self-interest in the wealth of nations and the theory of moral sentiment. Hist Polit Econ 40(2):365–382
Popper K (1994) In search of a better world: lectures and essays from thirty years. Routledge, London/New York
Raphael DD (2007) The impartial spectator: Adam Smith's moral philosophy. Clarendon Press, Oxford
Ricardo D (1817) On the principles of political economy and taxation. John Murray, London
Roscher WGF (1843) Grundriss zur Vorlesungen über die Staatswirthschaft nach geschichtlicher Methode. Druck und Verlag der Dieterichschen Buchhandlung, Göttingen
Schmoller G. v (1883/1987) Menger und Dilthey, Zur Methodologie der Staats- und Sozialwissenschaften. Gustav schmoller Kleine Schriften zur Wirtschaftsgeschichte Wirtschaftstheorie und Wirtschaftspolitik. Wolfram Fiedler und Rolf Kard (Hrsg.), Teil6. DDR: Zentralantiquariat der DDR
Schumpeter JA (1934) The theory of economic development: an inquiry into profits, capital, credit, interest, and the business cycle (trans: Redvers O). Harvard University Press
Smith A (1759/1981) The theory of moral sentiments. Liberty Fund, Indianapolis
Smith A (1776/1984) An inquiry into the nature and causes of the wealth of nations. Liberty Fund, Indianapolis
Tokumaru N (2009) Popper's analysis of the problems of induction and demarcation and Mises' justification of the theoretical social science. In: Cohen RS, Parusnikova Z (eds) Rethinking Popper, Boston studies in the philosophy of science, vol 272. Springer, Dordrecht, pp 161–174
Viner J (1927) Adam Smith and Laissez Faire. J Polit Econ 35(2):198–232
Weber M (1904/1922) Die "Objektivität" sozialwissenschaftlicher und sozialpolitischer Erkenntnis. In: Gesammelte Aufsätze zur Wissenschaftslehre von Max Weber, 1.Aufl., J.C.B. Mohr
Weber M (1913/1922) Ueber einige Kategorien der verstehenden Soziologie, in ibid
Wilkinson N (2008) An introduction to behavioral economics. Palgrave Macmillan, Hampshire/New York
Williamson O (1985) The economic institutions of capitalism. The Free Press, New York
Young J (1997) Economics as a moral science: the political economy of Adam Smith. Edward Elgar, Cheltenham

Chapter 2
Fairness Ideals, Hidden Selfishness, and Opportunistic Behavior: An Experimental Approach

Abstract Economic experiments have shown that human incentives are not limited to the profit-maximizing principle but also motivated by fairness. Such studies presuppose that individuals commit to fixed value systems and that experimental institutions invoke fairness ideals. By performing a distributive experiment followed by production, this research shows that participants strategically select fairness ideals that are advantageous to themselves in terms of self-distribution. Participants whose relative earnings exceed those of their partners in their assigned experimental pairs adhere to a liberalist fairness ideal, whereas those whose relative earnings are lower than their partners prefer an egalitarian distribution of money. This reflects that individuals behave opportunistically as a result of resolving a cognitive dissonance between material utility and fairness.

Keywords Fairness ideals • Cognitive dissonance • Hidden selfishness • Opportunistic behavior

2.1 Introduction

Studies involving economic experiments such as the dictator game, or the ultimatum game, which require participants to distribute a fixed amount of money among various participants, have shown that human incentives are not limited to the profit-maximizing principle but also include other ethical values such as reciprocity, consideration for others, or ideals of fairness (Kahneman et al. 1986; Forsythe et al. 1994; Levine 1998; Fehr and Schmidt 1999). Those studies show that limited numbers of participants conform to the *homo economicus* prediction; in most experiments, less than one-third of participants distributed all the money to themselves, while the remainder left money for distribution to the partners they were paired with.

Some studies performed experiments consisting of distribution and production stages, which were revisions of dictator games. Those studies are interesting in that they enable experimenters to observe how the experimental settings of a production stage affect subjects' decisions or fairness ideals in a subsequent distribution stage and how subjects have varied fairness ideals. For instance, experiments by Hoffman and Spitzer (1985) and Cappelen et al. (2007) showed that participants'

N. Tokumaru, *Social Preference, Institution, and Distribution*, Evolutionary Economics and Social Complexity Science 3, DOI 10.1007/978-981-10-0137-6_2

decision-making is influenced by various fairness ideals such as egalitarianism, liberalism, or utilitarianism. According to their studies, a strictly egalitarian participant would divide team income 50:50 with the partner they were paired with, whereas a strictly liberal participant would base the distribution on the earnings of each team member during the production process. Liberal egalitarians distribute team earnings according to the amounts each team member could control and thus take responsibility for (e.g., investment amount) and do not consider amounts that depend on chance (e.g., lottery winnings). Finally, a strict utilitarian would distribute the entire sum to themselves and leave nothing for the partners they were paired with.

Basically, the studies mentioned above presuppose that (1) each individual first commits to a certain *fixed value system* and (2) an *experimental institution* invokes a certain fairness ideal as a distribution principle, according to which individuals distribute money to those they are paired with.[1] Here it is presumed that, under a certain type of experimental institution (e.g., game rules, environments, payment procedures), a certain participant will *always* commit to a specific fairness ideal such as an egalitarian distribution. In that sense, subjects' fairness ideals are fundamentalist forms that remain constant under the same experimental settings.

Because it is presupposed that experimental institutions trigger fairness ideals in each subject, previous studies attempted to examine which factors definitively influence a participant's commitments to fairness ideals. This was done by changing the experimental institution and comparing the results with those where the institution is unchanged. For instance, Hoffman and Spitzer (1985) states that a participant tends to justify a larger distribution to themselves if a production method satisfactorily reflects their own ability and efforts. Experiments by Cherry et al. (2002) revealed that when anonymity is maintained, and when participants earn money through their own ability and effort (measured by GMAT score), most of them (more than 90 %) distribute all the money to themselves and leave nothing to their partners. However, questions arise as to whether individuals always follow a given value system in a fundamentalist way under a given experimental institution. Specifically, an important question is whether any wiggle room exists in which individuals can balance different fairness ideals or self-interests in a given situation.

By performing a distribution experiment involving production, this paper aims to show that some individuals tend to pursue opportunistic behavior, specifically the strategic selection of more advantageous distribution principles from among a range of possible options (i.e., opportunity sets) under constant experimental settings. Williamson (1975) suggests that individuals commit to opportunism, which does not follow an established or coherent ethical standard, but rather exploits opportunities inherent in a given transaction process. Opportunists do not deviate from social norms or rules (social reputation can be an important incentive), but are strategic

[1]Hoffman and Spitzer (1985) states that participants "would concur with a particular concept of fairness in distribution" before the experiments and that a participant "perceives the experimental institutions as triggering a particular aspect of his concept of justice" and then "implements his perceptions of a fair distribution" (p. 260).

and try to exploit opportunities in given social situations—a behavior that can be described as "self-interest seeking with guile" (p. 26).[2] Williamson proposed the term opportunism to explain the emergence of transaction costs in external markets, and his work was derived from empirical investigations based on observations of enterprises that focus on transactions, contracts, and hierarchical controls. The behavioral presuppositions of opportunism given by Williamson are very intrinsic, but should be confirmed through concrete observation of individual behaviors.

According to the experimental results of this paper, a significant number of participants whose relative earnings are lower than those of their partners tend to commit to an egalitarian distribution, while participants with higher relative earnings than their partners tend to commit to a liberalist distribution. This tendency comes from subjects' opportunistic way of committing to specific fairness ideals that result in a better distribution to themselves: for example, an egalitarian distribution brings higher income to participants with lower relative earnings, and vice versa, while a liberalist distribution brings higher income to participants with higher relative earnings. These experimental results imply that participants recognized two possible distributional opportunities, based on egalitarian and liberalist fairness ideals, respectively, and strategically "select" that which is more advantageous to themselves. Through such opportunism, subjects simultaneously satisfy both the "social norm" and their "self-interest."

The structure of this paper is as follows: I first explain the concept of opportunism and its theoretical connotations as given by Williamson (Sect. 2.2). Then in the next section (Sect. 2.3), I explain the experiment design. In Sect. 2.4, I first analyze previous models and clarify their premises; then, I present the hypothesis and predictions of this research. After reporting on the experimental results in Sect. 2.5, I discuss the opportunistic behavior and cognitive dissonance in the experimental results in Sect. 2.6. Finally, I present conclusions in Sect. 2.7.

2.2 Opportunism and Its Theoretical Connotations

Williamson (1985) introduced the concept of opportunism to explain transaction costs in external markets, as well as why enterprises developed internal markets and hierarchical regulations. For him, the existence of opportunism combined with bounded rationality explained why transactions in external markets are sometimes more inefficient than those in internal markets or organizations. Let me suppose a case involving an auto company trying to conclude a consignment contract with a part manufacturer to produce a specific car part. Because the part manufacturer has more information on part production than does the auto company, and because

[2] Williamson (1975) approaches the concept from a theoretical perspective, explaining the internal market in terms of transaction costs and opportunistic behaviors. However, this paper does not go into detail on this point.

the number of manufacturers that can produce the part is limited, the contract is likely to set transaction costs. In this situation, the part manufacturer may propose high part prices, decrease quality to reduce costs, or seek advantage through a contract that delays contract delivery. William called these cheating behaviors by the part manufacturer opportunistic behaviors, defined as "self-interest seeking with guile." These opportunistic behaviors become possible because the auto company cannot know the most appropriate completion price or time because of limited information and moreover lacks options in terms of consigning production to other manufacturers in the limited part production market. Restated, the part manufacturer uses available "opportunities" to create a situation advantageous to itself.

By presupposing opportunism as well as bounded rationality,[3] Williamson develops theories relating to transaction costs and the development of internal markets. According to Williamson, because of the existence of transaction costs, which exist because of opportunistic behaviors like cheating by part manufacturers and the bounded rationality of enterprises, transactions in external markets become more uncertain and risky. Enterprises thus tend to develop internal markets and shift those contracts to internal organizations with hierarchical regulations that involve less uncertainty. For instance, an auto company may establish a part manufacturing division through the acquisition of a part manufacturer to stabilize the production process and reduce its cost relative to external consignment. Although Williamson successfully explained opportunistic behaviors as purposive action to achieve an objective under given social situations and their institutional outcomes, he does not satisfactorily explain why individuals or companies behave opportunistically. One may complement Williamson's ideas regarding opportunistic behaviors by inquiring into individuals' motivations and their behavioral mechanisms.

Opportunistic behaviors may be complementarily explained based on individuals' psychological levels, as dialectic solutions to the problem of balancing different individual incentives: self-interest oriented and social norm oriented. Obviously, individuals seek to pursue their interests based on their self-preservation instincts, but we also observe that most individuals conform to the social norms of the society or organization they inhabit. According to Commons (1934), because interdependencies among people have increased in modern social systems, "working rules" that prevail in "going concerns" include various kinds of organizations or institutions, such as markets, enterprises, nations, families, and so on, and have become increasingly important to individual decision-making or behaviors. For instance, a market transaction process involves a set of rules or business customs that are broadly accepted by participants. Most participants in market transactions follow those "working rules" to avoid being removed from the transaction process in the market relevant to their interests. Thus, we can say that individuals have norm-oriented incentives, namely, tendencies to follow working rules that regulate the transaction process as well as self-interest-oriented incentives.

[3]This behavioral assumption is originally proposed by Simon (1991).

Based on these two directions of individual incentives, one may explain the psychological mechanisms of an opportunistic behavior: as discussed above, these two orientations may superficially appear to involve conformance to social norms on the one hand, while on the other they seek to satisfy self-interest on a fundamental level. If one recalls the case of the part manufacturer, it becomes hard to accuse the manufacturer of cheating behaviors because superficially it does not deviate from social norms or market rules. Simultaneously though, the manufacturer is maximizing their self-interest under the limitations imposed by social rules. One may characterize opportunism as involving dual orientations of social norms and self-interest at the motivational levels.

2.3 Experimental Design

To examine the opportunistic behaviors discussed above, I modified the experiments of Cappelen et al. (2007). In the experiments, participants were asked to play a one-shot game involving both production and distribution. During the game, each participant was randomly matched with a partner to form teams of two players. Participants knew that they each had another team member, but the experiment was designed such that no participants, including the experimenter, were aware of the identity of their partners both during and after the experiment. The details of the game are as follows:

Production Stage In the production stage, participants were asked to earn a certain amount of points, and the total income earned by team members during this stage formed the team earnings. Each participant was given an initial endowment of 300 points. Participants were asked to invest their endowment in units of 100 points (i.e., they could invest 0, 100, 200, or 300 points). Points not invested were counted in a final payoff to the relevant participant. After deciding the investment amount, each participant automatically obtained a lotto number from a computer program, which attributed "2" with a probability of 50 % and a "4" with a probability of 50 %. Each income event at this production stage was counted by multiplying each investment amount by the lotto result. If a participant invested a_1 ($\in$ [0, 100, 200, 300]) and derives a lottery win q_1 ($\in$ [2, 4]), their production earning was $\pi_1 = a_1 q_1$ ($0 \leqq \pi \leqq 1200$). If the partner with whom a participant was paired invested a_2, derived a lotto win of q_2, and received production earnings $\pi_2 = a_2 q_2$, then the team's combined income became $\Pi = \pi_1 + \pi_2$ ($0 \leqq \Pi \leqq 2400$).

Distribution Stage In the distribution stage, a participant was asked to furnish a distribution proposal that separated total team income into two shares, one for each individual in the pair. After the production stage, each participant was informed of the relevant figures on the screen: his investment a_1, his lottery result q_1, his earnings $\pi_1 = a_1 q_1$, the investment of his partner a_2, the lottery result of his partner q_2, the earnings of his partner $\pi_2 = a_2 q_2$, and the earnings of the team $\Pi = \pi_1 + \pi_2$. Then, as in the dictator game, the participant was asked for a distribution proposal that divided the team's earnings between himself and his partner. After the proposals were given, one of the proposals offered by each member was randomly selected for implementation, and each individual's final profit was decided accordingly.

Payment The total points of the individual's distributed final profit were added to a non-invested endowment that was converted based on 1 point = 1 yen (100 yen is approximately $1) and paid to each participant after the experiment.

2.4 Models, Hypotheses, and Predictions

In this section, I wish to explain the hypothesis of this chapter by summarizing the premises that form the basis of previous models on decision-making regarding distribution. I first describe the five premises of models from previous experimental studies regarding individuals' decision-making and then explain my hypothesis for this research.

2.4.1 Previous Models and Premises

To explain the results of distribution experiments such as the dictator or ultimatum games, Fehr and Schmidt (1999) developed a model of value function, consisting of individuals' utility function and social utility function. In those experiments, subjects were asked to distribute a given amount of money (e.g., $10) with their team members. Most distribution experiments saw many subjects share the available pies with the partners in their pairs equally instead of taking the maximum possible for themselves, contradicting classical utilitarian predictions. Thus, they regarded individuals as having a tendency to avert inequality and as having negative utility owing to a deviation from equal distribution. The model of Fehr and Schmidt (1999) presupposes that individuals try to maximize their value function, consisting of utility function and social utility function, by deciding the amount y_i to be distributed to themselves in the distribution process. That is, individuals decide distribution amounts for themselves and their colleagues to satisfy their material utility as well as their social utilities according to their model.

In their model, a function of the social utility of an individual i is expressed as a negative function of deviating from an egalitarian distribution where team income is split equally among team members. A social utility function is expressed as

$$S_i = -\lambda_s\left(y_i - \frac{\Pi}{n}\right)^2 \quad (0 \leq \lambda_s, 0 \leq y_i \leq \Pi),$$

where Π denotes total team income, λ_s denotes the loading factor for the social utility, and n denotes the number of team members. In a case involving two team members ($n = 2$) and where \$10 is the total amount available for distribution, denoted as Π, the ideal amount to be distributed to each team member should be \$5 $\left(= \frac{\Pi}{2}\right)$. In this case, if I distribute \$7 ($y_i = 7$) to myself, it must yield negative utility of $-\lambda_s\,(5-7)^2$ by deviating from the ideal distribution under egalitarianism. In this case, the optimal solution for maximizing S_i is to follow ideal egalitarianism in determining the appropriate distribution to oneself: $\left(y_i = \frac{\Pi}{2} = 5\right)$. Thus, we can derive the following premise:

Premise 1: Individuals hold a social utility function, which is expressed as negative utility in accordance with its deviation from a certain ideal social norm. [4]

According to the model of Fehr and Schmidt (1999), individuals try to maximize their value functions consisting of a utility function and a function of the social preference that decides the optimal allocation. The utility function increases with increasing self-distribution amount y_i, where $U_i = u\,(y_i)\ \frac{dU_i}{dy_i} > 0$, whereas the function of social utility is expressed as negative utility according to its deviation from the ideal social norm as expressed above. Individuals also assign a certain weight to each material utility and social utility expressed as a load factor for each function. That is, in each individual material utility and social utility exist in parallel and that individual has a preference between them. The value function is expressed as follows:

$$\max_{y_i} V_i = U_i + S_i = \lambda_m y_i - \lambda_s\left(y_i - \frac{\Pi}{n}\right)^2$$

where λ_m denotes the loading factor for material utility. Thus, we can derive the following premise:

Premise 2: Individuals try to maximize value functions. Individuals' value functions are expressed as linear combinations of utility function and social function, each with load factors of utility and social utility.

Additionally, some experimental studies showed a variety of fairness ideals rather than only egalitarianism as is described above, but also showed that some individuals adhere to other forms of distributive justice, such as liberalist or liberal egalitarian distributions. The basic experimental design of those studies was that subjects were required to earn a specific amount of money under a given set of production rules and to distribute the money earned between themselves and the individuals they were paired with. For instance, the experiments of Cappelen et al. (2007) showed that some individuals distributed according to the earnings of

[4]The original model of Fehr and Schmidt (1999) distinguished positive and negative deviation, with individuals having a stronger incentive to deviate on the positive side (e.g., in the case above the possibility exists of a positive deviation reaching as high as \$7 and a negative deviation reaching as low as \$3, representing a \$2 deviation on either side of the ideal of \$5), but for simplicity this difference is ignored here.

each team member in a production process, while others adhered to the distributive justice of liberalist egalitarianism, which considers factors individuals can control (e.g., sum invested) and ignores factors they cannot control (e.g., lottery results). Thus, we can derive the following premise:

Premise 3: Variety of fairness ideals or distributive justice. Individuals can hold different fairness ideals that can influence forms of distributive justice.

In the case of different fairness ideals, it is also presupposed that individuals keep premise 2, which holds that value function consists of utility function and social function, where $V_i = \lambda_m y_i - \lambda_s (y_i - F^k)^2$, whereas F^k denotes ideal distribution amounts according to a certain fairness ideal (e.g., egalitarian, libertarian, liberal egalitarian). Thus, we can identify the following premise:

Premise 4: Individuals adhere exclusively to one of the fairness ideals in a given situation. They try to maximize the value function, consisting of the utility function and the function of committed fairness. Thus, it is presupposed that individuals may be ambivalent between material utility and a certain fairness ideal, but not between different fairness ideals.

According to Hoffman and Spitzer (1985), the results of distribution experiments with production showed that experimental institutions, rules governing the game and payment, and the experimental environment strongly affected subjects' decision-making during the distribution process. They performed distribution experiments with different treatments in a production process that may reflect subjects' ability, efforts and moral consideration, and investigated how subjects' fairness ideals differed according to differences in production methods. To derive interpretations from given experimental results in different treatments, they simply summarized the premises related to preference and experimental institutions as follows: "i) Each subject concurs with a particular concept of fairness in distribution (also known as a theory of distributive justice). ii) Each subject perceives the experimental institutions as triggering a particular aspect of their concept of justice, and as indicating the distribution or set of distributions that is fair within that experiment. iii) The subject implements his perceptions of a fair distribution." (p. 260) Here, they presuppose that certain fairness ideals, which a subject potentially holds, emerge for certain given institutional conditions. This simple principle is logically expressed as $(\forall i)\,(P_i \wedge R_a) \rightarrow p_{ia}$ where P_i denotes a set of social preferences (or distribution justice) $P_i\left(p_{ik} \in P_i \middle| p_{ik} = p_{i1},\, p_{i2}, \ldots p_{in}\right)$ that an individual *i* potentially holds and R_a is a given experimental institution (rules of a game). I summarize the premise as follows:

Premise 5: Individuals hold a certain set of social preferences regarding distribution justice before the start of the experiment, and a certain set of experimental institutions (formal rules set in experimental design) invokes one of those preferences.

The option of distributing the entire pie to oneself is included among the fairness ideals because some individuals regard it as fair under certain situations.

2.4.2 Hypotheses

Based on the premises presupposed by the models of previous experimental studies, I here propose three hypotheses on individual incentives and behaviors in relation to distribution.

First, I shall discuss the tendency of individuals to be averse to the exposure of their own selfishness. The value function that presupposes individuals have both material utility and social utility, as explained in premises 1 and 2, is quite reasonable. We know that most individuals are neither fundamental idealists nor complete egoists, but rather are a mix of both. We live in a society that requires us to follow certain social norms (or risk social exclusion) and more or less have to be selfish to survive following the law of self-preservation. However, even given the social utility that coexists in the minds of individuals, individuals are nevertheless averse to exposing their selfishness to others, and hence we should consider the existence of a feeling of "shame." Because social norms in themselves are constituted or internalized through the eyes of others, how others evaluate one's behavior becomes important. Additionally, following social norms in itself may bring social advantage—such as long-term relationships based on trust or social cooperation—thus, individuals should have an incentive to be seen by others as "good" people and to try to hide their selfishness in public.

Hypothesis 1: Aversion to exposing selfishness. Individuals simultaneously hold social and utilitarian preferences. However, those who hold a certain degree of social preference (who are not completely selfish, but care to some extent about social norms) also have a tendency to be averse to the exposure of their selfishness and hence to have an incentive to hide it.

The second hypothesis is that individuals tend to use opportunities given within a range of formal rules to satisfy both their social and utilitarian preferences. Thus, only when they have opportunities to conceal their selfishness under given social norms do they tend to satisfy their selfishness. This kind of behavior is not apparently egoistic but belongs to what Williamson called "self-interest seeking with guile," as is discussed in Sect. 2.2.

Hypothesis 2: Individuals tend to use opportunity under a given set of social rules to get advantages from the given conditions. By doing so, they satisfy their material utility while hiding their selfish motivations under certain social rules.

The third hypothesis is that individuals' fairness ideals under certain experimental institutions are not fixed but rather shift according to opportunities they can exploit. The previous model presupposes that individuals exclusively adhere to a single fairness ideal if a certain form of distribution justice is invoked by an experimental institution, as explained in premises 4 and 5. Individuals potentially have various fairness ideals, as is indicated in premise 3, but these ideals change according to available opportunities, and individuals tend to commit to a fairness ideal that is advantageous to their material utility. By doing so, they can satisfy both social norms and material utility, and their selfishness is hidden by the social norms they choose to follow.

Hypothesis 3: Flexibility of fairness ideals. Individuals, who are not completely selfish, tend to change their fairness ideals according to the opportunities provided within a given set of rules.

The concept of flexibility of fairness ideals concerns whether individuals' social norms or justice are based on the classical distinction in ethics between deontology and consequentialism. Deontology regards justice as a universal principle that decides what should or should not be done in a given situation. In contrast, consequentialism considers whether an action results in a preferable outcome. For instance, if one believes that "an eye for an eye" reflects universal justice, as maintained by deontologists, one should follow this principle in any situation, even when the committer of a wrong is the strongest individual in a society and attempts at enforcing justice are certain to fail. In the case of a consequentialist, one would consider whether acting in such a way actually brings preferable consequences. Where individuals understand justice in the sense of deontology, giving only formal rules is important because such rules simply invoke individual convictions regarding justice in universal form. However, if individuals judge justice based on whether it yields preferable outcomes, it becomes more flexible, and they should consider opportunities provided within the social rules. I do not deny some individuals hold deontologistic ideas of justice and act in a more fundamentalist way by following universal moral principles. However, this hypothesis presupposes that individuals, who are not completely selfish and have an incentive to follow social norms, try to achieve their material utility and social preferences by changing their fairness ideals according to available opportunities.

2.4.3 Value Functions, Fairness Ideals, and Predictions

2.4.3.1 Value Function

Here, I shall explain the value functions and fairness ideals of the experiments conducted in this paper and also provide predictions based on the hypothesis above.

Following the models of Fehr and Schmidt (1999) and Cappelen et al. (2007), which are explained above, an individuals' value function for distribution is expressed as follows:

$$V_i = \lambda_m y_i - \lambda_s \left(\frac{y_i - F^{k(i)}}{\Pi} \right)^2 \quad \lambda_m + \lambda_s = 1, \quad 0 \leq \lambda_m, \lambda_s,$$

where $F^{k(i)}$ denotes a fairness ideal of a participant i, y_i is the amount distributed to participant i, λ_m is the load factor to his material utility, and λ_s is the load factor to his fairness ideal. The first term in the formula on the right is a utility function, and the second term expresses that negative social utility produced as the amount y_i that is distributed to the participant himself deviates from his fairness ideal $F^{k(i)}$. The self-distribution amount y_i^* that maximizes i's value function V_i is expressed as:

$$\max_{y_i} V_i : \frac{\mathrm{d}V_i}{\mathrm{d}y_i} = 0 \quad y_i^* = F^{k(i)} + \left(\frac{\lambda_m}{1-\lambda_m}\right) \Pi.$$

One's optimum self-distribution y^* can be understood as a total of the ideal amount based on fairness ideals $F^{k(i)}$, and the amount a participant may add by selfish material utility $\lambda_m / (1-\lambda_m)\ \Pi$. Because $\lim_{\lambda_m \to 0} y^* = F^{k(i)}$, the self-distribution amount y_i^* approaches the ideal fairness amount as a participant's personal load factor on material utility λ_m approaches zero.

2.4.3.2 Fairness Ideals

The self-distribution amount based on a fairness ideal $F^{k(i)}$ that a participant i may commit can be defined as follows (see Hoffman and Spitzer 1985; Cappelen et al. 2007)[5]:

- Utilitarian:
  A utilitarian is defined as an individual who pursues self-profit and tries to maximize personal utility. Thus, a strict utilitarian will distribute team earnings entirely to himself as $F^U = \Pi$.
- Egalitarian:
  An egalitarian believes total team earnings should be shared 50:50 with the partner she is paired with. Thus, the distribution for herself is $F^E = \Pi/2$
- Liberalist:
  A liberalist thinks it is fair to distribute total team earnings according to the earnings of each member in the production stage. Thus, a strict liberalist distribution is $F^L = \pi_1$.

Based on the value function and fairness ideals above, individuals can be classified into five types according to the difference in degree of load factor on material utility and fairness ideals, as follows:

- Complete utilitarian:
  This type of individual is simply understood as a completely selfish person, who monopolizes team earnings for themselves and leaves nothing for the partner he

[5]Cappelen et al. (2007) also refers to a "liberal egalitarian," who distributes team earnings according to the amount each participant invested: $m^{LE} = a_1\Pi/(a_1 + a_2)$. However, this chapter does not consider the liberal egalitarian concept because the experimental design produces little evidence to support it.

is paired with. Thus, his load factor to material utility is maximized ($\lambda_m = 1$) and he distributes all team earnings to himself ($y^* = \Pi$).

- Selfish liberalist:
  This type of individual carries out a liberalist distribution, but maintains some degree of material utility ($0 < \lambda_m < 1$). Thus, the amount she distributes to herself is expressed as the ideal liberalist distribution plus some amount $\left(\frac{\lambda_m}{1-\lambda_m}\right)\Pi$, stemming from material utility. That is, $y^* = \pi_1 + \left(\frac{\lambda_m}{1-\lambda_m}\right)\Pi$, where $0 < \left(\frac{\lambda_m}{1-\lambda_m}\right)\Pi$.
- Fundamental liberalist:
  This type of individual engages in a fundamental liberalist distribution, meaning the amount distributed to themselves is identical to that under the ideal liberalist distribution: $y = \pi_1, \lambda_m = 0$.
- Selfish egalitarian:
  This type of individual engages in an egalitarian distribution but preserves some material utility ($0 < \lambda_m < 1$). Thus, the amount she distributes to herself is expressed as an ideal egalitarian distribution plus some amount α, stemming from material utility. That is,

$$y^* = \frac{\Pi}{2} + \left(\frac{\lambda_m}{1-\lambda_m}\right)\Pi, \quad \text{where} \quad 0 < \left(\frac{\lambda_m}{1-\lambda_m}\right)\Pi.$$

- Fundamental egalitarian:
  This type of individual carries out a fundamentally liberalist distribution, meaning the amount distributed to themselves is the same as under the ideal egalitarian distribution: $y^* = \frac{\Pi}{2}, \lambda_m = 0$.

2.4.3.3 Relative Earnings and Opportunities

Based on premises 4 and 5, Cappelen et al. (2007) presuppose that given an experimental institution that invokes one of the fairness ideals of individuals also determines the load factor of material utility. Thus, it is presupposed that given three types of individuals having preference sets P_i, P_j, P_k and given a certain experimental rule R_a, three types of fairness ideals p_{ia}, p_{ja}, p_{ka} should be invoked in the experiments: $\left(\left(P_i \vee P_j \vee P_k\right) \wedge R_a\right) \rightarrow p_{ia} \vee p_{ja} \vee p_{ka}$. In this case, the difference of opportunity given to each individual in the game rules is ignored, and thus it is presupposed that the conditions remain the same across these differences in opportunities: $\left(\left(P_i \vee P_j \vee P_k\right) \wedge R_a \wedge o_1\right) \simeq \left(\left(P_i \vee P_j \vee P_k\right) \wedge R_a \wedge o_2\right)$, where o_1, o_2 denotes different opportunities. Thus, the invoked fairness ideals should also be almost the same $\left(p_{ia} \vee p_{ja} \vee p_{ka}\right)$.

However, the observed results of individuals' fairness ideals can differ significantly according to given opportunities that affect individuals' implementation of distributive justice. For example, $(R_a \wedge o_1) \rightarrow p_1$ and $(R_a \wedge o_2) \rightarrow p_2$ are observed relatively frequently. Suppose examinations for students. The formal rules are simple and almost identical everywhere: students are expected to solve problems through their own efforts and without cheating. Those who achieve higher scores are rewarded (e.g., by obtaining permission for enrollment). Taking examinations in either room A or room B is an opportunity given to each student incidentally. If the scores of students in room A significantly exceed those of students in room B, even when the students are randomly allocated between the two rooms, teachers should consider the possibility that students in room A are cheating. In that case, students in room A may use an opportunity given to them (e.g., inadequate test monitoring) to achieve higher scores.

Here I distinguish three groups according to their situation in relation to relative earnings and identify them with respect to whatever opportunity they have or lack. These conditions are decided using given rules and incidentally also through individual decision-making and luck, as well as the partners they are paired with. Here, I identify "opportunity" as resulting in higher self-distribution, by changing (or shifting) fairness ideals.

- *Group without opportunity: relative earnings are neutral.* In this group, the earnings of individual team members are the same, and thus relative earnings are neutral. Moreover, the ideal egalitarian and liberalist distributions are the same, in this case $\frac{\Pi}{2} = \pi_1 = \pi_2$. This group lacks opportunity to obtain a higher distribution amount for themselves by changing their fairness ideals.
- *Group with an opportunity to shift from a liberalist to an egalitarian distribution: the relative earning for the subject controlling the distribution is lower.* In this group, the earnings of the subject *controlling* the distribution are lower than those of the partner he/she is paired with, $\pi_1 < \pi_2$. Thus, the ideal egalitarian distribution always results in the distributive actor receiving more than under the liberalist distribution $\pi_1 < \frac{\Pi}{2}$. Thus, even if one invokes his preference for a liberalist distribution by experimental institutions, one can receive more by shifting his fairness ideal to egalitarianism.
- *Group with an opportunity to shift from an egalitarian to a liberalist distribution, where the relative earnings of the subject controlling the distribution are higher.* In this group, an individual's earnings exceed those of the partner he/she is paired with $\pi_1 > \pi_2$. Thus, under the ideal liberalist distribution the distributing partner always receives more than under the egalitarian distribution $\pi_1 > \frac{\Pi}{2}$. Thus, even if an individual invoked his preference for an egalitarian distribution by experimental institutions, that individual can receive more for themselves by adopting a liberalist fairness ideal.

Based on the above classification and hypothesis, I propose three predictions of the experimental results.

First, individuals whose relative earnings are neutral tend to adhere to either an ideal utilitarian or ideal liberalist (=egalitarian) distribution. As discussed in Hypothesis 1, individuals who are not completely utilitarian have a tendency to be averse to their selfishness being exposed. They also do not have the opportunity to shift from one fairness ideal to the other and so commit to the ideal amount. Second, as explained in groups with opportunities, those with higher relative earnings have an opportunity to increase the distribution amount they receive by shifting from egalitarian to liberalism. Third, those with lower relative earnings have an opportunity to increase the distribution amount they receive by shifting from liberalism to egalitarianism and vice versa. These predictions come from Hypotheses 1, 2, and 3, which refer to individuals making use of their opportunity to change their fairness ideals and satisfy their material utility without exposing it. These predictions are summarized as follows:

Prediction 1: Individuals who are not completely selfish and whose relative earnings are neutral tend to be fundamental liberalists (egalitarians).

Prediction 2: Individuals who are not completely selfish and whose relative earnings are higher tend to uphold liberalist ideals of fairness as this brings them a higher distribution amount than egalitarianism.

Prediction 3: Individuals who are not completely selfish and whose relative earnings are lower tend to uphold egalitarian fairness ideals because these ideals bring them a higher distribution amount than being liberalist.

2.5 Experimental Results

I performed experiments consisting of a production stage and a distribution stage six times from November 2011 to July 2013 in the laboratory of Kyoto Sangyo University in Japan. This experiment is performed using an experimental program z-tree (Fischbacher 2007). Participants were assembled from undergraduate students attending Kyoto Sangyo University, including all departments, and the total number of participants was 134. Each experiment took approximately 30 min, including instructions. Before the game started, an experimenter read aloud an introduction describing the rule (see Appendix), after which the participants were free to ask questions. The experiment started once all participants understood the rules.

2.5.1 Statistical Description

Table 2.1 shows a statistical description of the experimental results. Three participants invested nothing, 32 invested 100 points, 53 invested 200 points, and 46 invested 300 points. Participant earnings ranged from a minimum of 0 points to a maximum of 1200 points, with an average of 622.38 points, and a mean of 600 points. The minimum for total team earnings was 400 points, the maximum was 2000 points, the average was 828.9 points, and the mean was 800 points. The average payment participants received was 716.42 yen. In Japan, the average

Table 2.1 Statistical description

	a	Π	Π	y
Min	0	0	400	200
Max	300	1200	2000	2000
Average	206	622.38	1245	828.9
Mean	200	600	1200	800

payment to students for an hour of work is approximately 1000 yen (almost $10), and thus the game result fully satisfied participants' opportunity costs.

2.5.2 Distribution in Group Without Opportunity

Graph 2.1 shows the correlation between self-earnings π_1 and the self-distribution amount y for a group with neutral relative earnings. The sloping line designates points where $y = \pi_1 = \frac{\Pi}{2}$. Note that relative earnings are the same for the neutral group. For $\pi_1 > \pi_2$, one cannot distinguish participant preferences for liberalist versus egalitarian ideals because in this case the distribution amounts are the same for both. Interestingly, and in line with prediction 1, the distribution amounts for all subjects who are not completely selfish (16 subjects) precisely matched the ideal liberalist-egalitarian amount. Most of the remaining subjects committed to a utilitarian distribution were also committed to an ideal utilitarian distribution in terms of actual distribution amount (one slight exception involved a utilitarian who distributed 1500 to himself given team earnings of 1600).

The results do not seem to match the previous model consisting of material utility and fairness discussed in premise 2, because in this study individuals are either fundamental utilitarians or fundamental liberalists-egalitarians. That is, individuals' load factors on material utility and fairness are all or nothing rather than combining both. $(\lambda_m, \ \lambda_s) = (0, 1) \vee (0, 1)$. Interestingly, including the case where relative earnings are different, 85 % of subjects committed to the ideal amounts under utilitarianism, liberalism, or egalitarianism. Thus, we propose the following:

Proposition 1: Most subjects committed to ideal distribution rates under utilitarian, liberalist, or egalitarian distributions. That is, most subjects were complete utilitarians, fundamental egalitarians, or fundamental liberalists, rather than selfish egalitarians or selfish liberalists.

2.5.3 Distribution in Groups with Opportunity

Graph 2.2 shows the correlation between the predicted value according to a liberalist distribution and the observed values from self-distribution. The sloped

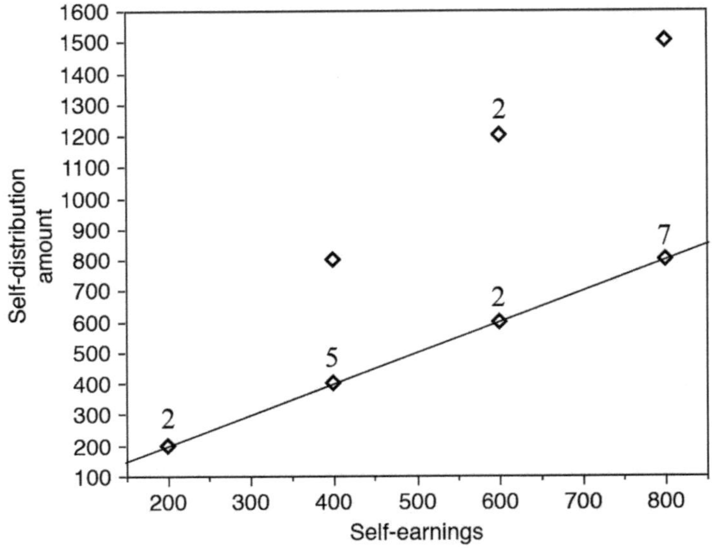

Graph 2.1 Correlation between self-earning and self-distribution amounts in the group with neutral relative earnings

line designates where the liberalist distribution rate matches the self-distribution rate. The horizontal line designates where the observed value of distribution rate is 0.5, that is, the ideal egalitarian distribution. The point where the sloped and horizontal lines meet designates where relative earnings are neutral, as explained above.

In line with predictions 2 and 3, we can see many subjects with lower relative earnings (+) were plotted on the horizontal line that designates the egalitarian distribution (27 participants), while many subjects with higher relative earnings (○) were plotted on the sloped line that designates the liberalist distribution (18 participants). A few subjects with lower relative earnings who committed to the liberalist distribution (5 participants) were also observed. Similarly, a few subjects with higher earnings committed to the egalitarian distribution (5 participants), but their number was relatively low. We can also observe a few subjects with higher relative earnings plotted between the egalitarian and liberalist distributions (7 participants), though their earnings were nearer to the liberalist distribution.

2.5.4 Fairness Ideals by Opportunities

Here, I examined the correlations between different opportunities identified in relative earnings and occurrence frequencies of different fairness ideals. Because most subjects implemented an ideal distribution according to a certain fairness ideal,

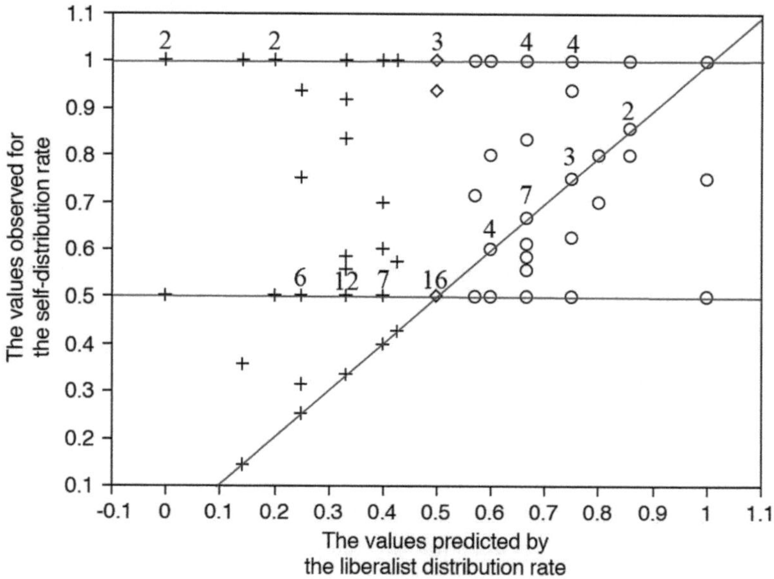

Graph 2.2 Correlation between the values predicted by the liberalist distribution rate and the values observed for the self-distribution rate. ○ Higher relative earning + lower relative earning ◇ neutral relative earning. **Diagonal line* designates points where the predicted and observed values are the same

I classified each subject according to a fairness ideal, where the residual norms become the minimums. That is, most subjects were either complete utilitarians, fundamental liberalists, or fundamental egalitarians, and few selfish egalitarians or selfish liberalists were observed. Thus, the load factor on material utility is estimated as zero (for egalitarian and liberalist) or one (for utilitarian) ($\lambda_m = 0, 1$) in this classification. Then, I examined the occurrence frequency of the fairness ideals based on participant relative earnings, as shown in Table 2.2.

As is described in Graph 2.1, 80 % of participants, who belong to the neutral group, committed to an egalitarian–liberalist distribution, while the remaining 20 % distributed their entire earnings to themselves. This result is in line with previous distribution experiments that excluded production and suggests that the participants' group, or experimental environment, does not significantly differ from previous studies, in which 20–35 % of subjects implemented selfish distributions (Forsythe et al. 1994).

As is shown in Graph 2.2 a sharp contrast was observed between liberalist and egalitarian participants in terms of their relative earnings. Participants with lower relative earnings significantly preferred the egalitarian distribution compared with participants whose relative earnings were higher. In contrast, participants with higher relative earnings preferred the liberalist distribution, while those with lower relative earnings tended not to. Interestingly, a few subjects were observed to

Table 2.2 Occurrence frequency of fairness ideals by relative earnings

Relative earnings	Fairness ideals				p-value[d]
	Utilitarian $N = 36$	Egalitarian $N = 49$	Liberalist $N = 26$	Ambivalent[a]	
High ($N = 57$)	16(28.1)[b]	**14(24.6)**	**21(36.8)**	6(10.5)	<0.0001
Low ($N = 57$)	16(28.1)	**35(61.4)**	**5(8.8)**	1(1.8)	
Neutral[a] ($N = 20$)	4(20)	16(80)	[16(80)][c]	0	

[a]Ambivalent describes participants who implement distributions that fall into the middle ground between egalitarian and liberalist, egalitarian and utilitarian, or liberalist and utilitarian distributions

[b]Numbers in brackets denote percentages

[c]Participants in the neutral group overlap with those in the egalitarian and liberalist distribution groups. To estimate the occurrence frequencies of the utilitarian, egalitarian, and liberalist groups, neutral participants are deselected from the population

[d]Estimated by Pearson's chi-squared test

implement an ambivalent distribution, and these ambivalent distributions clustered around the middle ground between the two fairness ideals.

Regarding utilitarianism, I could not find a significant difference in its occurrence rate in terms of relative earnings. Participants who committed to a utilitarian distribution, i.e., those who left nothing to the partners they were paired with, were observed to act independently of their relative earnings.

From these results, I could derive the following propositions:

- *Proposition 2*: No correlation exists between implementation of utilitarian distributions and the relative earnings of the individual implementing the distribution.
- *Proposition 3*: Individuals whose relative earnings are high compared with those they are paired with tend to implement a liberalist distribution.
- *Proposition 4*: Individuals whose relative earnings are low compared with those they are paired with tend to implement an egalitarian distribution.

2.6 Discussion

As summarized in Proposition 1, the experimental results of this study show that most participants (85 %) proposed distribution amounts completely compatible with either one of ideal utilitarianism, liberalism, or egalitarianism. Seven percent of participants committed to a median amount between two of these three ideals. This result is not congruent with the expectations of previous models summarized in premise 4, which describes individuals' value functions and consists of a linear combination of material and social utility and the load factor held by each individual

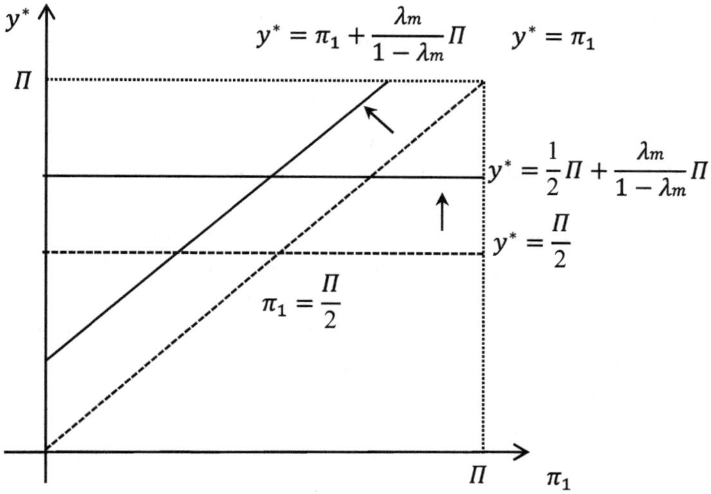

Fig. 2.1 Distribution of the previous model

to each utility.[6] In this model, the optimum distribution is a total of the ideal amount of fairness and the amount considering the "amount added owing to selfish incentives," $y^* = F^{k(i)} + \frac{\lambda_m}{1-\lambda_m}\Pi \; (0 < \lambda_m < 1)$. Thus, the distributions implemented by individuals who are not completely selfish should be observed in forms of selfish liberalism or selfish egalitarianism, as explained in Sect. 2.3.

Figure 2.1 shows that the optimal distribution for the actor implementing the distribution y^* expected by previous models, as amounts of an ideal fair distribution (egalitarian or liberalist) with additional selfish amounts. The dotted horizontal line in Fig. 2.1 expresses egalitarian ideal amounts: $y^* = \frac{\Pi}{2}$ egalitarian participants are expected to implement a distribution that gives themselves the amounts on the upward diagonal line $y^* = \frac{1}{2}\Pi + \frac{\lambda_m}{1-\lambda_m}\Pi$. Similarly, liberalist participants are expected to implement a distribution that gives themselves the amounts on the diagonal line shifted from the dotted diagonal line $y^* = \pi_1 + \frac{\lambda_m}{1-\lambda_m}\Pi$, which expresses liberalist ideal amounts, with these additional amounts taken based on selfish incentives, as is shown in Fig. 2.1. However, those additional amounts are observed in few participants in the experiment, and this phenomenon should be explained.

Do the experimental results mean that most subjects were either completely selfish or fundamental idealists? I think the premises of the previous model that presupposes that individuals hold both material and social utility are quite reasonable. However, the model overlooks another incentive of individuals, namely, that they are averse to the exposure of their selfishness as explained in Hypothesis

[6]Fehr and Schmidt (1999) themselves admit the linear model is not completely compatible with experimental observations (p. 847).

1. Because a social norm in itself is explained as an internalization of other people's views (cf. Smith 1759), it is strongly associated with a sense of shame. The "additional amounts by selfish incentives" described above imply the exposure of individual selfishness even in individuals whose behavior is consistent with a certain social norm. However, even if individuals are averse to the exposure of their selfishness through behavior consistent with certain social norms, their incentives to material utility will remain.

According to Festinger (1957), individuals that hold contradictory beliefs and consequently experience mental discomfort reflect what he calls "cognitive dissonance." Moreover, individuals experiencing cognitive dissonance try to resolve psychologically uncomfortable situations *by changing their beliefs*. For instance, the fox in Aesop's fables, having failed to obtain a grape, tried to resolve the cognitive dissonance between his desire for grapes and his frustration by changing his belief from "grapes are sweet" to "grapes are bitter." Experimental results show that the commitment of an individual to a given distribution principle can be understood as an outcome of an attempt to resolve their "cognitive dissonance" stemming from contradictory cognitions between material and social utility. Committing to a certain distribution principle may be followed by personal efforts to resolve cognitive dissonance.[7]

Propositions 2 and 3 summarize the experimental results that show a participant's commitment to liberalist or egalitarian fairness ideals significantly depend on their relative earnings. In the experiments, participants whose relative earnings were higher than those they were paired with displayed a significant tendency to commit to a liberalist distribution, whereas those whose relative earnings were lower tended to implement an egalitarian distribution. This result contrasts with previous studies that presuppose individual fairness ideals are invoked by experimental institutions, as summarized in premise 5. Because relative earnings incidentally give opportunities to subjects, not experimental institutions, if experimental institutions only affect the fairness ideals of subjects, they should be independent from relative earnings.

The experimental results show that individuals who engaged in opportunistic behaviors, namely, those who selected more *advantageous* fairness ideals (to satisfy distributive justice and their selfishness), did so because of their resolution of cognitive dissonance. Figure 2.2 describes the relation between relative earnings and fairness ideals. The left half of Fig. 2.2 indicates the range of lower relative earnings, whereas the right half indicates the range of higher relative earnings. Where relative earnings are lower, the egalitarian distribution $y = 1/2\Pi$ always brings a higher self-distribution than the liberalist distribution $y = \pi_1$; where relative earnings are higher, a self-distribution based on liberalist principles is always higher than one based on egalitarian principles and vice versa. As shown by

[7]Rabin (1994) states that cognitive dissonance decreases people's commitments to reciprocity because they cannot be completely ethical and then commit to selfish behavior without cognitive dissonance. For discussion on material utility and individual decision-making, see Konow (2000).

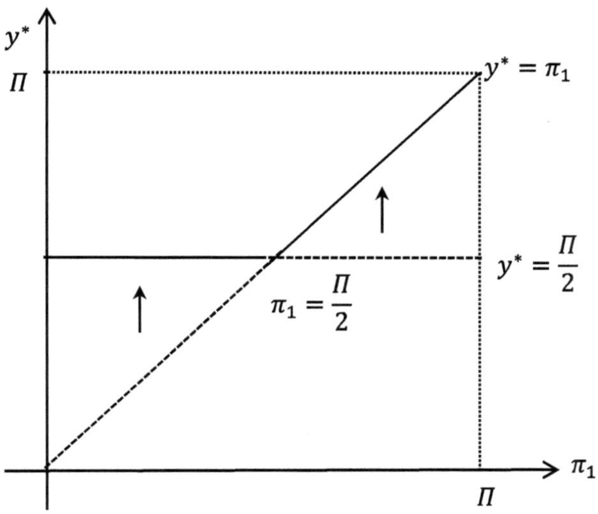

Fig. 2.2 Distribution of the opportunist model

the arrows in Fig. 2.2, participants have shifted their fairness ideals from liberalist to egalitarian given lower relative earnings and from egalitarian to liberalist under higher relative earnings. If participants' fairness ideals are coherent and independent of their relative earnings, those participants committed to egalitarianism should always distribute their team earnings 50:50, whereas participants committed to liberalism should implement an earning-based distribution. Such fundamentalist behaviors can be observed but are rare. Many participants prefer fairness ideals that bring them higher relative earnings: individuals with higher relative earnings display a significant preference for a liberalist distribution, whereas those with lower relative earnings prefer an egalitarian distribution.

As discussed in relation to the group without opportunity in Sect. 2.2, Williamson (1975) describes opportunistic behavior in terms of individuals seeking self-interest "with guile" while following social norms or rules. If a participant determines the self-distribution amount by adding a "selfish amount" to the ideal fair amount, as shown in Fig. 2.1, then that added amount exposes his selfishness. However, if an individual "commits" to a more advantageous fairness ideal, as expressed in Fig. 2.2, then her selfishness becomes hidden. On the surface, she seems to be a strict liberalist or egalitarian individual. In this sense, the premise of the previous model consisting of material and social utility is correct, but opportunities such as prevailing conditions and the flexibility of individuals' fairness ideals should be taken into consideration.

Interestingly, all subjects who were not utilitarian in the group with neutral relative earnings committed to precise liberalist-egalitarian distributions. As proposed in Hypothesis 1, this should come from those subjects in this group that lack opportunity to change their fairness ideals to increase their material utility.

In this group, the risk of exposure of selfishness is higher than in those groups with opportunities. Because if a subject who implements an earning distribution that is neutral to herself is being a selfish egalitarian (liberalist) such as $\Pi/2 + \alpha$ ($0<\alpha$), it is obvious that this addition of α is the result of their selfishness. On the contrary, the actions of subjects who implement distributions that see themselves receive a larger "additional amount" may be justified by liberalist fairness ideals rather than selfishness. Such subjects may believe that an egalitarian distribution is appropriate in this situation but based on liberalist ideas may also believe that they can legitimately add some amount for themselves over and above what they would receive under an equal distribution. The beliefs of such an individual may be motivated by having earned more than his partner. The logic is the same for a subject with lower earnings who is originally liberalist but shifts to become egalitarian. In Graph 2.2, we find a few subjects plotted in the triangle zones between egalitarian and liberalist. Thus, we could conclude that not only experimental institutions matter but opportunities also matter for the decision-making of subjects regarding distribution.

A possible criticism is that a group with higher relative earnings is likely to be classified as liberalist because "added material utility" lacks validity. This is because all non-selfish subjects that belong to a group with neutral relative earnings concentrated on precise amounts of fairness. Sixteen subjects were plotted at the point where the horizontal and slash lines are closest—the point relative earnings are the same in Graph 2.2. These data do not match the previous model described in Fig. 2.1, in which individuals add some selfish amount to the ideal fair amount. Even if we admit that each individual has a different degree of material utility, that amount should be distributed equally among subjects if it is independent of difference of opportunity. However, if we interpret the data as indicating that individuals with opportunities are more selfish than those without opportunities, we should conclude that the opportunities are conditions that cause individuals to add their material utility to the ideal amount of fairness.

As argued by Levitt and List (2007), besides morals, social norms are another important motivator of individual behavior. If an individual exposes his selfishness to others in an obvious way, he may be afraid of receiving a social sanction for violating norms. Individuals with different directional incentives related to fairness and selfishness might strategically "select" a more advantageous fairness ideal from among two possible distribution opportunities, rather than expose their selfishness by adding "selfish amounts" to their ideal fair share. Here, we can discover behavior that does not deviate from distributive justice, but statistically uses opportunities through *hidden and selfish incentives*. Opportunistic behavior allows an individual to satisfy his selfish incentives to an extent, without deviating from social norms. The previous models presupposed that an individual's optimum distribution amount can be defined such that "extra amounts resulting from selfish incentives" are added to the ideal amount according to a certain fairness ideal. However, the experimental results obtained in this paper show that individuals have a significant tendency to exclusively commit to a single distribution principle—whether strict utilitarianism or some other fairness ideal—and thus the value function of the previous model cannot satisfactorily explain the result. According to the experiments presented in this research, this tendency is an outcome of individuals' efforts to resolve the cognitive dissonance between their desire to maximize their material utility and fairness ideals through opportunistic behavior.

Applying the experimental results to real situations of opportunism, we could see the same mechanisms of satisfaction with both selfishness and a social norm utilizing opportunity. Suppose that a company requires a worker to perform a certain task until a specific deadline. To maintain task performance at a high level of quality until the given deadline requires that the worker do his best, but the worker always has selfish incentives to reduce his burden. If this was a case in which the company imposed a penalty for work delays, the worker may neglect his work by reducing his work quality to maintain work speed and avoid being penalized. If the company strictly checks quality, the worker may instead neglect his work by slowing down and extending deadlines. In this case, we regard the worker as strict about neither punctuality nor quality, but rather as an opportunist. Both actions are understood in terms of the worker making use of the opportunities available to him to satisfy his selfishness within the terms of the formal contract and social framework. In case a task delegation transaction occurs within a company with which that worker has longer relations, there should be less room for opportunism. In this way, transaction cost should be explained as strongly related to opportunistic behavior.

2.7 Conclusions

In this chapter, I demonstrated that many individuals do not fundamentally commit to a certain fairness ideal invoked by a certain experimental institution; instead, they strategically select an advantageous option from among several possible "fair" distribution principles. If an individual is not a strict utilitarian, willing to ignore social norms and pursue selfish behavior, he tends to hide his selfish motivation. Such an individual may strategically "select" a fairness ideal that is personally profitable without making any further selfish additions, thus hiding his selfishness and satisfying ethical (or social) justifications—all to resolve the cognitive dissonance between material utility and fair distribution.

Figure 2.3 summarizes three individual behaviors that emerged from fairness ideals and material utility. Behavior A describes some participants as fundamentally liberalist or egalitarian and as remaining faithful to a given form of distributive justice and then distributing earnings according to a coherent set of fairness ideals regardless of the situation. Behavior B reveals the more opportunistic behavior of individuals who opportunistically change their fairness ideals according to relative earnings. Their incentives arise from both fairness ideals (adhering to social norms) and hidden selfishness (to satisfy their material utility). Behavior C describes those who are purely motivated by material utility and who are not reluctant to hide their selfish incentives.

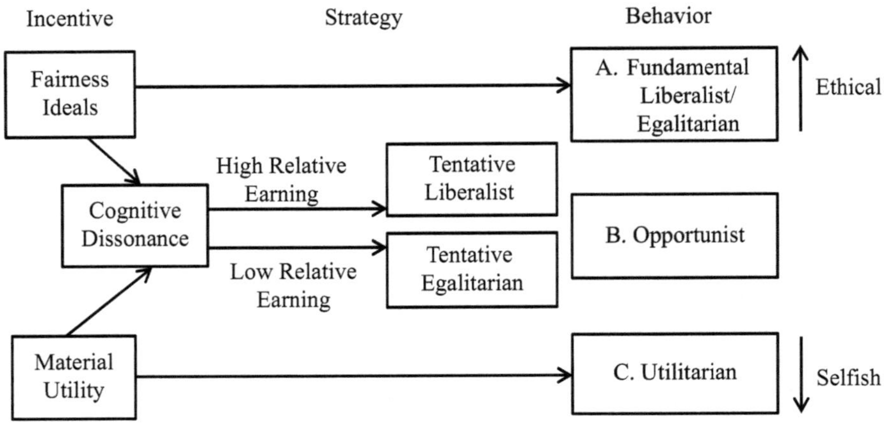

Fig. 2.3 Incentives and behaviors

Opportunists should not be classified as purely selfish or purely ethical because both these incentives are simultaneously present and individuals strategically hide their selfish incentives and assume "fair" behavior. Those who pursue opportunistic behaviors may suffer cognitive dissonance between distributive justice and selfishness and then strategically exploit different opportunities. By behaving opportunistically, individuals may be able to satisfy their selfishness within the contexts of social norms or given institutional conditions.

Appendices

- Experiment instructions

> Thank you very much for attending this economic experiment. An experimenter will now explain the rules of the game. Please read the instructions below carefully to ensure you understand the rules of the game. You can raise your hand to ask a question at any time should anything be unclear.

1. Endowment

   You will be given 300 points as an initial endowment in this game. You can invest the points in a lotto game in units of 100 points. You can choose to invest either all, some, or none of the initial endowment points in this way. That is, you can select among investment amounts of 0 point, 100 points, 200 points, and 300 points. Points that are not invested will be counted when calculating your final profit.

2. Lotto

   You will receive the winnings of the lotto game should you choose to invest in this way. There is a 50 % probability of receiving winnings that total either four times your investment ("very lucky") or two times your investment ("lucky") and a 50 % chance of receiving no winnings. Any points earned through the lotto game are counted toward your final score.

   For example, if you invested 100 points and won a "very lucky" lotto prize, your earnings would total: $100 \times 4 = 400$ 400 points.
3. Pair (two-member team)

   You are randomly matched with another participant to form a two-member team. The identity of your partner is unknown to you, as well as to other participants and experimenters both during and after the experiment.
4. Team earnings

   You and your partner's earnings are summed to form the earnings of your team. The team earnings are shown to you and your partner on each screen, together with information on the investment points, lotto results, and total earnings for each team member.
5. Distribution proposal

   After team earnings are shown on the screen, please make a distribution proposal regarding the sharing of team earnings between you and your partner. The total of the points you distribute to yourself plus those distributed to your partner should equal the total team earnings.

   For example, for total team earnings of 1000 points:

   Distribution for myself, 500; distribution for my partner, 500
6. Final profit

   Of the two distribution proposals, the one you made and the one your partner made, one is randomly chosen. The team earnings are then distributed according to the chosen distribution proposal. Any points you did not invest are counted toward your final profits.
7. Points conversion and payments

   Points are counted as 1 point equaling 1 yen and are paid at the conclusion of the experiment.

If there is anything you do not understand about the game, please raise your hand to ask.

References

Cappelen AW, Hole AD, Sorensen EO, Tungodden B (2007) The pluralism of fairness ideals: an experimental approach. Am Econ Rev 97(3):818–827

Cherry TL, Frykblom P, Shogren JF (2002) Hardnose the dictator. Am Econ Rev 92(4):1218–1221

Commons JR (1934) Institutional economics: its place in political economy. Macmillan, New York

Fehr E, Schmidt KM (1999) Theory of fairness, competition, and cooperation. Q J Econ 114(3):817–868

Festinger L (1957) A theory of cognitive dissonance. Stanford University Press, Stanford
Fischbacher U (2007) z-Tree: Zurich toolbox for ready-made economic experiments. Exp Econ 10(2):171–178
Forsythe R, Horowitz JL, Savin NE, Sefton M (1994) Fairness in simple bargaining experiments. Games Econ Behav 6(3):347–369
Hoffman E, Spitzer ML (1985) Entitlements, rights, and fairness: an experimental examination of subjects' concepts of distributive justice. J Leg Stud 14:259–297
Kahneman D, Knetsch JL, Thaler RH (1986) Fairness and the assumptions of economics. J Bus 59(4):285–300
Konow J (2000) Fair shares: accountability and cognitive dissonance in allocation decisions. Am Econ Rev 90(4):1072–1091
Levine DK (1998) Modeling altruism and spitefulness in experiments. Rev Econ Dyn 1(3):593–622
Levitt SD, List JA (2007) What do laboratory experiments measuring social preferences reveal about the real world? J Econ Perspect 21:153–174
Rabin M (1994) Cognitive dissonance and social change. J Econ Behav Organ 23(2):177–194
Simon H (1991) Bounded rationality and organizational learning. Organ Sci 2(1):125–134
Smith A (1759) The theory of moral sentiments. (1981). Liberty Fund, Indianapolis
Williamson OE (1975) Markets and hierarchies, analysis and antitrust implications: a study in the economics of internal organization. The Free Press, New York
Williamson O (1985) The economic institutions of capitalism. The Free Press, New York

Chapter 3
What Is "Fair" Distribution Under Collaboration?: Evidence from Lab Experiments

Abstract In recent decades, increasing numbers of enterprises and organizations are introducing performance-based pay systems to increase labor productivity. However, some empirical studies show that this style does not always have the intended effects and can even trigger adverse outcomes such as declining teamwork. Some studies note that failures of performance-based pay systems may be attributed to a mode of collaborative production, wherein each production process is mutually connected, and each worker's output depends on that of others; thus, it is hard to accurately measure individual performance. By performing distribution experiments followed by production, we examined which fairness ideals or distribution principles—selfish (take-all), performance based, or egalitarian—individuals prefer to commit to in different production modes (collaborative or independent working style) and different conditions of performance information. Our experimental results showed that a significant number of subjects engaged in the collaborative working style preferred to perform egalitarian distribution and were less selfish than those engaged in the independent working style. We also observed that a significant number of participants who were informed of each team member's performance preferred performance-based pay, whereas those without such information preferred egalitarian distribution. The results imply that in the collaborative working style, wherein individual performance information is opaque, workers tend to support egalitarian fairness ideals. This may partly explain recent failures in implementing performance-based pay systems.

Keywords Mode of production • Distribution • Fairness ideals • Performance-based pay • Egalitarianism

---

This chapter is a joint work with Hiroyuki Uni.

N. Tokumaru, *Social Preference, Institution, and Distribution*, Evolutionary Economics and Social Complexity Science 3, DOI 10.1007/978-981-10-0137-6_3

3.1 Introduction

In recent decades, an increasing number of enterprises have introduced performance-based pay[1] with the aim of increasing productivity. According to a survey based on data from the European Working Conditions Surveys (2000–2005) and the General Social Survey (2002–2006), almost 50 % of private enterprises in the USA and more than 15 % of those in the EU have introduced performance-related pay (Boeri et al. 2013). Even in Japan, where seniority-based wages have traditionally been dominant, many enterprises introduced annual salary systems that incorporated performance-based characteristics from the 1990s. According to the survey on Japanese human recourse management by the Japan Productivity Center, the number of enterprises implementing such annual salary systems increased from 10 % in 1996 to 40 % in 2002.

Performance-based pay is usually introduced in the expectation that it will increase labor productivity by linking worker output and wages, thus giving workers an extrinsic incentive to increase their productivity. Some empirical studies corroborate these assumptions, especially in the case of simple labor work. Shearer's (2004) field experiment in a tree-planting firm in Canada showed that increases in piece rate pay increased worker productivity by at least 20 % relative to workers on a fixed wage. Lazear (2000) investigated approximately 3000 workers in an auto glass company that changed its payment regime from hourly pay to piece rate pay in 1994 and 1995 and found that this change increased average output per worker by approximately 44 %, half of which can be attributed to incentive effects (other reasons for the increase include that the change helped the firm hire more productive workers).

However, many empirical studies report that the reality of performance-based pay does not always match expectations based on theory and can even have adverse effects (Lawler 1987; Perry et al. 2009), especially in situations that involve *organizational labor work*. Some studies (Drago and Garvey 1998; Burks et al. 2009) report that workers become less cooperative with their colleagues under performance-based pay. Others (Lawler 1987; Milgrom and Roberts 1992; Freeman and Kleiner 2005) report difficulties in evaluating individual performance in complex and organizational production processes.[2] In fact, few organizations implement pure performance-based pay; in most cases, performance-based pay is introduced in a mixed form that combines incentive pay with a fixed wage range (Boeri et al. 2013). The survey on labor conditions by Japan's Ministry of

[1]In this research, we exclusively present the information in terms of individuals' performance-based pay or piece rates, which link worker performance to remuneration. Group performance pay or other forms of financial participation by employees are beyond the scope of this paper.

[2]A case study by Freeman and Kleiner (2005) showed that a shift from a piece rate to fixed pay in a US shoe company in the early 1990s increased profitability despite worker productivity being higher under the former system. This apparent contradiction is explained by the fact that the costs associated with monitoring worker performance required by the piece rate pay system offset the increase in productivity.

Health, Labour and Welfare reported that the number of enterprises implementing performance-based pay has been gradually decreasing since the 2000s.

The characteristic contrast between simple labor work and organizational labor work should explain why performance-based pay tends to succeed in the former and fail in the latter, from the perspective of worker fairness ideals and motivations. Consider a worker engaged in the solitary production of violins. The entire production process, including wood cutting, parts assembly, and body staining, is done by the worker himself. The worker will be satisfied with receiving 1000 dollars for the ten violins he has made, based on a price of 100 dollars per violin. In this case, he regards performance-based pay as fair reward for his own work, because the link between wages and production is clear. However, in contrast to the simple individualistic working style, since the twentieth century, most job tasks have come to be performed collaboratively rather than independently. Workers must work cooperatively with their colleagues, and the outcomes achieved by individual workers depend to different degrees on those achieved by their colleagues. In the case of automobile production at Toyota, each production process, such as welding, assembly, painting, and checking, is strongly connected with other processes, all of which are necessary to car production. The Kaizen system of Toyota, which improves the quality and productivity of each production process, requires worker collaboration. Thus, organizational performances are not mere aggregations of individual worker performances but rather the product of interactions and cooperation with other workers. If one worker receives 100 dollars while another receives 70 dollars for their different "performance" contributions to the production of a car that sells for 1000 dollars, the second worker may become dissatisfied. In this case, workers may regard a performance-based payment as "unfair" and lose motivation because much of their individual performance depends on the performance of others. Workers may also see it as reasonable to focus solely on certain tasks most relevant to their personal performance while neglecting tasks that support others.

A collaborative working style also finds it intrinsically difficult to evaluate the performance of individual workers in situations where worker motivations are also involved. Because under a collaborative working style each production process is closely connected with others, it becomes increasingly difficult to distinguish which output belongs to which worker and accurately evaluate individual worker performance. Thus, the introduction of performance-based pay in a collaborative working process always carries risks of improper performance evaluation. Workers may regard their wage as "unfair" based on a feeling that it does not correctly reflect their efforts and may suffer a loss of motivation as a consequence. Actually, the survey on human resource management and worker attitudes under a diversified working style conducted by the Japan Institute for Labour Policy and Training in 2005 reports that workers dissatisfied with their wage as determined by their companies (36 %) outnumbered satisfied workers (23 %). The top reason for worker dissatisfaction was that "their efforts are not properly evaluated," while the second reason was "their performance is not properly evaluated." According to Kessler (1994), the necessary condition for improving worker motivation through performance-based pay is the existence of a clear link between the achievement of performance goals and pay (see also Guzzo and Katzell 1987). It is reasonable for workers to lose their incentives if managers fail to measure their performance correctly. A recent empirical study by Brenčič and Norris (2010) discussed how employers are less likely to offer performance-based pay in multitasking, quality control, or teamwork because of difficulties in appropriately evaluating employee performance in such jobs. Because of this difficulty in measuring performance in collaboration situations, performance pay may contradict workers' sense of fairness, which in turn may trigger dissatisfaction with their payment or poor work motivation.

If managers introduce a payment system without considering worker fairness ideals, resulting in a gap between the payment system and those fairness ideals, workers will become dissatisfied and demotivated. Thus, the fairness ideals workers support under a certain working environment matter to the introduction of a payment system in that they incentivize workers to be more productive. Additionally, if a difference in working style (simple or collaborative) relates to worker fairness ideals, we should identify the effects on those differences and fairness. Bregn (2013) observed that employee norms are significant in a payment system. Moreover, Brown and Walsh (1994) discussed the significance of notions of fairness for worker motivation owing to their connections with worker self-esteem: if workers' fairness ideals are such that they believe they are not appropriately compensated for their work, those workers may become demotivated. Performance pay may improve employees' job commitment provided they believe the payment scheme is more "fair" than fixed pay. Thus, the fairness ideals that workers possess in a specific working condition are key to ensuring a successful payment system.

By performing lab experiments consisting of both production and distribution stages, this study examines three types of fairness ideals—(1) selfish (take-all), (2) performance based, and (3) egalitarian—to determine which type individuals prefer across different production modes of independent/collaborative working style and different conditions of access to performance information. In our experiment, subjects were paired a partner, worked to earn money on behalf of their team, and finally were tasked with distributing team earnings with their partner. We set up four treatments, each with a different production process: (1) an independent production style with information on each team member's performance, (2) an independent production style without performance information, (3) a collaborative production style with performance information, and (4) a collaborative production style without performance information. We classified each of the subject distribution proposals as belonging to one of the three possible fairness ideals, (1) selfish (take-all), (2) performance based, and (3) egalitarian, and examined the coefficient between these four treatments and the occurrence rate of each fairness ideal.

Notably, this study does not intend to clarify a link between a certain payment system and its positive/negative consequences on factors such as productivity[3] but to clarify the fairness ideals that individuals uphold and are triggered by specific

[3]Dohmen and Falk (2011) performed a laboratory experiment in which subjects were asked to choose between fixed or variable payment, with piece rate payment being an example of the latter.

production processes. Taking individuals' spontaneous norms into consideration is important because fairness ideals matter for both financial reasons and in terms of their motivation.

We also attempt to contribute to the literature on experimental studies examining individual distribution behavior by introducing a set of new experimental designs in the production stage, specifically designs that involve a collaborative working style. Several previous experimental studies have contributed to clarifying subjects' distribution of behavioral changes in terms of justice or selfishness under different experimental conditions, such as social context, anonymity, or production style (Kahneman et al. 1986; Forsythe et al. 1994; Hoffman and Spitzer 1985; Cherry et al. 2002; Cappelen et al. 2007). In those experiments, subjects were asked to distribute a sum of money that was either given as an endowment or produced independently from other members. However, these behaviors have not been examined in the context of a collaborative production style. To examine how a collaborative working style affects individuals' fairness ideals, we designed a production stage in which subjects can communicate and collaborate with their team members through the chat function of a computer program.

The results of our experiment are intriguing. A significant number of participants engaged in collaboration preferred an egalitarian distribution, whereas subjects engaged in an independent working style preferred a performance-based distribution. Those who were notified of team member performance information chose performance-based pay, whereas a significant number of participants without such information preferred an egalitarian distribution. Furthermore, it is interesting to note that the increase of labor dependency on other team members as well as the transparency of performance information significantly impacts subjects' use of a selfish distribution pattern. The results of our experiment show that individuals favor an egalitarian distribution under circumstances of collaboration with insufficient performance information. This finding may partly explain some of the failures of performance-based pay under collaboration, wherein individual output is closely linked to the output of others, and it is hard to measure individual performance.

This study is organized as follows. Section 3.2 explains the historical discussions of piece rate remuneration by Marx, Webbs, and Cole. Section 3.3 describes the experimental design, game rules, and treatments. The models and hypothesis are proposed in Sect. 3.4, while the experiment results are described in Sect. 3.5. Finally, after having discussed on the results in Sect. 3.5, Sect. 3.7 gives conclusions.

The experimental results indicated that subject productivity was significantly higher under a piece rate than under fixed payment.

3.2 Marx, Webbs, and Cole: Studies on Two Types of Payments

Marx (1887), in *Capital* (Vol. 1, Parts 1–6), analyzes the historical transformation of labor activity from simple cooperation to mechanized industry by way of the division of labor; identifies patterns accompanying changes in labor productivity, wage, and working hours; and then discusses wages. One of the major conclusions of his analysis on labor process is that such transformation leads to an increase in labor productivity owing to stronger interdependency among workers and stronger dependency of workers on machinery. In other words, according to Marx, a quantitative increase in labor productivity brings a qualitative change in labor formation. Rather than products being direct reflections of the individual productive power of each worker, they become realizations of the "social productive power" (ibid., p. 230) of total workforce and total machinery, which are closely related. As a result, the relation of individual labor to its output becomes obscure.

However, he did not extend his analysis on qualitative transformation in labor formation to consider enhanced interdependency among workers, and thus his analysis of income distribution and sages obscured individual worker output. Most of Marx's discussion is based on the premise that the relation of individual labor to output is self-evident, and each worker's labor productivity becomes known to capitalists and workers through experience. Marx sees the issue largely from the viewpoint of capitalists' wage policy, saying, "piece-wage is the form of wages most in harmony with the capitalist mode of production" (ibid., p. 392) because, according to him, "superintendence of labor becomes in great part superfluous," promotes "sub-letting of labor," and "enables the capitalist to raise more easily the normal degree of intensity of labor." (ibid., p. 391) Marx points out the coexistence of piece wages and time wages but does not understand this as related to fairness ideals.

Regarding fairness ideals in relation to wages, Marx's analysis on the transformation of labor process would be complemented by the empirical study conducted by S. Webb and B. Webb (1897) on trade unions under two different types of payment. According to research conducted by the Webbs in 1894, the opinions of trade unions were split with regard to the form of payment preferable as a basis for the standard wage rate. At that time, 44 % of trade unions supported piece wages—with examples including the unions for miners and textile workers—and 57 % of union members belonged to such unions. Meanwhile, 34 % of trade unions preferred time wages—with examples being the unions for mechanics, carpenters, and brick builders—and 29 % of union members belonged to such unions (ibid., pp. 286–287). This situation, where not merely capitalists but almost half of the trade unions supported piece wages, seems to contradict the thesis of Marx (1887) on piece wages as "the form of wages most in harmony with the capitalist mode of production" (ibid., p. 392). Webb and Webb gave a detailed analysis to explain this seeming paradox and the reason for the divergence of opinions among workers.

Following the studies by Webb and Webb, G.D.H. Cole (1918) clearly explained the split of opinion among workers regarding different payment types—time wages versus piece wages. Referring to the measurability of outputs, he states:

> In trades in which the unit of output is highly standardized, so that output is as a rule commensurate with effort, systems of payment by results are for the most part accepted without serious question. In other trades in which either there is no ready unit of measurement, or at least output varies widely from time to time and from case to case, owing to causes which cannot easily be reduced to mathematical formulae, the Trade Unions, wherever they are strong enough, usually offer strong opposition to the adoption of payment by results instead of time-work. (p. 108)

Thus, Cole as well as Webb and Webb concluded that different fairness ideals of workers in relation to payments reflect differences in the discernibility of the contributions of individual workers to the whole output, which led to differences in the opinions of trade unions emerging on occupational lines. However, Cole did not endorse the idea that this divergence of opinions caused by differences in the technological nature of occupations influenced trade unions. He argued that workers in sectors where individual payment by results was already established should seek a transition to collective payment by the results option under the collective control of workers. He made this argument based on the judgment that "the fruits of the common labour of all should be equitably shared among all" (p. 112).

However, Webb and Cole overlooked a fact pointed out by Marx: interdependency among workers also affects their fairness ideals. Thus, their analysis of the effects of mechanization on workers' fairness ideals is one-sided. They inferred that mechanization promotes the adoption of payment based on results because it contributes to increasing numbers of standardized and repetitive jobs that can be performed at a fixed speed and also increases the discernibility of individual worker contributions (Webb and Webb 1897, p. 302; Cole 1918, p. 9). The history of the twentieth century contradicted this inference: whereas mechanization greatly advanced, the number of workers paid according to results significantly decreased. The forecast of Webb and Cole may reflect they are missing the way in which mechanization influenced workers' fairness ideals: as Marx already pointed out, mechanization deepens interdependency between workers, which in turn drives change in worker fairness ideals by increasing opposition to payment based on results.

3.3 Experimental Design

Based on the discussions in the previous section, I have designed economic experiments to clarify how different degrees of labor independency and performance information in production processes affect individuals' fairness ideals. My experiment is a modification of previous distribution experiments involving production (Hoffman and Spitzer 1985; Cappelen et al. 2007). The experiment is designed to examine individuals' preferences regarding certain fairness ideals under different production modes and levels of access to performance information. The details of the experimental design are as follows.

Every participant is randomly paired with another by computer, but partner identities were kept hidden from participants and experimenters both during and after the experiment. Each experiment consists of two stages: a production stage and a subsequent distribution stage. In each production stage, participants are required to earn points by performing a numerical calculation task. Each subject's answers are scored, and this score determines his/her individual income. The individual incomes of both team members are then combined to yield total team earnings. After completing a production stage, each subject is required to submit a distribution proposal that separates total team income into two shares, one for themselves and one for their partner. A computer randomly selects one of the two proposals from each team, and total team earnings are then distributed according to the selected proposal. A final profit for each participant is then calculated by summing whatever points they did not invest in the production stage with the distributed team earnings.

The four treatments in our study differ in terms of production modes and performance information, thus enabling comparison of the impact of these factors. The four treatments are as follows:

- IW *with*-PI treatment: An independent working style where the performance information of each team member is available to all team members.
- In this treatment, during each production stage, each subject is required to work with 100 numerical calculations, independently of his/her team member. Random double digits are displayed in odd-numbered questions (e.g., Q1.12, Q3.34, Q5.56, etc.), and subjects can get a correct answer to the question by multiplying 8 by the double digits. In even-numbered questions (Q2, Q4, Q6, etc), characters like AQX (AQ1, AQ3, AQ5, etc), meaning a correct answer of QX, are displayed. Here, subjects can correctly answer even-numbered questions by multiplying 8 by AQX. Subjects receive 4 points for each correctly answered odd-numbered question and 16 points for each correctly answered even-numbered question. Subjects are allocated 15 min for answering questions. The maximum subject earnings are 1000 points if all questions are answered correctly.

  After the production stage, individual performance information is displayed on the subjects' screens. Specifically, this information comprises a subject's point earnings, the point earnings of the pair to which he/she belongs, and total team earnings calculated by aggregating the earnings of each team member.
- IW *without*-PI treatment: An independent working style *without* access to individual performance information.

  In this treatment, subjects are engaged in the same tasks as in IW *with*-PI treatment, but subjects are not shown individual performance information. Instead, after the production stage, subjects can only see total team earnings on their screens.
- CW *with*-PI treatment: A collaborative working style *with* access to performance information for each team member.

  In this treatment, a subject is required to work with 100 numerical calculations similar to those in the independent working style. However, during the production process, each subject must collaborate with his/her partner. Half of the given questions are designed to be unanswerable without knowing the answer of one's

Table 3.1 Example of collaborative work

Questions of team member A	Correct answers of team member A	Questions of team member B	Correct answers of team member B
Q1. 12	Q1. 96 (=12 × 8)	Q1. A1	Q1. 768 (=96 × 8)
Q2. A2	Q2. 2176 (=272 × 8)	Q2. 34	Q2. 272 (=34 × 8)
Q3. 56	Q3. 448 (=56 × 8)	Q3. A3	Q3. 3586 (=448 × 8)
Q4. A4	Q4. 4992 (=624 × 8)	Q4. 78	Q4. 624 (=78 × 8)

partner to a certain question. As shown in Table 3.1, random double-digit numbers are displayed in the odd-numbered questions (Q1, Q3, etc.) for team member A, whereas random double-digit numbers are displayed in the even-numbered questions (Q2, Q4, etc.) for team member B. Like the independent working style treatment, subjects can correctly answer the question by multiplying these two-digit numbers by 8. Team member A's even-numbered questions show characters like AX (A2, A4, A6, etc.), which means an answer of QX is displayed for team member B. Team member A must answer by multiplying 8 by AX for the even-numbered questions, while team member B must answer similarly for the odd-numbered questions. To obtain AX information from one's partner, a chat box is displayed on the left side of each participant's screen. Each participant can communicate with his/her team member via the chat box during the production stage. Subjects get 4 points for correctly answering a double-digit question and 16 points for correctly answering an AX question. All participants are given 20 min to answer the questions. Following the production stage, individual performance information, namely, points earned by each individual participant, points earned by his/her partner, and total team point earnings as calculated by aggregating each team member's individual earnings, are shown on the subject's screen.

- CW *without*-PI treatment: A collaborative working style *without* each team member's performance information.

  In this treatment, subjects performing under a particular working style are engaged in a process similar to that in the CW *with*-PI treatment. In this treatment, each individual's performance information is given to their partners, but only total team earnings are shown on their screens after the production stage.

The final profit in terms of the number of points each subject earned in an experiment is converted into yen and paid in cash. Following the experiments, we performed a short anonymous questionnaire survey to determine participants' views regarding the experiments.

3.4 Models, Hypothesis, and Predictions

The three possible fairness ideals that subjects may choose in the distribution stage are assumed to be (1) *selfish* (take-all), (2) *performance based*, and (3) *egalitarian*. Under the strict selfish distribution, all team earnings go to the proposer himself, leaving nothing to his partner. The strict performance-based distribution sees team earnings distributed according to the individual earnings of the team members during the production stage. Finally, the strict egalitarian proposal distributes team earnings equally between team members. Naturally, not all subjects strictly follow these fairness ideals. In the next section, we will explain the classifications applied to those who slightly deviated from strict fairness ideals.

Now, let us consider a value function V_i of an individual i, whose self-earnings in the production stage are π; belongs to a team with total earnings of Π and distributes to himself/herself an amount y ($0 \leq y \leq \Pi$). We assume person i has a given endowment vector $\lambda_i = (\lambda_i^S, \lambda_i^P, \lambda_i^E)$, $(0 \leq \lambda_i^S, \lambda_i^P, \lambda_i^E \leq 1, \lambda_i^S + \lambda_i^P + \lambda_i^E = 1)$, which designates the loading factor for each fairness ideal, where λ_i^S denotes *selfish*, λ_i^P represents *performance based*, and λ_i^Edenotes *egalitarian*. Person i maximizes his value function by deciding self-distribution y as follows:

$$\underset{y}{\text{Max}}\ V_i = V_S + V_P + V_E = \lambda_i^S\left(\frac{y}{\Pi}\right)^2 - \lambda_i^P\left(\frac{\pi - y}{\Pi}\right)^2 - \lambda_i^E\left(\frac{\Pi/2 - y}{\Pi}\right)^2$$

Where $V_s = \lambda_i^S\left(\frac{y}{\Pi}\right)^2$ is the material utility that person i can get from self-distribution, $V_P = -\lambda_i^P\left(\frac{\pi-y}{\Pi}\right)^2$ designates the negative utility triggered by a deviation from the ideal performance-based distribution π; and $V_E = -\lambda_i^E\left(\frac{\Pi/2-y}{\Pi}\right)^2$ designates the negative utility triggered by a deviation from ideal egalitarian distribution $\Pi/2$. Suppose that we have three extreme types of individual s, namely, *S*, *P*, and *E*, who exclusively prefer one of the three fairness ideals: strictly selfish, strictly performance based, or strictly egalitarian. The value function and optimum distribution of each extreme can be expressed as follows:

- Strictly selfish

$$\lambda_S = (1,\ 0,\ 0) \qquad V_i = V_S = \left(\frac{y}{\Pi}\right)^2 \quad y^* = \Pi$$

- Strictly performance based

$$\lambda_P = (0,\ 1,\ 0) \qquad V_i = V_P = -\left(\frac{\pi - y}{\Pi}\right)^2 \quad y^* = \pi$$

- Strictly egalitarian

$$\lambda_E = (0,\ 0,\ 1) \qquad V_i = V_E = -\left(\frac{\Pi/2 - y}{\Pi}\right)^2 \quad y^* = \frac{\Pi}{2}$$

With respect to production conditions, let us define the degree of performance information disclosure as θ $(0 \leq \theta)$ and the degree of labor dependency with the other team member in the production process as δ $(0 \leq \delta)$. Degree of performance information disclosure refers to the intensity of performance information disclosure regarding individual earnings in the production process. As explained in Sect. 3.2, it reaches a maximum for the "*with*-PI" (performance information) treatment and a minimum for the "*without*-PI" treatment. Degree of labor dependency means the degree to which an individual's productivity depends on that of another team member. This reaches a maximum under the collaborative working style (CW) treatment and a minimum under the independent working style (IW) treatment.

Regarding the degree of performance information disclosure θ and individuals' fairness ideals or distribution incentives, we offer the following three hypotheses:

Hypothesis 1A: If the degree of performance information disclosure increases, individuals' incentives to choose selfish distribution decrease: $\frac{\partial V_S}{\partial \theta} < 0$.

Hypothesis 1B: If the degree of performance information disclosure increases, individuals' incentives to choose performance-based distribution increase: $\frac{\partial V_P}{\partial \theta} > 0$.

Hypothesis 1C: If the degree of performance information disclosure increases, individuals' incentives to choose egalitarian distribution decrease: $\frac{\partial V_E}{\partial \theta} < 0$.

Hypothesis 1B is clear because individuals choose performance-based distribution more easily in situations offering transparency of performance information than situations where performance information is lacking. If performance information is disclosed, individuals are less likely to choose an egalitarian distribution, as Hypothesis 1C designates. Incentives to leave nothing to others should decrease if individuals know the outputs or contributions to team earnings of other team members, as Hypothesis 1A expresses.

Regarding degree of labor dependency between team members in production process δ, we offer the following three hypotheses:

Hypothesis 2A: If the degree of labor dependency between team members increases, individuals' incentives to choose selfish distribution decrease: $\frac{\partial V_S}{\partial \delta} < 0$.

Hypothesis 2B: If the degree of labor dependency between team members increases, individuals' incentives to choose performance-based distribution decrease: $\frac{\partial V_P}{\partial \delta} < 0$.

Hypothesis 2C: If the degree of labor dependency between team members increases, individuals' incentives to choose egalitarian distribution increase: $\frac{\partial V_E}{\partial \delta} > 0$.

If labor dependency increases, individuals' output during production largely depends on cooperation with other team members. In such cases, it becomes hard to differentiate one's own performance from that of team members. Thus, in this condition, individuals avoid a performance-based distribution as indicated in Hypothesis 2B and instead favor an egalitarian distribution as designated in Hypothesis 2C. If the majority of a team's earnings are attributable to collaboration between members, then selfish distribution should decrease, consistent with Hypothesis 2A.

Table 3.2 Predictions for maximum and minimum load factors

	Load factor of fairness ideal			
Type of treatment	Selfish (take-all) ($1/\alpha\delta\theta$)	Performance based ($\theta/b\delta$)	Egalitarian ($\delta/c\theta$)	Prediction
IW with-PI		Max	Min	2A, 3B
IW without-PI	Max			1A
CW with-PI	Min			1B
CW without-PI		Min	Max	2B, 3A

Taking the above six hypotheses on production conditions into consideration, we assume for simplicity that individuals have compound fairness ideals expressed by the following vector of loading factors: $\lambda = \left(\frac{1}{a\delta\theta}, \frac{\theta}{b\delta}, \frac{\delta}{c\theta}\right)$, where a, b, and c are positive constants. Accordingly, individuals' value function V can be expressed as follows:

$$V = \frac{1}{a\delta\theta}\left(\frac{y}{\Pi}\right)^2 - \frac{\theta}{b\delta}\left(\frac{\pi - y}{\Pi}\right)^2 - \frac{\delta}{c\theta}\left(\frac{\Pi/2 - y}{\Pi}\right)^2.$$

Information disclosure intensity approaches a maximum ($\theta \to \infty$) under the *with*-PI (performance information) treatment and approaches a minimum ($\theta \to 0$) under the *without*-PI treatment. Similarly, labor dependency intensity approaches a maximum under the CW treatment and a minimum under the IW treatment. Taking those relationships into consideration, one can infer maximum and minimum load factors for each treatment, as shown in Table 3.2.

From these considerations, the above six hypotheses can be converted into the following six predictions (see also Table 3.2):

Prediction 1A: From Hypotheses 1A and 2A, selfish distribution is maximized in the IW *without*-PI treatment.

Prediction 1B: From Hypotheses 1A and 2A, selfish distribution is minimized in the CW *with*-PI treatment.

Prediction 2A: From Hypotheses 1B and 2B, performance-based distribution is maximized in the IW *with*-PI treatment.

Prediction 2B: From Hypotheses 1B and 2B, performance-based distribution is minimized in the CW *without*-PI treatment.

Prediction 3A: From Hypotheses 1C and 2C, egalitarian distribution is maximized in the CW *without*-PI treatment.

Prediction 3B: From Hypotheses 1C and 2C, egalitarian distribution is minimized in the IW *with*-PI treatment.

The hypotheses and predictions proposed here will be examined in depth in the next section.

3.5 Results

3.5.1 Overview

The experiments were performed in a laboratory at Kyoto University, Japan, in July 2014, and 130 participants were recruited from among undergraduate students across all faculties at the university. Approximately 20 % of the subjects were female. This almost matches the ratio of females among undergraduate students at Kyoto University. Experiments were performed nine times, and an average of 14.4 subjects participated in each experiment. At the beginning of each experiment, an explanation of the game rules was read aloud by an experimenter. Participants could ask questions if anything was unclear. Each experiment commenced only after all participants sufficiently understood the rules. Each experiment took an average of around 45 min, including the instruction and payment periods. All experiments were performed using the experimental software *z-tree* (Fischbacher 2007).

Table 3.3 shows the average figure for each parameter by treatment type. The table reveals that the average for self-production in the IW treatment group (844.58) was clearly higher than that in the CW treatment group (486.29). This finding indicates that tasks were easier in IW than in CW, which required subjects to calculate questions and communicate with their partners simultaneously. In fact, in the anonymous questionnaire survey administered after the experiments, 57 % of subjects from the CW treatment groups answered that the calculation tasks made them feel tired (responses of "very tired" or "tired" to a question that allowed them to select one of five answers expressing degree of feeling), in contrast with 47 %

Table 3.3 Parameter averages by treatment type

	Averages of parameters			
Type of treatment	Individual production (π)	Team production (Π)	Self-distribution (y)	Self-distribution rate (y/Π)
IW with-PI ($N = 32$)	850.4	1700.8	1147.5	0.679
IW without-PI ($N = 30$)	838.4	1676.8	1265.2	0.763
CW with-PI ($N = 30$)	500.0	1000.0	570.5	0.585
CW without-P ($N = 38$)	475.5	950.9	613.6	0.655
CW total ($N = 68$)	486.3	972.6	594.6	0.624
IW total ($N = 62$)	844.6	1689.2	1204.5	0.720
With-PI total ($N = 62$)	680.8	1361.7	868.3	0.633
Without-PI total ($N = 68$)	635.6	1271.2	901.1	0.703

of subjects from the IW treatment group who answered similarly.[4] Interestingly, despite the average size of the profit available for distribution (i.e., team production) being somewhat smaller in the CW treatment group (972.5882) than the IW group (1689.161), the average self-distribution rate in the CW treatment group (62.4 %) was almost 10 % lower than in the IW group (72.0 %).[5]

Participants in the CW treatment group were paid an average of 1286.29 yen, while those in the IW treatment group were paid an average of 1644.58 yen, totals determined by converting final profit points including the show-up fee to yen (100 yen is roughly equal to 1 US dollar). In 2014, the average hourly wage in urban areas of Japan was 956 yen according to a survey by the Recruit Jobs Research Center (2014); thus, the payment in our experiment, which took an average of 45 min to complete, sufficiently satisfied participants' opportunity cost. Almost 70 % of participants across all treatments responded to our questionnaire survey that they were satisfied (responses of "very satisfied" or "satisfied" to a question allowing them to select one of five responses expressing degree of feeling) with their final payments.

3.5.2 Classification of Fairness Ideals

As discussed in the previous section, we assumed three possible fairness ideals and judged which of them each subject chose according to two classification criteria: (1) divergence rate of subject self-distribution from their individual production (μ), defined as $\mu = \frac{|y-\pi|}{\pi}$, ($\mu \geq 0$), and (2) distance of subject self-distribution from an egalitarian distribution (d), defined as an absolute value of the difference between 0.5 and the self-distribution rate (y/Π, a proportion of self-distribution out of total team earnings), expressed as $d = |0.5 - y/\Pi|$, ($0 \leq d \leq 0.5$). The second criterion resembles the Gini coefficient, which is used to measure income inequality. Using these two criteria, we classify each subject's fairness ideal as follows:

- Selfish (take-all): ($\mu > 0.25$ and $d \geq 0.25$) or ($\mu \leq 0.25$ and $d > 0.49$)
- Performance based: $\mu \leq 0.25$ and $0.01 \leq d \leq 0.49$
- Egalitarian: ($\mu > 0.25$ and $d < 0.25$) or ($\mu \leq 0.25$ and $d < 0.01$)

[4]This inference is partly based on the free descriptions by subjects contained in the questionnaire. Some CW treatment participants wrote that they felt pressured by the tasks in the production stage because of the need to communicate with their partner. Almost no IW treatment participants offered such comments.

[5]We do not consider a difference of team production between the CW and IW treatments in our analysis as previous experimental studies reported a change in the stakes only weakly affects subjects' distribution rates (Cf. Camerer 2003).

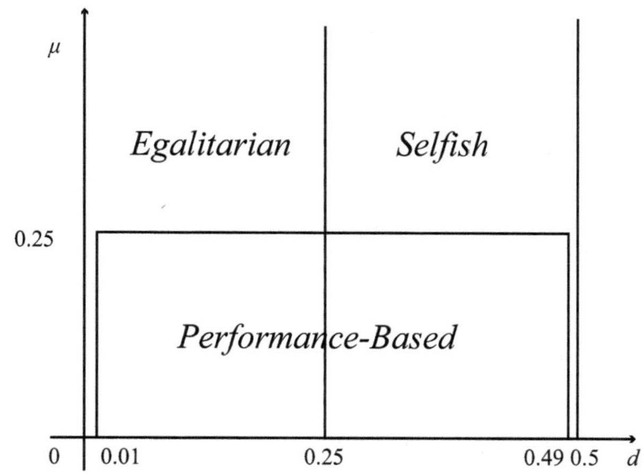

Fig. 3.1 Classification of fairness ideals

Table 3.4 Component ratio of fairness ideals for each treatment type

	Component ratio of fairness ideals %			P-value[b]
Type of treatment	Selfish (take-all)	Performance based	Egalitarian	
IW with-PI ($N = 32$)	34.38(11)[a]	46.88(15)	18.75(6)	0.0068
IW without-PI ($N = 30$)	50.00(15)	26.67(8)	23.33(7)	
CW with-PI ($N = 30$)	13.33(4)	56.67(17)	30.00(9)	
CW without-PI ($N = 38$)	31.58(12)	23.68(9)	44.74(17)	
IW total ($N = 62$)	41.9(26)	37.10(23)	20.97(13)	0.0362
CW total ($N = 68$)	23.53(16)	38.24(26)	38.24(26)	
With-PI total ($N = 62$)	24.19(15)	51.61(32)	24.19(15)	0.0073
Without-PI total ($N = 68$)	39.71(27)	25.00(17)	35.29(24)	

[a]Figures in parentheses indicate numbers of subjects
[b]Estimated by Pearson's chi-square test

If we place the divergence rate μ on the vertical axis and the distance from egalitarian distribution d on the horizontal axis, three fairness ideals can be mapped, as in Fig. 3.1.

3.5.3 *Fairness Ideals by Treatment*

Following the classification criteria above, we determined the occurrence ratios of the three fairness ideals in each type of treatment. Table 3.4 shows the numbers and occurrence rates of each fairness ideal on a treatment basis. Our main findings here were threefold, as described below.

Interestingly, the results of our experiments showed that 50 % of subjects in the IW *without*-PI treatment group chose a selfish distribution versus 13.33 % of subjects in the CW *with*-PI treatment group, consistent with our Predictions 1A and 1B. These figures are statistically significant and also corroborate Hypotheses 1A and 2A. As we can see from comparing the total rates of selfish (take-all) choices for subjects in the CW groups (23.53 %) versus the IW groups (41.9 %), labor dependency on other workers significantly contributes to reduced occurrence of selfish distribution. Similarly, performance information disclosure seems to significantly decrease selfish (take-all) distribution, as shown by comparing its occurrence between the groups *with*-PI (24.19 %) and *without*-PI (39.71 %). Thus, we can derive the following thesis:

Thesis 1: Increase of labor dependency significantly decreases selfish (take-all) distribution, and increase of performance information disclosure significantly decreases selfish (take-all) distribution.

Second, we found that providing performance information significantly increases the occurrence rate of performance-based distribution, while labor dependency does not affect the occurrence rate of the performance-based fairness ideal. More than half of the subjects in the *with*-PI treatment group adhered to the performance-based fairness ideal (51.61 %) versus only a quarter of those in the *without*-PI group (25.00 %). This result is in line with Hypothesis 1B, which assumes that information disclosures increase the occurrence of the performance-based fairness ideal. However, it is interesting to note that labor dependency does not decrease the occurrence of performance-based fairness ideals, as becomes clear if we examine the rates of adherence to performance-based pay between the CW treatment group subjects (38.24 %) and IW treatment group subjects (37.10 %). This result is inconsistent with the predictions of Hypothesis 2B. Thus, our second thesis is as follows:

Thesis 2: Increase of performance information disclosure significantly increases the occurrence of performance-based distribution, whereas intensity of labor dependency does not affect the increase of performance-based distribution.

Third, we found that labor dependency significantly contributes to the increased occurrence of egalitarian distribution, and lack of performance information significantly increases adherence to the egalitarian fairness ideal. As predicted in Hypotheses 3B and 3A, only a small number of subjects with IW in the *with*-PI treatment group chose an egalitarian distribution (18.75 %) versus nearly half of the subjects with CW in the *without*-PI treatment group (44.74 %). These results are compatible with our Hypotheses 1C and 2C, which we can also confirm through our finding of a significant numerical difference in egalitarian behavior between the whole of the IW cohort (20.97 %) and the CW cohort (38.24 %), as well as through the difference between the whole of the *with*-PI cohort (24.19 %) and the *without*-PI cohort (35.29 %). Our third and final thesis is as follows:

Table 3.5 Maximum and minimum occurrence ratios of each fairness ideal

	Fairness ideal			
Type of treatment	Selfish (take-all)	Performance based	Egalitarian	Prediction
IW with-PI			Min*	2A, 3B
IW without-PI	Max*			1A
CW with-PI	Min*	Max		1B
CW without-PI		Min*	Max*	2B, 3A

Note: Each asterisk (*) indicates a confirmed prediction

Thesis 3: Increase of labor dependency significantly increases the occurrence rate of egalitarian distribution, and decreased disclosure of performance information also increases egalitarian distribution.

The results of our experiments were consistent with the predictions made in Sect. 3.3, except for prediction 1B, based on Hypotheses 1B and 2B, as indicated in Table 3.5. As explained above, Hypothesis 1B was confirmed by the coefficient data between the participants that completed PI treatment and those that did not, as well as the occurrence rate of performance-based fairness. Thus, we can conclude that our experiments disprove Hypothesis 2B, which assumes labor dependency increases the occurrence of performance-based distribution, whereas the other five hypotheses were confirmed.

3.6 Discussion

As revealed by the experimental results presented in the previous section, our primary findings were that both labor dependency and the disclosure of performance information have significant effects in terms of decreasing selfish behavior, as described by Thesis 1. In the CW *with*-PI treatment, the rate of selfish (take-all) subjects who retained all team earnings for themselves and left nothing to their partners remained less than 15 %, whereas half the subjects in the IW *without*-PI treatment were selfish (take-all). These figures significantly deviate from the results of previous distribution experiments without a production stage, which found a selfish (take-all) distribution rate range of 20–30 % (Cf. Camerer 2003).

This result related to selfishness may stem from participants' enhanced awareness of other workers belonging to the CW group as well as conditions regarding performance information. Subjects from the IW group had no opportunity to directly recognize their partner during the production stage. Subjects only know that their partner seems to have contributed to team earnings via a screen displaying information on the team's production results before distribution. In contrast, subjects belonging to the CW group always recognize their partner during the production stage and communicate via chatting. We further confirmed this assumption in our postgame questionnaire survey, in which some subjects from the IW group described their reason for retaining all the team's earnings for themselves as "not knowing their partner." The same description was extremely rare among CW subjects. Similarly, subjects informed of individual performance information were more conscious of their partner than those informed only of total team earnings, based on a recognition that both they and their partner contributed to total team earnings. These results on refrained selfishness are consistent with previous studies, implying that subjects' selfish incentives are further enhanced under experimental conditions where they experience a social distance from other subjects due to factors such as heightened anonymity (Hoffman et al. 1996; Cherry et al. 2002).

Our second thesis posited that whether or not subjects are informed of an individual's performance before deciding on a distribution proposal is crucial to their adherence to the performance-based fairness ideal, whereas labor dependency does not influence adherence to performance-based distribution. Under both the independent and collaborative working styles, subjects with individual performance information were considerably more likely to choose performance-based distribution than subjects without such information. This result implies that, in the case of a performance-based pay system, transparency and appropriate measurement of individual performances are necessary requirements to uphold workers' fairness ideals. Even in the treatment of a collaborative working style, incentives to choose performance-based fairness were maintained in subjects who were informed of individual performances since our Hypothesis 2B was disproved. This finding suggests that individuals tend to prefer performance-based payment under conditions where their own output and that of their colleagues is clearly known. This explains that piece rate pay schemes effectively increase worker productivity when output is easily measurable.

However, while conditions of performance transparency could be realized in our artificially constructed laboratory and may also be possible in some of the simplest production systems, ensuring transparency could prove difficult in most modern workplaces, in which processes are more complex, interconnected, and integrated across many workers, as discussed in previous studies (Cf. Milgrom and Roberts 1992; Freeman and Kleiner 2005; Brenčič and Norris 2010). If an individual's performance cannot be measured and disclosed appropriately in a workplace, workers will naturally be unsatisfied with performance-based pay, viewing it as "unfair" and hence feel demotivated. This difficulty in measuring individual performances explains some of the unsuccessful results seen for performance-based pay, as already explained (Cf. Perry et al. 2009).

Our experiment also shows that labor independence significantly strengthens adherence to the egalitarian fairness ideal, as described in Thesis 3. Further, participants in the collaborative working style groups tend to choose a strong egalitarian distribution: many of them distribute team earnings 50:50 even in cases involving marked variation in individual earnings. This result is consistent with a theoretical study by Lazear (1989) that showed an egalitarian wage system is better than a performance-based pay system, which may reduce incentives for cooperation. In the collaborative working style, individual performance achievement strongly depends on partner cooperation, and effective teamwork improves team performance. Because one cannot achieve better performance without cooperation, a participant naturally takes an equal distribution with his/her partner for granted. In fact, some CW participants indicated in the comments in our questionnaire survey that they split the money evenly "because they worked together." Thus, we can conclude that collaboration in the workplace enhances egalitarian fairness ideals among workers.

Thesis 3 further indicates how lack of performance information promotes adherence to an egalitarian distribution. Taking into consideration the above result that disclosure of performance information increases performance-based fairness ideals, we can assume that in a workplace where individuals' performances cannot be correctly measured, workers tend to prefer egalitarian distributions over performance-based pay. This finding suggests that correctly measured performances or collaborative evidence for each performance is indispensable to garner worker support for the performance-based fairness ideal.

As previously discussed, most modern jobs require collaboration with others, implying it is difficult to precisely measure individual worker output. In this sense, it can be said that the CW *without*-PI treatment is the best approximation to common workplace conditions, and it is interesting to note that the egalitarian distribution was mostly supported in that treatment. However, neither the collaborative working style nor the scenario without performance information promotes adherence to performance-based pay but rather to egalitarian pay. Almost half the subjects in the CW *without*-PI treatment group distributed their team's earnings 50:50 with their partner, whereas less than one fifth of subjects in the IW style *with*-PI treatment group were egalitarian. From these results, we could assume that introducing performance-based pay in a workplace where work is carried out collaboratively, and therefore where accurately measuring performance is difficult, may contradict workers' fairness ideals and hence demotivate them.

From the discussion of the experimental results, we conclude that egalitarian distribution would be more compatible with the fairness ideals of individuals working under collaboration. Correctly measured performance information is required as a basis to support performance-based pay, but gathering this information may be difficult in situations where a collaborative working style is used. Additionally, workers cooperating with others have a significant tendency to distribute earnings equally with others. These results may partly explain recent failures of performance-based pay, given that recent collaborative and complex working conditions do not satisfy conditions where the performance-based fairness ideal is supported.

3.7 Conclusions

Collaboration with colleagues is the most frequently observed working style in many modern workplaces. Under such collaboration, goods or services are produced through cooperation between workers; thus, correctly measuring individual contributions to an outcome becomes difficult. Additionally, workers may feel an outcome is due not only to themselves but also to their colleagues, and hence that total team earnings should be equally distributed.

The results of our experiments showed that disclosure of correctly measured performance information is key to gaining support for performance-based distribution, but achieving such a measurement is difficult in most real workplace conditions. Our experiments further revealed that under collaboration, individuals were less selfish and preferred to divide total team earnings 50:50 with their teammates. From these results, we can conclude that egalitarian distribution is mostly compatible with workers' fairness ideals when they are working under collaboration.

These results partly explain the success of piece rate pay systems in situations that involve a simple independent working style and where performance measurement is easier. The results also partly explain the failure of performance-based pay in workplaces using a collaborative working style where the problem of performance measurement exists. Whether a specific payment principle or group performance-based pay will increase workers' productivity is beyond the scope of this paper but should be examined in future research.

Appendices

Instructions for IW with-PI Treatment

Thank you very much for participating in this economic experiment. A leader will now explain the rules of the game. Please read the instructions below carefully to understand the rules. You can raise your hand to ask a question at any time if you find anything unclear.

- Handouts

  Please check that all handouts are on the table in front of you: an instruction page, a blank sheet of paper, and a sheet for writing a distribution proposal.
- Participation fee

  You will receive 800 points (equivalent to 800 yen) as a participation fee, simply by attending and participating in this game. This show-up fee will be paid to all participants regardless of the total points they earn in the game.
- Pairs (two-member team)

  You will be pair-matched with another participant (in a two-member team) and will play a game. A computer will randomly select an individual to become your partner. No participants, including the experimenters, will know who is paired with whom during or after the experiment.

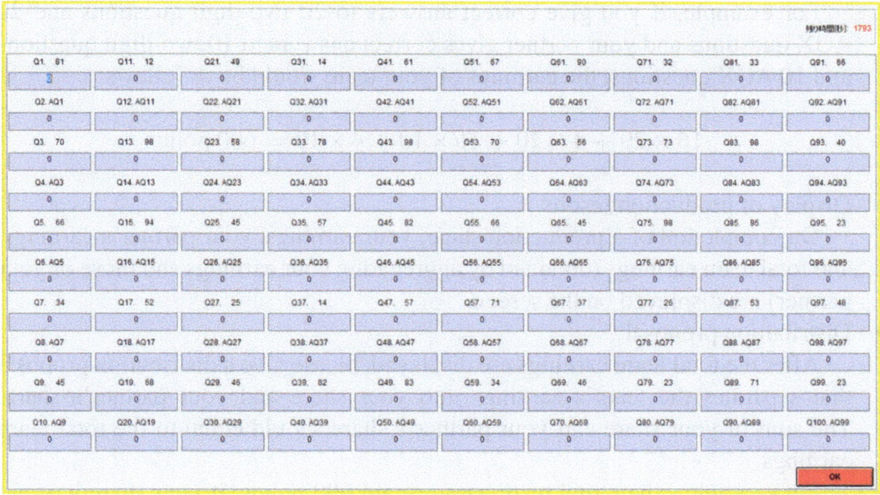

Fig. 3.2 Calculation task

Production (Calculation Task)

The game begins with the display of 100 questions on a screen. The question types alternate, with a two-digit question (Q1, Q3, Q5, etc.) being followed by an AQX question (Fig. 3.2).

These example questions differ from those that will be displayed in the actual task.

For two-digit questions, the correct answer is the figure obtained by multiplying 8 by every two-digit number. For AQX questions, the correct answer is the figure obtained by multiplying 8 by the correct answer to a previous question (i.e., the figure given by multiplying 8 by a two-digit number). Please input the appropriate data into each answer column on the screen. You can move the cursor to the next answer column by pressing the tab key.

Ex. Q1. 38 Correct answer: 304 $(=38 \times 8)$ Q2. AQ1 Correct answer: 2432$(=304 \times 8)$

You will receive 4 points for correctly answering a two-digit question and 16 points for correctly answering an AQX question. You can use the blank sheet of paper on the desk for your calculations.

The time allowed is 15 min. When an experimenter indicates, "15 min have passed. Please stop work and press the OK button at the lower right of the screen," please stop working and press the OK button on the screen. *Please do not press the OK button until an experimenter gives the signal.*

- Team earnings

  A team's total earnings are given by aggregating your earnings and the earnings of your partner (the other member of your team) in the production stage.

For example, if you give correct answers to 20 two-digit questions and 20 AQX questions and your partner gives correct answers to 10 two-digit questions and 10 AQX questions, the earnings of your team would be as follows:

$$16 \times 20 + 4 \times 20 + 16 \times 10 + 4 \times 10 = 600 \text{ points}$$

- Display of production results
  On completion of a production stage, your earnings, your partner's earnings, and total team earnings (obtained by aggregating your earnings and those of your partner) are displayed on the screen.
- Distribution proposal
  After the total team earnings are displayed, please give a distribution proposal that separates the team's earnings into your share and your partner's share. The sum of your share and your partner's share should equal to the total team earnings.
  For example, when total team earnings are 600 points, if your share is x and your partner's share is y in your distribution proposal, then $x + y = 600$. Please fill in your distribution proposal sheet, and then enter your distribution proposal after an experimenter gives the signal.
- Final profit of a game
  A computer randomly selects one distribution proposal out of those proposed by you and your partner. Total team earnings are distributed according to the selected proposal. These distributed earnings are added to the 800 show-up fee points to obtain the final profit points of each participant.
- Point conversion and payment
  Points are converted on the basis that 1 point = 1 yen and are paid to each participant upon conclusion of the game.

If you feel anything is unclear, please raise your hand.

Instructions for the IW Without-PI Treatment

All contents except for item 6 (display of production results) are similar to the instructions above for the IW *with*-PI treatment. However, item 6 in the IW *without*-PI treatment differs as follows:

- Display of production results
  After completing the production stage, total team earnings, which are obtained by aggregating your earnings and those of your partner, are displayed on the screen.

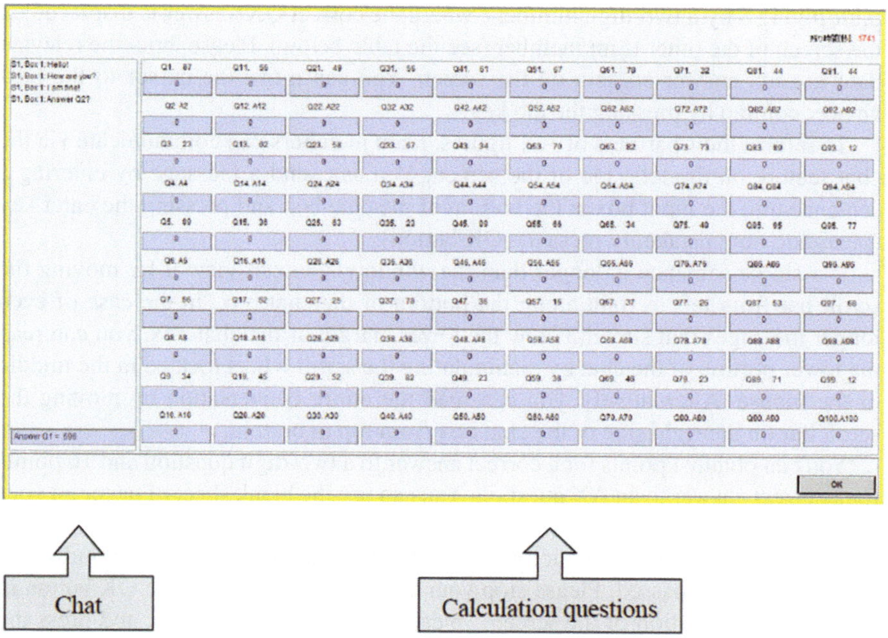

Fig. 3.3 Calculation task

Instructions for the CW with-PI Treatment

Contents except for item 4 (production [calculation task]) are the same as in the instructions for the IW *with*-PI treatment above. Item 4 in this treatment is as follows.

Production (Calculation Task)

At the beginning of a game, a chat is displayed on the left side of the screen, and 100 calculation questions are displayed on the right side of the screen (Fig. 3.3).

There are two types of questions, which differ by team member. On one member's screen, two-digit numbers are displayed for odd-numbered questions (Q1, Q3, Q5, etc.), and characters like AX (A2, A4, A6, etc.) are displayed for even-numbered questions (Q2, Q4, Q6, etc.). On the other team member's screen, two-digit numbers are displayed for even-numbered questions (Q2, Q4, Q6, etc.), and characters like AX (A1, A3, A5, etc.) are displayed for odd-numbered questions (Q1, Q3, Q5, etc.). The correct answer for two-digit number questions is obtained by multiplying the two-digit number by 8. The correct answer for AX questions is obtained by multiplying 8 by a correct QX answer (which in turn is obtained by multiplying 8 by a two-digit number), where the correct QX answer is displayed on the screen of the other team member (see the table below). Please input the relevant data to each answer column on the screen. You can move the cursor to the next answer column by pressing the tab key.

To inform their partners of AX figures, team members can communicate via the chat feature on the left side of the screen. You can send a message by entering a sentence into the input box at the bottom of the chat box and pressing the enter key (please do not mistakenly press the OK button).

If a single sentence is longer than the window, you can view it by moving the scroll bar from left to right along the bottom of the chat box. In the case of even longer messages that stretch below the lower margin of the chat box, you can read the lower portion of the chat by manipulating the scroll wheel located in the middle of the mouse. Alternatively, you can read the entire conversation by moving the scroll bar on the right side of the chat box from top to bottom.

You can obtain 4 points for a correct answer to a two-digit question and 16 points for a correct answer to an AX question. You can use the blank sheet of paper on your desk for your calculations.

The total available calculation time is 20 min. When an experimenter indicates, "20 minutes have passed. Please stop your calculations and press the OK button in the lower right portion of the screen," please stop your calculations, and press the OK button on the screen. *Please do not press the OK button until an experimenter gives the signal.*

Instructions for the CW Without-PI Treatment

Contents except for item 6 (display of production results) are the same as in the instructions for CW *with*-PI treatment above. Item 6 in this treatment is similar to item 6 in IW *without*-PI treatment.

- Your final profit

  The game has finished. Thank you very much for your participation in this economic experiment. We are going to hand out a questionnaire sheet and receipt. Please fill out the questionnaire sheet while we hand out your payment. You can leave the room after having received an envelope and confirmed your payment.

References

Boeri T, Lucifora C, Murphy KJ (2013) Executive remuneration and employee performance-related pay: a transatlantic perspective. Oxford University Press, Oxford

Bregn K (2013) Detrimental effects of performance-related pay in the public sector? On the need for a broader theoretical perspective. Publ Organ Rev 13(1):21–35

Brenčič V, Norris JB (2010) On-the-job tasks and performance pay: a vacancy-level analysis. Ind Labor Relat Rev 63(3):511–544

Brown B, Walsh J (1994). Managing pay in Britain. In: Personnel management. Blackwell, Oxford, pp. 437–464
Burks S, Carpenter J, Goette L (2009) Performance pay and worker cooperation: evidence from an artefactual field experiment. J Econ Behav Organ 70:458–469
Camerer CF (2003) Behavioral game theory: experiments in strategic interaction. Princeton University Press, Princeton
Cappelen AW, Hole AD, Sorensen EO, Tungodden B (2007) The pluralism of fairness ideals: an experimental approach. Am Econ Rev 97(3):818–827
Cherry TL, Frykblom P, Shogren JF (2002) Hardnose the dictator. Am Econ Rev 92(4):1218–1221
Cole GDH (1918) The payment of wages: a study in payment by results under the wage-system. The Fabian Research Department/G. Allen and Unwin, Westminster/London
Dohmen T, Falk A (2011) Performance pay and multidimensional sorting: productivity, preferences, and gender. Am Econ Rev 101:556–590
Drago R, Garvey GT (1998) Incentives for helping on the job: theory and evidence. J Labor Econ 16(1):1–25
Fischbacher U (2007) z-Tree: Zurich toolbox for ready-made economic experiments. Exp Econ 10(2):171–178
Forsythe R, Horowitz JL, Savin NE, Sefton M (1994) Fairness in simple bargaining experiments. Game Econ Behav 6(3):347–369
Freeman RB, Kleiner MM (2005) The last American shoe manufacturers: decreasing productivity and increasing profits in the shift from piece rates to continuous flow production. Ind Relat 44(2):307–330
Guzzo RA, Katzell RA (1987) Effects of economic incentives on productivity: a psychological view. In: Nalbantian HR (ed) Incentives, cooperation, and risk sharing: economic and psychological perspectives on employment contracts. Rowman & Littlefield, Totowa, pp 107–119
Hoffman E, Spitzer ML (1985) Entitlements, rights, and fairness: an experimental examination of subjects' concepts of distributive justice. J Leg Stud 14:259–297
Hoffman E, McCabe K, Smith VL (1996) Social distance and other-regarding behavior in dictator games. Am Econ Rev 86(3):653–660
Kahneman D, Knetsch JL, Thaler RH (1986) Fairness and the assumptions of economics. J Bus 59(4):285–300
Kessler I (1994) Performance pay. In: Sisson K (ed) Personnel management. Blackwell, Oxford, pp 465–494
Lawler EE III (1987) Pay for performance. In: Nalbantian HR (ed) Incentives, cooperation, and risk sharing: economic and psychological perspectives on employment contracts. Rowman & Littlefield, Totowa, pp 69–86
Lazear EP (1989) Pay equality and industrial politics. J Polit Econ 87:1261–1284
Lazear EP (2000) Performance pay and productivity. Am Econ Rev 90(5):1346–1361
Marx K (1887/1967) Capital: a critique of political economy, vol I. Engels F (ed), Moore S, Amd Aveling E (trans). Progress Publishers, Moscow
Milgrom P, Roberts J (1992) Economics, organization and management. Prentice-Hall, London
Perry JL, Engbers TA, Jun SY (2009) Back to the future? Performance-related pay, empirical research, and the perils of persistence. Public Adm Rev 69(1):39–51
Recruit Jobs Research Center (2014) 「2014年7月度アルバイト・パト募集時平均時給調査」(An average hourly payment survey for part-time job workers in 2014 July). jbrc. http://recruitjobs.co.jp. Accessed 8 Sept 2014
Shearer B (2004) Piece rates, fixed wages and incentives: evidence from a field experiment. Rev Econ Stud 71:513–534
Webb S, Webb B (1897/1920) Industrial democracy, 2nd edn. Green and Co, Longmans

Chapter 4
Income Sharing Between Workers and Investors: Economic Experiments on Functional Income Distribution

Abstract Since the 1980s, declines in labor wage rates accompanied by increases in dividend yields or stock prices have become a global tendency and denote significant changes in functional income distributions between capital and labor. In this research, I performed economic experiments involving investment, production, and distribution and examined fairness ideals in functional income distributions. All participants are pair matched to form two-player teams, each comprising a worker and an investor, where each team member is required to present a proposal for the division of team earnings. The findings of this research are threefold: First, a few libertarian proposals were made, meaning proposals for dividing production according to ownership of the means of production. Second, labor-value theory seems to significantly impact individuals' fairness ideals: in the with-labor treatment, both investors and workers tend to be unselfish, whereas in the without-labor treatment, investors do not need to work and both investors and workers tend to exhibit take-all behavior. Third, investors show a significant tendency to favor income-based egalitarian proposals, which enable them to hold the rest of their investment funds as an asset, whereas workers show a significant tendency to favor radical egalitarian proposals, which enable them to redistribute investors' assets. The experimental results partly explain recent declines in labor wage rates that have accompanied institutional changes.

Keywords Functional income distribution • Labor value theory • Income-based egalitarian • Radical egalitarian

4.1 Introduction

Rising capital profit distribution rate accompanied by decreasing labor wage rate has been a worldwide phenomenon since the 1980s. According to Lavoie and Stockhammer (2013), the labor income distribution rate—which was 68.2 % between the early 1980s and early 1990s in the USA—declined to 65.87 % from 2000 to 2008. Simultaneously, the same trend occurred in Germany—where the

---

This chapter is a joint study with Hiroyuki Uni.

N. Tokumaru, *Social Preference, Institution, and Distribution*, Evolutionary Economics and Social Complexity Science 3, DOI 10.1007/978-981-10-0137-6_4

labor distribution rate declined from 67.11 to 63.37 %.[1] Even Japan, known for its employee-oriented management style (cf. Yoshimori 1995), was no exception and saw its labor distribution rate decline from 72.38 % to 65.75 % during the same period. In contrast to the decline in labor income, the capital profit distribution rate, as in dividends, clearly increased after 2002, with a survey on incorporated enterprises showing that it rose to two or three times its 1990s level. The background to these changes has been the implementation of market-focused deregulation of the financial and labor market, with many enterprises witnessing a shift from stakeholder- to shareholder-oriented governance. These growing gaps between capital and labor share have been accompanied by growing economic imparities.[2]

According to some empirical studies, the above tendencies involving growing capital share and declining labor share stem from macro-level structural and institutional changes since the 1980s. In other words, changes in the *functional distribution of income*[3] for different production elements (e.g., capital and labor) were caused by change in the structure of international labor, change in the power balance in industrial relationships, extension of neoliberalistic ideology, and labor deregulation. For instance, Stockhammer (2013) performs double regression analysis setting technological change, globalization, financialization, and the decline of the welfare state as explanatory variables and the labor distribution rate as the explained variable. According to his analysis, the most important factors behind the decline of the labor income distribution rate are financialization, the decline of the welfare state, and globalization in developed countries.

Although both empirical and theoretical analyses on functional income distribution at the macro-level have been developed, a few studies analyze this distribution from a micro-level perspective. However, macro-level institutions cannot be separated from the norms or consciousness of economic agents at the micro-level. Mail surveys of middle managers conducted during 1990–1992 in five countries by Yoshimori (1995) show a clear contrast between shareholder-oriented corporate governance in Anglo-Saxon countries and stakeholder-oriented corporate governance in Japan and Germany. Among responses to a survey question asking respondent assumptions on the management orientation of large companies, more

[1]While the trend is less extreme, declining labor income share has also been observed in developing countries (Stockhammer 2013, p. 42).

[2]The income of the top 1 % of earners as a share of total income increased from the mid-1970s to the 2000s in most G20 countries: it increased 4.7 % in Australia, 1.7 % in Germany, 2.1 % in Japan, 8.2 % in the UK and 10.1 % in the USA (Stockhammer 2013, p. 5).

[3]Discussion of functional income distribution stems from classical economic literature such as Ricardo (1817). In the preface to *On The Principles of Political Economy and Taxation* Ricardo wrote: "the produce of the earth . . . is derived from its surface by the united application of labor, machinery, and capital . . . " and " . . . to determine the laws which regulate this distribution, is the principal problem in Political Economy" (1817, p. 5). Thus, strictly, functional income distribution comprises not only the distribution of worker and investor income but also that of other production income such as rent and land. For simplicity, this study focuses solely on income distribution between workers and investors.

than 97.1 % of valid responses in Japan and 82 % of those in Germany were that "A firm exists for the interest of all stakeholders"; in contrast, 75.6 % of valid responses in the USA were that "shareholder interest should be given the first priority."[4] Here I could see clearly reflected both fundamental differences in institutions and awareness with respect to corporations. Thus, micro-level analysis of functional income distribution is necessary to understand changes in labor distribution rates at the macro-level.

If macro-level changes in functional distribution occur parallel with micro-level consciousness of economic agents, the factors that decide principles of distribution between labor and capital should be analyzed to understand these institutional changes. Relevant questions include a just distribution of total income between workers and investors when both contribute to the creation of that income; the existence of differences in fairness between workers and investors in functional distribution; and institutional factors that decisively influence the fairness of workers and investors in income distribution. Those questions directed at the micro-level analysis of individual behavior and consciousness in functional distribution should be scrutinized.

This chapter aims to clarify fairness ideals in relation to the distribution of production income between workers and investors and their determinative factors through economic experiments. The experiments are a revised version of experimental studies comprising both the production and distribution stage (Hoffman and Spitzer 1985; Cappelen et al. 2007).[5] Experiments in these previous experimental studies saw subjects pair matched to form two-player teams and required to distribute team income earned in the production stage with their partners. The present experiment differs from those in previous studies in that each pair-matched team member contributes to the production by performing different roles—either investor or worker—whereas previous experimental designs saw participants engage in the same production task. I have designed two versions of the experimental treatment—in the first version investors must earn their investment funds through their own labor, while in the second they receive investment funds automatically as an endowment. I have further examined whether roles played in the production process and investors' laboring for investment funds versus receiving endowments affect fairness ideals in the distribution process.

This paper is structured as follows. In Sect. 4.2, I identify factors that may affect distributive justice between workers and investors and propose models that may explain fairness ideals in functional income distribution. In Sect. 4.3, I explain the experimental design and present fairness ideals, classifications, and our models

[4]The question was "Under which of the following assumptions is a large company in your country managed?" (Yoshimori 1995, p. 34). The contrast was also clear in another question asking suppose a CEO must choose either to maintain dividends or to lay off a number of employees. In your country which of these alternatives would be chosen? 97.1 % of valid responses in Japan were "Job security," as were 59.1 % of those in Germany; whereas in the USA 89.2 % of valid responses were "Dividends" (Yoshimori 1995, p. 35).

[5]See also Chaps. 2 and 3 of this book.

and hypothesis. In Sect. 4.4, I analyze the results of the experiments, and in Sect. 4.5, I discuss those results. Finally, Sect. 4.6 contains a summary and presents conclusions.

4.2 Background: Different Models in Functional Income Distribution

Discussion on functional income distribution has its roots in classical economics. Ricardo (1817), in the preface to *On The Principles of Political Economy and Taxation*, states that, "the produce of the earth [is] derived from [the] united application of labour, machinery and capital, thus [the] principal problem in political economy should be to determine a law regulating distributions among production factors: that is, the proprietor of the land, the owner of the stock or capital, and the labourers" (p. 5). Thus, the following question may arise: what are the determining factors that regulate the functional distribution of income among different production factors, such as labor and capital, which contribute to a production process? That is, what is a fair distribution principle for splitting production income among different production factors? Here I propose three models of fairness in functional distribution.

4.2.1 Model 1: Libertarian

Libertarians, such as L. v. Mises, F. V. Hayek, and M. Friedman, believe that a fair distribution is basically one based on the contribution of each individual to production, whether through capital, labor power, ownership of the means of production, and so on. This ideal is summarized by Friedman (1962) as follows, "The ethical principle that would directly justify the distribution of income in a free-market society is. . . To each according to what he and the instruments he owns produces" (pp. 161–162). According to this view, fair shares should be calculated by multiplying the inputs of the production factors (e.g., labor, capital, and land) that an individual owns and the marginal productivity of each production factor. Thus, each individual worker should receive wages according to their marginal labor productivity and hours worked; similarly, each investor should receive profit according to the amount yielded through means of production (such as machinery) in which they invested.

Libertarians basically believe that the appropriate distribution based on the marginal productivity of each production factor is achievable via free-market transactions. According to libertarians, individuals may lose their incentive to increase their labor productivity or invest their capital if they do not expect to receive a share (i.e., income) equal to what they have produced by their own production measures. Through seeking outcomes that reflect the production measures of each individual involved, libertarians believe total social welfare is best enhanced, consistent with the ideal of "the greatest happiness of the greatest number of people." Thus, libertarians believe that redistribution in general should be avoided as much as possible, and both appropriate resource allocation and economic efficiency can be achieved via market mechanisms. Based on their trust of market mechanisms, libertarians justify what is called laissez-faire policies; that is, individuals' liberties are given the utmost respect, with minimum government intervention via such means as setting basic transaction rules. Thus, individuals' property rights, whether inherited from previous generations, obtained as profits from investments, or gained through hard work, should be protected, and economic disparities in society should not be rectified by coercive political measurements such as progressive taxation. If not, the poor may stop working and thus become dependent on social welfare, and the rich may decrease investments that accelerate market growth. Thus, we can summarize two libertarian theses on income distribution as follows:

1. Distribution should be determined according to what an individual has produced by using a production measure that the individual owns, including the individual's labor power, capital, or other production measurement.
2. Whatever the individual owns should be protected as their property and should *not* be redistributed to others.

4.2.2 Model 2: Labor-Value Radicalist

Unlike libertarians, classical economists, such as Smith, Ricardo, and Locke, have regarded the *labor* that an individual invests as the basis of property rights. In a chapter on property in the *Second Treatise of Civil Government*, Locke (1690) states:

> ... every man has a property in his own person; this nobody has any right to but himself. The labour of his body and the work of his hands, we may say are properly his. Whatsoever, then, he removes out of the state that nature hath provided and left it in, he hath mixed his labour with, and joined to it something that is his own, and thereby makes it his property. (p. 15)

From the labor-value theory of Ricardo and the classical economists, socialists, such as Hodgskin and Thomson, developed the theory of *labor's claim to the whole product of industry* (*Das Recht auf den vollen Arbeitsertrag*), which states that labor should be entitled to all property (cf. Menger 1904). According to Hodgskin (1825), fixed capital is primarily an outcome of labor, because "fixed capital consists of the tools and instruments the labourer works with, the machinery he makes and guides, and the buildings he uses either to facilitate his exertions or to protect their produce. Unquestionably, by using these instruments, man adds wonderfully to his power" (p. 52). Furthermore, he maintains that the machineries or instruments workers use for production cannot be separated from the skilled manpower using them, and thus fixed capital should be considered the same as a skilled labor force (ibid., p. 108). Therefore, for a labor-value radicalist such as Hodgskin, all production elements—including fixed capital, machineries, and so on—stem from labor, and all income from the production process should be distributed to workers. However, the realization that "every laborer should receive all the value he produces," as A. Menger (1904) highlights, depends on both the form of production means used (private or common use) and the form of ownership (private or common property). A combination of private use of production means and common ownership of property only allows such a distribution, and other combinations of production means use and ownership prevent an individual from achieving labor's claim to the whole product.

Regarding ownership of fixed capital, Marx discussed "transition of the laws of property" in *Capital* (1867, p. 609). According to Marx, if a fixed amount of capital is produced by a capitalist's own labor, the property right to that capital is based on the capitalist's own labor. Thus, the profit that a capitalist can earn using fixed capital is an outcome of that capitalist exchanging their own labor to appropriate the labor of others. However, according to Marx, characteristics of capital stock change as capital accumulation progresses. Thus, if a capitalist earns profits using capital gained from earlier production profits and the labor of others, this represents the appropriation of others' labor without any equivalent investment of labor by the capitalist. Marx illustrates the change in the characteristics of capital stock using the example of a spinner. A spinner, who has accumulated £10,000 from his "primitive labor" to serve as his first capital, invests £8000 of this money in machinery and cotton and invests the remaining £2000 as wages. He then receives £12,000 from producing yarn that is sold on the market. At the end of this first stage in the investment process, the spinner thus has earned £2000 from his labor; however, if the spinner buys more labor with that £2000 and earns a profit, this would cease to be the outcome of the spinner's labor and instead would be capital. Here, Marx identified a clear distinction between the first stage of an investment, which uses money derived from the labor of the investor, and subsequent stages where the invested capital no longer originates from investor labor.

Based on the discussion above, we can summarize the position of a labor-value radicalist as follows:

1. Income distribution should be decided only according to whether individuals contribute production via their own labor.
2. Whether investment capital is earned by investor labor or is received by the investor as an endowment represents a clear distinction to a labor radicalist in terms of distributive justice.

4.2.3 Model 3: Egalitarianism

The last model is egalitarianism, which believes all production earnings should be equally distributed among members regardless of their contribution to production. This position appears very simple and easy to understand. However, we need to consider the basic unit of the pie that is to be equally distributed between the parties.

Regarding redistribution, Bowles and Gintis (1998) classify four dimensions, each with high/low market-determined income flows and assets. In laissez-faire capitalism, as explained in the libertarian model above, the level of redistribution is low for both income flows and assets. The most radical redistribution model is represented by market socialism, which regards both income flows and assets as objects of redistribution. According to their classification, the other two forms of redistribution are asset-based redistribution and income-based redistribution, for which the representative political regime is social democracy (pp. 56–58).

Following the redistribution classifications explained above, I propose distinguishing egalitarianism into two types according to the object of distribution. First is radical egalitarianism, which considers the basic unit of the pie to comprise both the assets each individual owns and market-determined income flow. Second is income-based egalitarianism, which believes that while assets owned by individuals should not be redistributed, market income flow is a pie to be distributed on a 50:50 basis. Asset-based egalitarianism, which could be a third option according to the classification, is omitted here for the practical reason that it cannot be applied in our experimental setting. Concrete forms of these two varieties of egalitarianism are explained in detail in the following section.

Based on the discussions above, I summarize the fairness ideals of egalitarianism as follows:

1. Income should be equally distributed among members, regardless of how each contributes to production.
2. According to different distribution objectives, we can distinguish two types of egalitarianism: radical egalitarian, which distributes both the income flow and assets of members equally, and income-based egalitarianism, which only distributes income flow equally.

4.3 Methodology: Experimental Design, Treatments, Fairness Ideals, and Classifications

4.3.1 Experimental Design

To identify the fairness ideals of investors and workers and decisive factors in functional distribution, I designed experiments comprising investment, production, and distribution that revise and extend previous experiments (Hoffman and Spitzer 1985; Cappelen et al. 2007). All participants are randomly pair matched by a computer, preserving their anonymity and constituting two-player teams with multiple participant pairings. Each pair participates in a one-shot game. One member of the team is assigned the role of the investor, while the other is assigned the role of the worker. Thus, in this experimental design, each member contributes to team production differently: either by investing in a means of production or inputting their labor power as a worker. After the production stage, participants are asked to share team production in the distribution stage, according to the fairness ideals they followed. This is the main focus of the analysis in this paper. The experiment details are as follows.

In the first investment stage, the participants assigned to the investor role decide whether to invest in production equipment, specifically a calculator that costs 150 points, equivalent to 150 yen (approximately 1.2 US dollars). In the next stage, the other members of each two-player team—the participants assigned to the worker role—engage in production; that is, they complete computational problems to earn money. In this stage, workers whose partners invested in the production equipment can use the purchased calculator (displayed on their computer screens) to solve computational problems, whereas those whose partners did not invest (i.e., purchase the calculator) must perform the same work without this calculation tool. The computational problems the workers complete are scored and converted to points that constitute team production. A perfect score is 1000 points, equivalent to 1000 yen (approximately 8.2 US dollars).

In the final distribution stage, team production is displayed on the screen of each participant, and both team members are asked to propose a distribution of team production income between themselves and their partners. An example distribution proposal would be to distribute 300 points to oneself and 200 points to one's partner when team production is 500 points. The computer then randomly selects one of the proposals and the team profits are distributed to each team member accordingly. Final profit points are converted to cash (yen) and paid to participants after the experiment together with a participation fee.

For comparison, I performed the following two experimental treatments, which differ in whether the investment funds were earned through investor work (see Table 4.1).

- Treatment *with* investor labor (hereafter *with*-labor)

  In this treatment, the investor participants are first required to earn investment funds a by completing computational problems for 10 min. The average score was around 230 points. Participants are then required to decide whether they should invest; that is, purchase the calculator at a cost of 150 points paid from the investment funds they have earned. This investment option was not available to those who earned less than 150 points. The final points score for those that invest in the production equipment is $a\text{-}150$ points (where a denotes the total points earnings of their investment fund) and is automatically added to their final payment. Meanwhile, the final points for those who do not invest are a points and again are added to their final payment. Other rules and procedures are the same as in the *without*-L treatment described above.
- Treatment *without* investor labor (hereafter *without*-labor)

  In this treatment, the investor participants are not required to complete any computations and instead are automatically given 250 points as an endowment to invest ($a = 250$). They must then decide whether to invest in a calculator at a cost of 150 points. The remaining points of those who choose to invest in the production equipment, namely, 100 points (250 endowment points minus the

Table 4.1 Game procedures

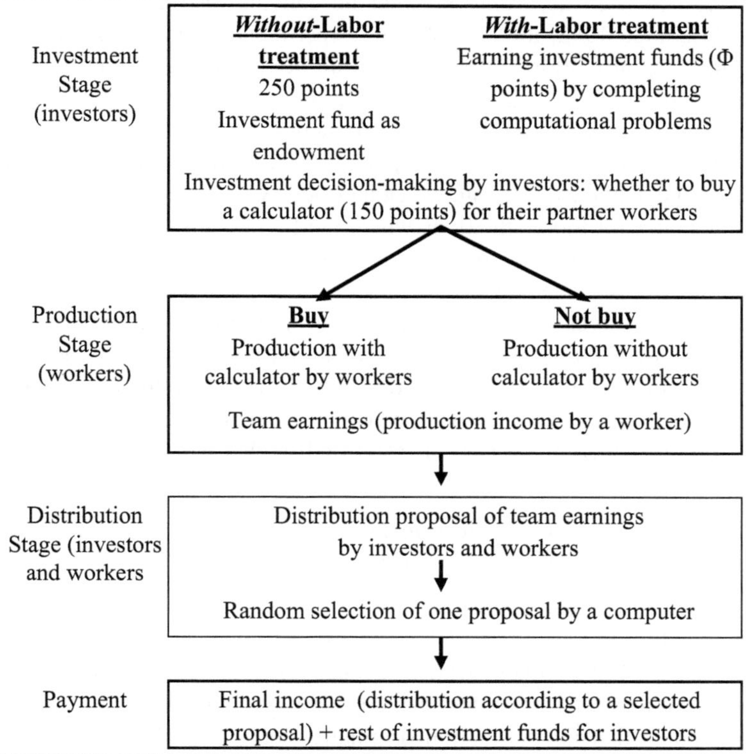

investment cost of 150 points), are automatically added to their final payments. For those who do not invest, their final point's total (250 points) is added to their final payment. In the next stage, workers completed computational problems for 10 min, working with or without a calculator depending on the investment decision of their investor partner.

4.3.2 *Fairness Ideals*

Based on the discussion of functional income distribution described in Sect. 4.2 as well as the experimental design above, I propose four fairness ideals to which participants may adhere: (1) libertarian, (2) take-all (partly labor-value radicalist), (3) income-based egalitarian, and (4) radical egalitarian. These fairness ideals are detailed as follows:

1. *Libertarian*

   As discussed in Sect. 4.2, what libertarians regard as a "fair" share should be decided according to the amount each individual contributes to production, via their labor, capital, or some other measurement of production, as expressed by the phrase "To each according to what he and the instruments he owns produces" (Friedman 1962, ibidem.). In this experimental setting, the amount of an investor's "contribution" to production can be quantified as the increase in team production using a calculator relative to production without such a tool; similarly, worker's "contribution" to production can be quantified as the production in the case where workers performed calculation tasks without calculators. In the actual experiment, we cannot observe the production amount without a calculator for those situations where workers perform the calculation task with a calculator, because it is a one-shot game. Thus, I designed the experiment such that an "average production amount without using a calculator" is displayed on the screens of all participants during the distribution stage, to enable them to count the contribution of either investors or workers according to an ideal libertarian distribution. If we denote the production amount using a calculator as Π and that without using a calculator as Π_{without}, the ideal libertarian distribution for each investor and worker can be expressed as follows:

- Ideal libertarian distribution for investor: $y_I = \Pi - \Pi_{without}$
- Ideal libertarian distribution for worker: $y_W = \Pi_{without}$

2. *Take-all or labor-value radicalist*

   Individuals who hold strict take-all positions distribute the team's income entirely to themselves.[6] Workers who distribute all of the team's income to themselves in the *without*-L treatment can be said to be labor-value radicalists: this position holds that all production originally stems from labor, and thus only labor imputed in a production process justifies distribution, as discussed in Sect. 4.2. However, I call this position simply the take-all position for descriptive purposes. The ideal take-all distributions for investor and worker are identical and can be expressed as follows:

   - Ideal take-all distribution for investor and worker: $y_I = y_W = \Pi$

3. *Income-based egalitarian*

   Income-based egalitarians believe that an individual's assets—investor's investment funds in this experiment—should not be considered for redistribution but regard market income flow as a pie that should be distributed 50:50. As I discussed in Sect. 4.2, Bowles and Gintis (1998) classify four dimensions regarding redistribution, each with high/low market-determined income flows and assets as two parameters for classification. Income-based egalitarianism can be classified as a position that involves high redistribution

[6] In the previous distribution experiments without production, the proportion of participants committing to take-all (selfish) distributions ranges widely, according to different experimental conditions such as anonymity or subject attributes. For the results of dictator games with different experimental settings, refer to Camerer (2003, pp.48–59).

of income flows and low redistribution of assets. In this experimental setting, a strict income-based egalitarian redistributes team earnings 50:50, without consideration of differences in investment funds (assets). For instance, consider the case where an investor earns 250 points via the investment fund and invests in the calculator (at a cost of 150 points); their partner worker then earns 600 points during the production stage in the *with*-L treatment. A strict egalitarian would separate team earnings into two shares of 300 points each. The final earnings of the investor, according to the proposal, would then be 400 points, with 300 points for the worker. The investor's remaining investment funds are regarded as their property according to this position and thus are not considered for distribution. The ideal income-based egalitarian distributions for the investor and worker are identical and can be expressed as follows:

- Ideal income-based egalitarian distribution for the investor and worker: $y_I = y_W = \Pi/2$

4. *Radical egalitarian*

   The other version of the egalitarian distribution is the radical egalitarian distribution, which involves the 50:50 distribution of all team assets, including the investor's investment funds. A strict radical egalitarian redistributes team earnings to achieve equality of final profits among team members, and in determining the redistribution further considers remaining investor funds. For instance, consider the case where an investor is left with 100 points of investment funds after purchasing the calculator, while the worker earns 600 points for the team; here the radical egalitarian distributes 250 team points to the investor and 350 to the worker, leaving both with 350 points. Here, the distribution to the investor is discounted based on their existing investment funds. The radical egalitarian distribution thus could be interpreted as a form of property redistribution (from the investor to the worker). This position describes the same labor-value radicalist model explained above in the *with*-L treatment, where both worker and investor contribute production through their labor. If we denote the investor's investment funds by a, the total investment funds remaining after purchasing a calculator becomes a-150, and the ideal income-based egalitarian distributions for investor and worker can be expressed as follows:

- Ideal radical egalitarian distribution for the investor:

$$y_I = (\Pi - (a - 150))/2$$

- Ideal radical egalitarian distribution for the worker:

$$y_W = (\Pi + (a - 150))/2$$

4.3.3 Classification Criteria for Fairness Ideals

As discussed above, I assumed four possible fairness ideals: (1) libertarian; (2) take-all (labor-value radicalist); (3) income-based egalitarian; and (4) radical egalitarian. However, as discussed later, few subjects adhered to the libertarian ideal in the experimental settings, and thus I focus on the latter three fairness ideals here. Because the distribution amounts proposed by individual subjects do not always precisely match any of the three fairness ideals, I made classification criteria comprising two indices, d_1 and d_2, and their combinations. Index d_1 indicates distance from the income-based egalitarian distribution, defined as follows:

$$\text{Index } d_1 : d_1 = \left| 0.5 - \frac{y}{\Pi} \right| \ (0 \leq d_1 \leq 0.5)$$

where Π indicates team earnings (production by the worker) and y indicates the individual's self-distribution amount. Here, the pie is redistributed 50:50 and is assumed to equal team earnings from the worker's labor in the production stage. As d_1 of an individual decreases, the distance between the self-distribution rate and the income-based egalitarian distribution rate decreases, which implies the individual is closer to the income-based egalitarian position. In contrast, individuals who distribute team earnings entirely to themselves and leave nothing to their partners are take-all and in that case $d_1 = 0.5$.

Index d_2 indicates distance from the radical egalitarian distribution and is defined as follows:

$$\text{Index } d_2 : d_2 = \left| 0.5 - \frac{y}{\Pi + \mathrm{a}} \right| \ (0 \leq d_2 \leq 0.5)$$

where a indicates remaining investor assets, namely, those assets that the investor in a team leaves uninvested. Here, the entire pie is to be distributed 50:50 and is assumed to comprise the sum of both the team earnings and the investment funds retained by the investor. As d_2 decreases for an individual, so too does the distance between the self-distribution rate and that of the radical egalitarian distribution, implying the individual is closer to the radical egalitarian position. In contrast, individuals who distributed both their team earnings and remaining investment funds entirely to themselves, leaving nothing to their partners, favor a take-all distribution and in that case $d_2 = 0.5$.

For classification, I plot individual distribution proposals on a plane, where d_2 is the horizontal axis and d_1 is the vertical axis, and classify take-all, income-based egalitarian, and radical egalitarian proposals using the following criterion values:

(a) Take-all: $0.5 \leq d_1 + d_2$
(b) Income-based egalitarian: $0 \leq d_1 + d_2 < 0.5$ and $d_1 \leq d_2$
(c) Radical egalitarian: $0 \leq d_1 + d_2 < 0.5$ and $d_2 < d_1$

These classification criteria are arranged in a plane in Fig. 4.1.

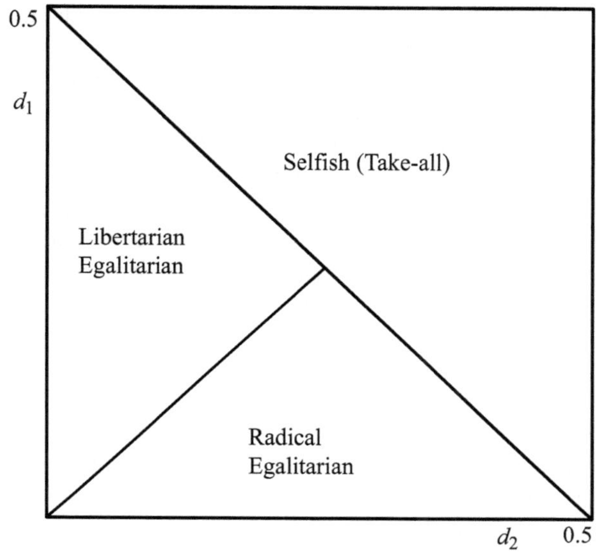

Fig. 4.1 Classification of fairness ideals by indexes d_1 and d_2

4.3.4 *Models, Hypothesis, and Predictions*

Based on the classifications above, I assume an individual i has a vector loading factor on each fairness standard $\lambda_i = (\lambda_{iS}, \lambda_{iL}, \lambda_{iR})$ $(0 \leq \lambda_{iS}, \lambda_{iL}, \lambda_{iR})$, where λ_{iS} designates a loading factor for selfishness, λ_{iL} for income-based egalitarianism, and λ_{iR} for radical egalitarianism. Each individual i tries to maximize the following value function $V_i(y)$ by determining self-distribution amount y.

$$V_i(y) = \lambda_{iS} y - \lambda_{iL}\left(0.5 - \frac{y}{\Pi}\right)^2 - \lambda_{iR}\left(0.5 - \frac{y}{\Pi + \mathrm{a}}\right)^2$$

where the load factor of the second member (λ_{iL}) of the right side of the equation designates a negative utility, triggered by deviating from the income-based egalitarian standard distribution; the third member (λ_{iR}) designates negative utility by deviating from the radical egalitarian standard distribution.

As is explained in the previous section, labor-value theory regards an individual's labor as the source of both their property rights and their inputs into a production process. As there are only two members per team in our game setting, relative labor can be a factor for each individual's fairness ideals for income distribution. That is, in the *with*-L treatment, the relative labor for both the worker and the investor is 1 because both are working equally in their production process. $(\delta_{\text{Investor}} = \delta_{\text{Worker}} = 1)$. In the *without*-L treatment, there are different labor roles: the workers alone contribute to production, while the investors do nothing $(\delta_{\text{Investor}} \to 0, \delta_{\text{Worker}} \to \infty)$.

Regarding investment funds, we should consider the "endowment effect," which may yield a gap in value recognition of funds between investors and workers. Kahneman et al. (1990) discuss the tendency of individuals to value what they already own more highly than that which they do not own, a tendency widely known as the "endowment effect." In their experimental studies, participants in one group were given souvenir cups from a particular university and then asked how much money they would accept in exchange for the mugs; meanwhile, participants in another group were instead asked how much money they would be willing to pay for the same mug. The results were interesting: in most cases, participants in the former group proposed higher sums than did participants in the latter group. The term endowment effect has been coined to describe the tendency of individuals to value more highly what they already own.

This endowment effect may influence our own experiment, specifically by occurring between investors and workers. Investors may value their investment funds more highly and wish to exclude them from distribution based simply on it being their endowment, whereas workers may value the same investment funds lower simply because they did not receive them as an endowment. Based on these hypotheses, I assume that the investors value their remaining investment funds more highly than their partner workers do. Thus, I set up a factor of endowment effect γ, which becomes higher for investors and lower for workers ($\gamma_{\text{Investor}} \rightarrow \infty, \gamma_{\text{Worker}} \rightarrow 0$).

Now, for simplicity, I assume that individuals have neutral loading factors for each fairness standard: $\lambda = \left(\frac{1}{3}, \frac{1}{3}, \frac{1}{3}\right)$. From the above discussion on the relative labor and endowment effect, value functions may be affected by these factors, and individual decisions are described as follows:

$$\max_{y} V = \frac{\delta}{3} y - \frac{\gamma}{3\delta}\left(0.5 - \frac{y}{\Pi}\right)^2 - \frac{1}{3\delta\gamma}\left(0.5 - \frac{y}{\Pi + \mathrm{a}}\right)^2.$$

Based on assumptions regarding relative labor and endowment effects, the optimum self-distribution amount y* for each group classified by treatments and roles is as follows:

$$y^* = \begin{cases} \frac{y}{\Pi} & \text{if } \delta = 1 \text{ and } \gamma \rightarrow \infty \\ \frac{y}{\Pi + \mathrm{a}} & \text{if } \delta = 1 \text{ and } \gamma \rightarrow 0 \\ \frac{y}{\Pi} & \text{if } \delta \rightarrow 0 \text{ and } \gamma \rightarrow \infty \\ \Pi & \text{if } \delta \rightarrow \infty \text{ and } \gamma \rightarrow 0. \end{cases}$$

Table 4.2 summarizes the fairness ideal predictions given using the value function and two factors concerning the treatments and assigned roles.

Based on the inferences above, I may be able to presume intensities of social preference by treatment and role. Thus, predictions on fairness ideals by treatment and function can be summarized as follows:

Table 4.2 Social preference intensity and prediction by treatment and role

	δ	γ	y^*	Predictions
With-labor/investor	$\delta = 1$	$\gamma \to \infty$	$\frac{\Pi}{2}$	Income-based egalitarian
With-labor/worker	$\delta = 1$	$\gamma \to 0$	$\frac{(\Pi + a)}{2}$	Radical egalitarian
Without-labor/investor	$\delta \to 0$	$\gamma \to \infty$	$\frac{y}{\Pi}$	Income-based egalitarian
Without-labor/worker	$\delta \to \infty$	$\gamma \to 0$	Π	Take-all (=labor-value radicalist)

Prediction 1: Investors in the *with*-L and *without*-L treatments may tend to adhere to income-based egalitarian positions as they experience a higher endowment effect that makes them prefer to keep their investment funds.

Prediction 2: Workers in the *with*-L treatment may adhere to radical egalitarian positions because they regard the production process as fair for both investors and workers based on a labor-value theory and equally distribute the sum of the team earnings and investment funds.

Prediction 3: Workers in the *without*-L treatment feel the production situation is unfair and uncomfortable as workers must work, whereas investors merely click a button to make their investment decision. Thus, those with a labor-value radicalist perspective will tend to distribute all team earnings to themselves.

4.4 Results of the Experiments

4.4.1 Overview

The experiments were performed 11 times between December 2014 and February 2015 in a laboratory at Kyoto University, using the z-tree experimental software (Fischbacher 2007). Participants were identified by the faculties of Kyoto University, and 100 undergraduate students from all faculties participated. An average of 9.3 individuals participated in each game. Each individual participated in either the *with*-L or *without*-L treatment, and the average experiment duration—including the instruction period, game period, and payment period—was around 50 min. At the beginning of the game, an instructor read some instructions aloud (see Appendix) and the game started after all participants understood the rules. The average payment made to participants was around 1168 yen (≅ 9.6 US dollars), a level sufficient to satisfy participants in terms of covering their opportunity costs.[7] Notably, in a questionnaire survey administered immediately following the experiments, over half of all participants reported being "very satisfied" or "satisfied" with the payments they received, these being the top two satisfaction levels in a five-level scheme.

[7] According to a survey on average hourly payment for part-time jobs conducted by the jobs research center, the average hourly payment in western Japan is 920 yen.

Table 4.3 Average team earnings, self-distribution, and self-distribution rate by treatment and role

	Average		
	Team earning	Self-distribution	Self-distribution rate[a] (%)
With-labor/investor ($N = 25$)	669.6	427.8	64.7
With-labor/worker ($N = 25$)	669.6	424.8	64.6
Without-labor/investor ($N = 29$)	575.2	365.9	64.2
Without-labor/worker ($N = 29$)	575.2	415.6	71.4

[a]Obtained by dividing the amount distributed to oneself by team earnings

Investors earned approximately 251 points on average in the with-L treatment, almost the same as the 250 point endowment in the without-L treatment. Of the 50 investors, 42 invested in calculators,[8] while 8 did not[9] (5 in the *with*-L treatment and 3 in the *without*-L treatment). This implies that the eight investors who did not invest in calculators recognized and sought to avoid the risk of their final profit suffering from their partners electing a "take-all" income distribution and this distribution proposal then being selected by a computer. As this study focuses on a situation where an investor contributes to production through investment, data from pairs where investors did not buy calculators were basically excluded from the analysis.[10]

Table 4.3 presents the average values of team earnings, self-distribution amounts, and self-distribution rates as indicated through treatment and roles. Interestingly, in both worker situations—*with*-L and *without*-L—the conditions of worker production were identical; however, the average team earnings under the two treatments differ by more than 110 points, and the *with*-L treatment scores 16.4 % higher than the *without*-L treatment. This result implies that worker motivation was dampened in the *without*-L treatment, where the investor partner does nothing for team production other than deciding whether to purchase a calculator, compared with the *with*-L treatment. From these experimental results, I derive the following thesis:

Thesis 1: Workers in the *with*-labor treatment exhibit a significant tendency to be more productive and generous than workers in the *without*-L treatment.

[8]In questionnaire surveys administered after the experiments, investors who bought calculators identified their reasons for doing so as "expecting a raise in productivity," and most workers who used calculators provided by their partner investors reported feeling grateful.

[9]On questionnaire surveys administered after the experiments, investors who did not buy the calculators reported their reasons for doing so as "productivity may not increase much" and "expecting the whole pie may be taken by workers." Most workers not bought calculators by their investor partners reported feeling angry.

[10]The average production income of the eight participants who completed calculation tasks without using calculators was 251 points. This, compared with the average of 625 points for participants using calculators, indicates that the calculator increased productivity by approximately 2.49 times.

Furthermore, workers in the *without*-L treatment had a higher self-distribution rate of 8 % compared with those in the *with*-L treatment. This can be interpreted as workers being more "uncomfortable" in the former situation than the latter and thus losing both their industriousness and their generosity. Interestingly, almost no difference was observed among treatments in terms of the average self-distribution rate of investors.

4.4.2 Libertarian

Graph 4.1 shows correlations between the predicted values of a libertarian distribution and observed values in the experiment and shows that almost no correlation existed. The transverse line indicates points where predicted and observed values are the same, and the horizontal line indicates points where the self-distribution rate is 0.5; that is, the horizontal line indicates values consistent with an income-

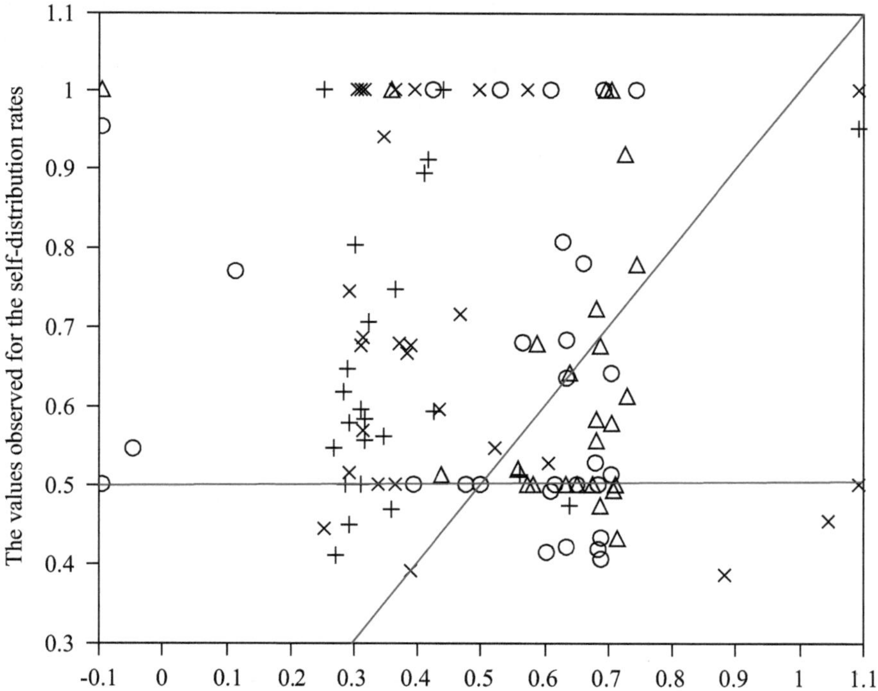

Graph 4.1 Relation between values predicted by libertarian self-distribution rates and the values observed for the self-distribution rates. + worker with-labor; Δ investor with-labor; × worker without-labor; ∘ investor without-labor * The *diagonal line* designates points where predicted values and observed values are the same

based egalitarian distribution. Some observed values are located on the line of a libertarian distribution but are not libertarian. Taking observed values exceeding 0.7 as belonging to the take-all distribution, we found that a few observed values correlated with predictions.

Interestingly, participants did not tend to consider their contribution to production. Moreover, this was the case despite it not being difficult to estimate their individual contribution under our experimental settings, as explained in the previous section. This may imply that individuals tend not to assess their own contributions and those of others on the same basis when they and those others have different roles in production. From this comparison, we could derive a second thesis, as follows:

Thesis 2: Libertarians are rarely observed in functional income distributions.

4.4.3 Fairness Ideals by Treatments and Roles

Graphs 4.2 and 4.3 show a scatter diagram between d_1, distance from income-based egalitarianism, and d_2, distance from radical egalitarianism, as defined in the previous section. In both treatments investors tend to be located above the diagonal line running from bottom left to upper right. This indicates that investors tend to be located nearer to income-based egalitarianism. Actually, 68 % of investors in

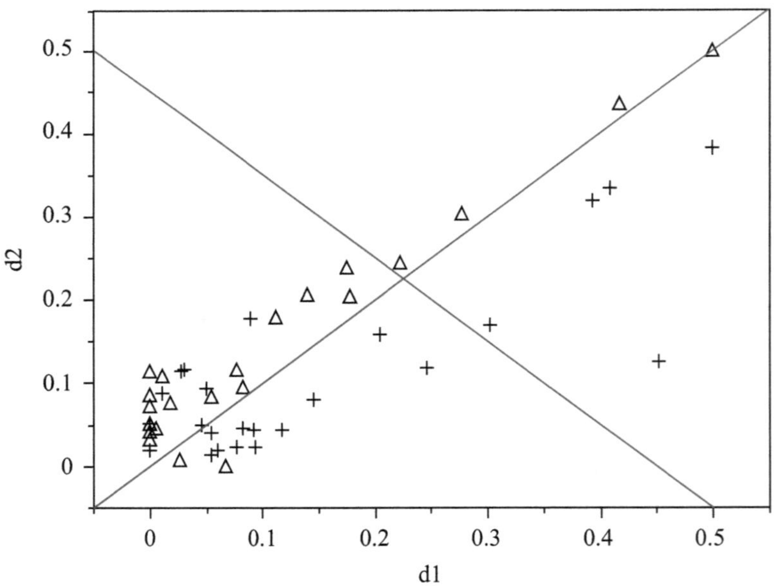

Graph 4.2 Scatter diagram between d_1 (distance from the income-based egalitarian position) and d_2 (distance from the radical egalitarian position) given the with-labor treatment. △ investor of *with*-labor treatment; +worker of *with*-labor treatment

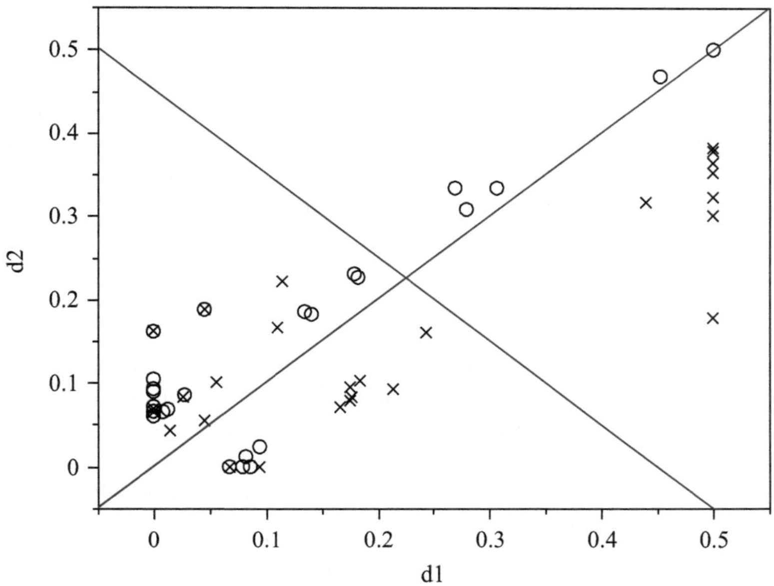

Graph 4.3 Scatter diagram between d_1 and d_2 for the without-labor treatment. ○ investor of *without*-labor treatment; × worker of *without*-labor treatment

the *with*-labor treatment and 51.72 % of those in the *without*-labor treatment were classified as income-based egalitarians, as shown in Table 4.3. The contrast becomes apparent if one compares the results with those for workers, only a few of whom adhered to the income-based egalitarianism. This result is consistent with prediction 1 as explained in the previous section.

Thesis 3: Regardless of whether investors work for their investment funds or not, compared with workers, they exhibit a significant tendency to favor income-based egalitarianism.

As is clearly shown in Graph 4.2, workers in the *with*-labor treatment are plotted below the diagonal line running from left-bottom to upper right and are on or near the line of the expected values of radical egalitarian. This designates that workers in this treatment are closer to radical egalitarianism, though a few elected the take-all distribution. Actually, 48 % of workers in this treatment were classified as radical egalitarians. This is in line with prediction 2 and can be summarized as follows: Table 4.4 shows that about half of the workers in the *with*-L treatment supported the radical egalitarian position.

Thesis 4: Workers in the treatment in which investors must work for their investment funds tend to be radical egalitarians.

Comparison of the two graphs reveals that the plotted points tend to shift from the bottom left in Graph 4.2 to the upper right in Graph 4.3 in both roles. This designates

Table 4.4 Fairness ideals by treatment and role[a]

	Income-based egalitarian	Radical egalitarian	Take-all	Total
Investor *with*-labor ($N = 25$)	17 (68.00 %)	2 (8.00 %)	6 (24.00 %)	25 (100 %)
Worker *with*-labor ($N = 25$)	8 (32.00 %)	12 (48.00 %)	5 (20.00 %)	25 (100 %)
Investor *without*-labor ($N = 29$)	15 (51.72 %)	5 (17.24 %)	9 (31.03 %)	29 (100 %)
Worker *without*-labor ($N = 29$)	10 (34.48 %)	9 (31.03 %)	10 (34.48 %)	29 (100 %)

[a]Teams in which investors did not purchase calculators were excluded

that both workers and investors tend to approach a take-all distribution in the *without*-labor treatment relative to the *with*-labor treatment. We can see in Table 4.3 that the number participants electing a take-all distribution nearly doubled under the *without*-labor treatment. The tendency of workers in the without-labor treatment group to favor take-all (or labor-value radicalist) distributions was predicted in the previous section (prediction 3), though this tendency did not apply to all investors. From these observed tendencies, I can derive the following thesis:

Thesis 5: Workers have a significant tendency to select a take-all distribution when investors do not contribute to production via their labor. Investors that do not contribute to labor are also significantly more likely to select a take-all position than investors that do contribute to labor.

As we can see, participants showed a clear difference in their ideals fairness in relation to treatments and roles. The results are discussed in detail in the following section.

4.5 Discussion

In the previous section, I showed the results of the experiments involving functional income distributions. The results showed that functional or positional difference in production also affects both investor and worker preferences in fairness ideals. I discovered interesting and significant findings from three perspectives. First, the experimental results described that functional income distribution has its own specific statistics compared with nonfunctional distribution: for example, functional distributions rarely coincide with libertarian distributions. Second, investors tend to adhere to income-based egalitarianism, which enables them to keep their investment funds as their endowment. Third, workers in the without-labor treatment are more likely to be radical egalitarians than are workers in other treatments and participants in other roles. Fourth, investment funds or capital being earned via investor labor strongly impacts participant fairness ideals for investors and workers. In the treatment where investors do not work to earn investment funds, participants exhibit a stronger tendency to seek a take-all distribution than in the treatment where they do work, regardless of participant roles. Additionally, worker productivity was significantly higher in the latter treatment. I will discuss the details of the results and attempt to derive implications in terms of actual economic situations in this section.

4.5.1 Functional or Nonfunctional

Consistent with Thesis 2, libertarian fairness ideals were rarely found in the functional distribution. In the previous experiment shown in Chap. 3, I performed similar experiments comprising production and distribution, where team members did not exhibit functional differences in production but performed the same work to produce team earnings. In the experiment with nonfunctional distribution, many participants adhered to a libertarian distribution (termed "performance-based" in this paper), if they were informed of their "contribution" to team earnings (46.88 % under the independent working style; 56.67 % under the collaborative working style). Even in the treatments where they were not provided precise information on their contribution, many adhered to a libertarian distribution (26.67 % under the independent working style; 23.68 % under the collaborative working style). Thus, it could be said that functional distribution matters to fairness ideals.

This difference implies that individuals do not strictly compare the amounts contributed by each team member to production when they and their partner undertake different production roles. From the results we could say the thesis of Friedman (1962) that "To each according to what he and the instruments he owns produces" (ibidem) does not work for distribution justice among workers and investors. Reflecting the actual market situation, few people consider "how much investment/labor contributes to increase profit" a relevant criteria when considering the validity of their income. As discussed in this paper, whether a given individual or their partner contributes via labor influences fairness ideals. Thus, in the functional distribution, it could be said that while the amount contributed by each investor or worker to production is not important, *whether individuals contribute by their own labor* is important.

4.5.2 Investor or Worker

The experimental results showed a sharp contrast in the roles of investors and workers. In both the *with*-L and *without*-L treatments, investors exhibit a significant tendency to adhere to the income-based egalitarian position. This means that production roles significantly influence individual decision-making: in other words, *functional roles (investor or worker) matter* for fairness ideals.

As is discussed in relation to predictions, the contrast seems to arise partly from the *endowment effect*, as investors evaluate investments made using endowments more highly, and income-based egalitarianism may be more strongly supported by those who already own property and do not want it to be redistributed. Conversely, few workers adhered to income-based egalitarianism, either because they do not highly value investor's investment funds or simply do not regard investors as having property rights.

This can be clearly understood in conjunction with the idea of self-serving bias or opportunistic behavior, as noted by Babcock and Loewenstein (1997) and as discussed in Chap. 2 of this book. According to them, individuals tend to make judgments that reflect a self-serving bias during a bargaining process, implying they consciously or unconsciously select advantageous distributions for themselves. Meanwhile, investors obtain a more advantageous distribution if they adhere to the income-based egalitarian position that respects their remaining investment funds as endowed property. From the workers' perspective, adherence to radical egalitarian fairness ideals clearly enables them to redistribute remaining investor funds and is more advantageous than income-based egalitarian distribution.

4.5.3 Whether Capital Is Gained via Investor Labor

The experiments show, in the case where both the investor and worker are engaged in production, that the interdependencies of their labor process make them more unselfish. As predicted in our hypothesis, workers in the *without*-L treatment displayed a significant tendency to commit to a take-all distribution; this may be natural as inequality between themselves and their partners makes them uncomfortable. It could be said that *whether capital is gained* via *investor labor matters* for fairness ideals in functional distribution.

With respect to workers, this tendency of committing to a take-all distribution may also be interpreted as indicating the adoption of labor-value radicalist positions. Here, I can see whether an individual's contribution to production via their labor is a significant factor for fairness in functional income distribution. In Graphs 4.2 and 4.3, I find relative plots of the distribution amounts of many workers in the *without*-L treatment in the upper space, far from the diagonal lines. This means the workers adhered to a take-all distribution without considering egalitarian fairness ideals. Worker behavior seems easily understandable in the context of the psychological situation in which workers found themselves: they felt "uncomfortable" and that their work was "unfair" when their partner simply had to click a button to decide whether to buy a calculator. It is reasonable to expect workers to lose production motivation and commit to a take-all distribution in the *without*-L treatment. As discussed above, although individuals have different roles in production, they may recognize the work as collaborative; however, the prerequisite condition for such recognition is that investor contribution is based on investor labor.

However, what is more interesting is that investors, who did not need to engage in work to earn investment funds, showed more take-all distributions than did investors engaging in labor. This contradicts the fairness ideals of the labor-value radicalist: investors who never contribute to production by their own labor expect more, while those who do contribute in this way expect less. Actually, all that investors in the without-labor treatment had to do for team production was "click" a button to purchase a calculator, but 31 % of them adhered to a take-all distribution. While we cannot say that this percentage is significantly higher than for other treatments and roles, it is high given their contribution to team earnings—clicking a button once, while their worker partners had to perform calculation tasks.

These investors' seemingly "unethical" behavior may be understood as resulting from their lack of "other-regarding" cognition. According to Bowles (2004), social preference results from other-regarding and process-regarding cognitions (p. 109). The experimental results imply that investor working experience enhanced "other-regarding" cognitions: more investors in the without-L treatment than the with-L treatment committed to a take-all distribution, because they lack work experience and found it harder to imagine worker hardship. Conversely, the "process-regarding" of workers in the without-L treatment condition seems to have increased as they can recognize the whole process and found it to be largely dependent on their labor.

4.5.4 Fairness in Functional Distribution and Implications for the Actual Economy

From these discussions based on the results of the experiments, I derive some implications of recent changes to macro-level functional distributions, meaning the decline in labor wages and the increase in stock dividends, accompanied by recent institutional changes in financial markets. Our experimental results imply that investors and workers tend to construct a cooperative relationship, and no significant gap in fairness ideals is observed between the two sides if both recognize each other's labor and contribution to production. In contrast, if investors do not contribute to the production process via their own labor, both workers and investors tend to commit to a take-all distribution.

Recent changes in market financialization and globalization may have undermined the relationship between investors and workers and led to imbalanced distributions. Due to radical deregulation in financial markets, long-term shareholders and/or banks have been replaced by an increasing number of foreign investors, individual investors, and/or corporate investors who seek short-term capital gains. This situation may be contributing to the growing gap in functional income distribution.

With respect to the situation in Japan, before the 1980s, when financial markets were relatively regulated and finance was not yet globalized, cross holdings among group companies ("Keiretsu") or main bank systems were the most prevalent form of financing for enterprises, contributing to harmonious management relationships. At that time, investors were limited to main banks or group company shareholders. Dividends were relatively low, but investors held shares long term without complaining as many became involved in enterprises and had a basis on which to recognize worker efforts or contributions to the company. From a worker's perspective, while wage rates remained relatively high in Japanese companies, Japanese business people were also known worldwide for being extremely hard workers and enormously loyal to their companies. As the CEO typically was selected from a pool of long-standing employees who had moved up the corporate ladder, the "other-regarding" attitude may have been easier to promote to investors and management on behalf of workers. Although these financial and management customs in Japan were condemned as "closed" by global markets, Japanese companies were also known for harmonious labor relations that contributed to the stable development of the Japanese economy.

However, the cooperative relationships between investors and workers gradually disintegrated following the arrival of financial market deregulation in the 1990s, which led to rapid capital inflow as the market was opened to foreign investors, individual investors, and other corporate investors. Foreign investors and/or individual investors sought short-term capital gains and became less concerned with workers; in some cases, shareholders implicitly threatened companies to declare higher dividends even at the expense of long-term value. These changes in the financial markets constitute one of the main causes of the decline in the labor income distribution rate at the macro-level, with corresponding growth in shareholder capital distribution rates.

Applying our experimental studies to the institutional change in the financial situation in Japan described above can effectively explain the cause of the shift from labor- to investor-weighted functional distribution at a micro-level. Most investors from corporations or main banks have working experience in similar domestic companies in Japan and often participate in management processes at such companies. Thus, it may be easy for them to recognize or imagine worker efforts, something that would be difficult for foreign or individual investors. Restated, investors from main banks or corporations face a situation that enables them to enhance their "other-regarding" attitudes toward workers and manage their investment without pressure for large short-term capital gain; meanwhile, foreign investors and individual investors face a situation where they require higher shareholder distribution rates. From the worker perspective, most managers or CEOs are selected from long-serving employees, and thus workers can easily imagine that both managers and CEOs, as well as investors from corporations and major banks, are contributing to the company's production through "their labor"; workers cannot see the same for foreign investors or individual investors. Harmonious relationships between employers and employees in traditional Japanese management styles were necessary outcomes of conditions that enhance the "other-regarding" and "process-regarding" social preferences of both groups. In contrast, financialization necessarily involves conditions that reduce "other-regarding" and "process-regarding" attitudes of both investors and workers, leading to lower wage rates and weakened worker bargaining power. Stockhammer (2013), referred to at the beginning of this paper, concludes from his correlation analysis at the macro-level that financialization is a significant cause of the decline in the labor income distribution rate in developed countries. Our experimental analysis corroborates his claim by looking at micro-level behaviors.

The other implications that I derive from our experiments concern the compromises between workers and investors in the income distribution process; these compromises largely depend on the characteristics of investment funds, specifically whether the funds originate from investor labor. The reason participants recognized the difference in capital in our experimental settings was clear: in our experiments participants only participate in one production and distribution process, meaning they can easily grasp the characteristics of capital in the game; participants clearly recognize the relationship between worker and investor. This may imply that conditions that allow recognition of the source of capital will affect individuals' perceptions of distributive justice.

In contrast to the understandable behaviors of workers, who become unmotivated and seek take-all distributions in the *without*-L treatment, it was intriguing that investors in the *without*-L treatment showed more take-all distribution patterns than did those in the *with*-L treatment. Although their only task in the production process was decide whether to buy a calculator, 36.4 % of investors chose to self-distribute all the production earnings and leave nothing to their partner workers. It could be said that investors who do not work had difficulty imagining worker hardships as the game did not provide them with this experience. In other words, an "other-regarding" attitude, which is a prerequisite for social preference according to Bowls, may be enhanced by sharing an experience with others and dampened by a lack of shared experiences. As investors in the *without*-L treatment did not share in the labor, their valuations of that labor may have been weakened by their lack of "other-regarding" attitudes.

Although a self-serving bias tended to make investors prefer an income-based egalitarian distribution, in which they kept property with which they were endowed, while workers preferred a radical egalitarian distribution, in which investor property was redistributed, those differences had a relatively small impact on preferred fairness ideals, implying that room exists for negotiating a compromise between the sides. However, in the case where investors receive investment funds as an endowment and do not engage in production, most workers and investors adhere to take-all distributions, which seem to make compromise difficult.

4.6 Conclusions

To examine individual fairness ideals under a functional income distribution, I have performed distribution experiments involving workers and investors, where each group performs different roles in the production process. I found different patterns of fairness ideals under a functional income distribution compared with a nonfunctional distribution. What was important to distributive justice in a functional income distribution was not how much an investor or worker contributed to production, but whether they earned their investment funds through their own labor. Both investors and workers tended to be unselfish and egalitarian when the former earned their investment funds by their own labor. On both sides, a difference in egalitarian direction was observed that may stem from self-serving bias; that is, workers were observed to prefer a radical egalitarian distribution, whereas investors preferred an income-based egalitarian distribution. However, this difference was not so extreme that workers and investors could not possibly find a compromise. In the case involving endowment of investment funds, where investors did not need to work to earn funds, the distribution gap between investors and workers seems so large as to preclude any compromise position. Our experimental results showed that both sides tended to be more take-all in that case, in addition to workers experiencing less motivation and productivity. Our experimental results and analysis may partly explain both recent declines in labor wages and increases in dividends accompanied by institutional change. Financialization may have created a situation where investors adopt a more take-all position and pay less regard to workers. Although our experimental studies were limited to artificial conditions in a laboratory, they nevertheless seem to have implications for recent macro-level situations. This experimental study, based on one-shot games, should be built on further using a repeated game to better approximate an actual situation over the longer term.

Appendix

Instructions for the with-Labor Treatment

> Thank you very much for attending this economic experiment. An experimenter will now explain the rules of the game. Please read the instructions below carefully and understand the rules. You can always raise your hand and ask a question should anything be unclear.

1. Handouts

   Please check that all handouts are on the table: an instruction page, a blank sheet of paper, an answer sheet, and a sheet for writing a distribution proposal.
2. Show-up fee

   Simply showing up to participate in this game earns you an 800 point (800 yen) participation fee. This participation fee will be paid to all participants on top of any income points they earn through the game.
3. Investors and workers

   Each participant is assigned the role of either investor or worker. Individual investors and workers are matched into pairs. Your partner is randomly decided by a computer. No participants, including any experimenter, can know who is an investor or a worker, or who is paired with whom, either during or after the experiment.

4. Investor's calculation task to earn investment funds

   At the beginning of a game, 100 questions comprising three-digit numbers (Q1, Q2, Q3 . . .) are displayed on the screens of participants assigned to the investor role. The correct answer to each question is obtained by multiplying the three-digit number by 37.

   Ex. Q1. 123 correct answer: 4551(=123 × 37)

   Investors earn their investment funds by engaging in this calculation task. Investors receive 10 points for each correct answer. Participants assigned to the investor role should please input their answers into each answer column on the screen. Pressing the Tab key moves the cursor to the next answer column. Please use the blank sheet of paper on the desk for your calculations. The time allowed for calculations is 10 min. When the experimenter indicates, "10 min have passed. Please stop your calculations and press the OK button in the lower right portion of the screen," please stop your calculations and press the OK button on the screen. Please do not press the OK button until the experimenter gives the signal.

   Those who are assigned the worker role, please wait during this time.

5. Investment decision by investors

   After investors have completed their work, the investment funds thus obtained are displayed on the screen of the investors that have earned them. Investors who have obtained more than 150 points in investment funds can purchase the right to use a calculation machine at a cost of 150 points paid out of their investment funds. Any remaining investment fund points automatically become part of the investor's final profit. Those assigned to the investor's role should answer the question "Do you wish to buy the right to use a calculation machine?" by simply pressing the "Yes" or "No" button on the screen. An investor that obtains less than 150 points cannot buy the right to use a calculation machine.

   Those who are assigned the worker role, please wait during this time.

6. Calculation task and calculation machine

   In the second game phase, 100 questions comprising triple digit numbers (Q1, Q2, Q3 . . .) are displayed on the screens of participants assigned to the worker role. Each question can be correctly answered simply by multiplying the triple digit number by 37.

   Ex. Q1. 123 correct answer: 4551(=123 × 37)

   Workers earn production income by engaging in a calculation task. Workers can earn 10 points of production income for each correctly answered question.

   The right-bottom of the screen of each worker whose partner bought the right to use a calculation machine displays a calculation button, together with a statement "you are a worker. Please engage in production. Since an investor of your team purchased the right to use a calculation machine, such a machine is available for your use. Please operate the machine using the calculation button at the right-bottom of the screen." Workers can operate the calculation machine using the numeric keypad on the right of their keyboards. Workers can release or implement the numeric keypad by pressing the Num Lock key.

Multiplication (×) is designated by the * key on the numeric keypad; All Clear is designated by the Esc button on the upper-left of the keyboard. Please do not press the OK button until an experimenter gives the signal. You can move the cursor to the next answer column by pressing the Tab key. You can use the blank sheet of paper for calculations.

The screens of workers whose partners did not buy a right to use the calculation machine display the statement "you are a worker. Please engage in production. Since the investor from your team did not buy the right to use a calculation machine, you cannot use a calculation machine."

Participants assigned the worker role, please work on the calculation tasks and enter your answers on the answer sheet. Workers with the right to use a calculation machine can use both the machine and the blank sheet of paper on their desks for their calculations. When the experimenter announces, "10 min have passed. Please stop your calculations and press the OK button at the lower right of the screen," please stop your calculations and press the OK button. Please do not press the OK button until the experimenter gives the signal.

Those who are assigned the investor role, please wait during this time.

7. Entry Screen

   After the calculation period ends, the entry screen is displayed to all workers. Those assigned to the worker role, please enter the answers to the calculation tasks displayed on the screen. The cursor can be moved to the next answer column by pressing the Tab key. Six minutes are allowed for entry. When the experimenter announces, "six minutes have passed. Please stop your calculations and press the OK button in the lower right portion of the screen," please stop your calculations and press the OK button. Please do not press the OK button until the experimenter gives the signal.

   Those who are assigned the investor role, please wait during this time.

8. Distribution proposal

   On completion of the worker production process, (1) average numbers of correct answers in the case without the use of a calculation machine is multiplied by 10; (2) production income of your team (= a worker's production income) will be displayed on the screens of both workers and investors. Please supply a distribution proposal that distributes the team's earnings between yourself and your partner. The sum of the two shares (your share and your partner's share) should equal total team earnings.

   For example, given total team earnings of 600 points, if your share is x, and your partner's share is y under your distribution proposal, then $x + y = 600$.

   Please fill in your distribution proposal sheet first and then enter your proposal after an experimenter gives the signal.

9. Final game profit

   A computer randomly selects one distribution proposal from those proposed by you and your partner. Total team earnings are distributed according to the selected proposal. Adding these to the 800 points paid as a show-up fee, the distributed team earnings constitute the final profit of each participant.

The remaining points that an investor has not invested are added to the investor's final profit points. For instance, for an investor who earned 230 points for use as investment funds, 80 points are added to their final profits in the case where they buy the right to use a calculation machine, while all 230 points are added in the case where they do not buy this right.

10. Points conversion and payment

Points are converted on a basis of 1 point = 1 yen and paid to each participant after the game finishes.

※ If you feel anything is unclear, please raise your hand.

Instruction for the Without-Labor Treatment

Items 1–3 and 6–10 are the same under the with-labor treatment. Items 4 and 5 are substituted as explained below.

4. Investment decision by investor

To participants assigned to the investor role, 250 points are given as their endowments. Investors can buy the right to use a calculation machine at a cost of 150 points paid out of their investment funds. The remainder of those investment funds, whether 100 points (given investment in the calculation machine) or 250 points (without investment in the machine), automatically become part of the investor's final profit. Those assigned to the investor role, please answer the question "Do you wish to buy the right to use a calculation machine?" by pressing the "Yes" or "No" button on the screen.

Those who are assigned the worker role, please wait during this time.

References

Babcock L, Loewenstein G (1997) Explaining bargaining impasse: the role of self-serving biases. J Econ Perspect 11(1):109–126

Bowles S (2004) Microeconomics: behavior, institutions, and evolution. Princeton University Press, Princeton

Bowles S, Gintis H (1998) Recasting egalitarianism: new rules for communities, states and markets. Verso, London

Camerer CF (2003) Behavioral game theory: experiments in strategic interaction. Russel Sage Foundation/Princeton University Press, New York/Princeton

Cappelen AW, Hole AD, Sorensen EO, Tungodden B (2007) The pluralism of fairness ideals: an experimental approach. Am Econ Rev 97(3):818–827

Fischbacher U (2007) z-Tree: Zurich toolbox for ready-made economic experiments. Exp Econ 10(2):171–178

Friedman M (1962) Capitalism and freedom. The University of Chicago, Chicago

Hodgskin T (1825) Labour defended against the claims of capital, or the unproductiveness of capital proved with reference to the present combinations amongst journeymen. Routledge, New York. Reprinted version. (1997)

Hoffman E, Spitzer ML (1985) Entitlements, rights, and fairness: an experimental examination of subjects' concepts of distributive justice. J Leg Stud 14:259–297

Kahneman D, Knetsch JL, Thaler RH (1990) Experimental tests of the endowment effect and the Coase theorem. J Polit Econ 98(6):1352–1375

Lavoie M, Stockhammer E (eds) (2013) Wage-led growth: an equitable strategy for economic recovery. The Palgrave Macmillan, Basingsoke

Locke J (1690/1948) Second treatise of civil government and a letter concerning toleration. Basil Blackwell, Oxford

Marx K (1867/1962) Das Capital. Buch I, Marx-Engels Werke, Band 23. Institut für Marxismus-Leninismus beim ZK der SED, Diertz Verlag, Berlin

Menger A (1904) Das Recht auf den vollen Arbeitsertrag in geschichtlicher Darstellung, Dritte verbesserteth edn. J.G. Cotta'sche Buchhandlung Nachfolger, Stuttgart

Ricardo D (1817) On the principles of political economy and taxation. John Murray, London

Stockhammer E (2013) Why have wage shares fallen? An analysis of the determinants of functional income distribution. In: Lavoie M, Stockhammer E (eds) Wage-led growth: an equitable strategy for economic recovery. Palgrave Macmillan, Basingsoke, pp 40–70

Yoshimori M (1995) Whose company is it? The concept of the corporation in Japan and the West. Long Range Plan 28(4):33–44

Chapter 5
Socially Responsible Investment: Distributive Experiment Among Investors, Companies, and Society

Abstract The last decade has witnessed growing public and academic attention being paid to socially responsible investment (SRI) as a new way of enhancing corporate governance and bringing institutional changes in financial markets. However, few studies have focused on interactions between investors and companies or the institutional settings that promote SRI. In this research, the author performed economic experiments that artificially recreate a financial market comprising investors and companies to observe which institutional settings of SRI—information disclosure, reward, and punishment—are effective for governing corporate activities that can harm or benefit society. The results of experiments showed that disclosure of information related to a company's social value somewhat reduces harmful corporate activities in relation to investor social preferences. However, it cannot exclude free-riding strategies of companies and investors and higher payment gaps among participants that result from such strategies. A rule of rewarding the company most beneficial to the public in addition to information disclosure had a significant effect in limiting public losses and narrowing payment gaps among participants. However, punishing the most harmful company had a stronger and stabilizing effect in limiting public losses and narrowing payment gaps. These experimental results imply that a combination of voluntary information disclosure to appeal to investor social preferences and compulsory punishment of harmful companies is a condition for successful SRI.

Keywords Socially responsible investment • Public goods game • Information disclosure • Punishment • Reward

5.1 Introduction

Since the 1990s, there has been a rapid increase worldwide in socially responsible investment (hereafter SRI). This is investment based on an evaluation that considers corporate activities in terms of their "social" or "sustainable" aspects. According to the survey of the Global Sustainable Investment Alliance, SRI has increased in capital terms from 13.3 trillion US dollars in 2012 to 21.4 trillion US dollars in 2014 (GSIA 2014, p. 7). This tendency has been observed in all areas of Europe, North America, Australia, and Asia, and the rate of SRI among professional investors

N. Tokumaru, *Social Preference, Institution, and Distribution*, Evolutionary Economics and Social Complexity Science 3, DOI 10.1007/978-981-10-0137-6_5

increased from 21.5 % in 2012 to 30.2 % in 2014 (ibid., p. 7). A typical form of socially responsible investment is to invest in stocks with higher ethical standards as measured by an SRI index (e.g., the Domini 400 Social Index or Dow Jones Sustainability Index), which evaluates and screens companies that match certain ethical requirements in terms of environment, working conditions, contributions to communities, and so on (cf. Renneboog et al. 2008).[1] Against the background of continuous misconduct, corruption, or environmental pollution, SRI seems to have attracted attention from an investor perspective as a new measure of govern corporate activities.

Several studies have contributed to clarifying the incentives of investors who consider social aspects of corporations in their stock investment decisions. This approach to investment still incorporates financial considerations, as such investors expect corporations with high ethical standards (CSR corporations) to achieve stable long-term returns. Some studies (Khanna and Damon 1999; Baron 2001; Tirol 2001) discuss enterprise commitment to CSR activities, specifically whether, based on consideration of stakeholders, SRI contributes to long-term firm value by decreasing conflicts with society and potential associated risks. Bollen (2007) claims SRI funds exhibit lower monthly volatility than conventional funds. Besides financial reasons, some studies (GraffZivin and Small 2005; Borghesi et al. 2014) discuss how altruism and social preference also motivate investors to follow SRI.

If investors consider the "social values" of enterprises in making investment decisions, it becomes important to ask whether SRI can substantially control corporate activities, whether socially harmful or beneficial. Does SRI contribute to limiting corporate activities that cause negative externalities for a society? Conversely, does it promote corporate activities that cause positive externalities? If so, what are the mechanisms through which SRI influences corporate governance and what factors are important to those mechanisms? Finally, in what institutional settings is it appropriate to apply SRI to the governance of corporate activities?

To answer those questions, I have designed SRI experiments involving investors and companies, who engage in several corporate activities that simultaneously bring both profits and negative/positive externalities. In the experiments of Consolandi et al. (2009), where subjects are required to allocate their endowments among corporate stocks, it is observed that subjects stock selections corresponded to ethical stock indexes. In my experiments, "ethical" or "unethical" standards are designed at the substantial rather than the hypothetical level, regardless of whether a corporate activity brings positive or negative earnings to all other participants. Thus, in this experiment, participants are more serious in their decision-making because their "unethical" decisions (e.g., investing in companies with higher externalities) actually decrease payments to other participants.

[1]There are several forms of SRI. Historically, SRI stems from religious origins and negative screening to exclude corporate stocks involved in alcohol, tobacco, or gambling. Recently, positive versions of SRI have emerged that are based on selecting ethically preferable companies according to certain standards, as well as mixed versions that employ both negative and positive screening.

To observe how companies change their strategies to balance stakeholder benefits—the distribution of profit among the company, investors, and society—in given institutional settings, the experiment is designed such that a trade-off exists in rate of returns from corporate activities and positive externalities to the public. According to this trade-off, if the rate of returns of a corporation increases, so too do negative externalities to the public (e.g., environmental pollution)—the model here is that "bad" companies have higher profitability. Conversely, if the rate of returns of a corporation decreases, positive externalities to the public (e.g., environmental protection) increase—the model here is that "good" companies have lower profitability. By creating a trade-off between profitability and positive externality, one can observe investment that is initially motivated by social incentives and its institutional effects. Real-world situations involve companies that create positive externalities while maintaining higher profitability, but such cases are omitted in this experiment as this paper aims to observe how certain institutions can control corporate strategies that can be either beneficial or harmful to themselves, investors, and society. From the perspective of sustainability, how to balance those stakeholders should also be taken into consideration.

This chapter is structured as follows: in the next section (Sect. 5.2) I explain the historical discussions on stock corporations and their social responsibility. Then, I describe the experimental design in Sect. 5.3 and explain models and predictions in Sect. 5.4. After describing experimental results in Sect. 5.5, I discuss the results and implications of SRI as an institution for corporate governance in Sect. 5.6 and finally present conclusions in Sect. 5.7.

5.2 Stock Corporations and Corporate Social Responsibility

It is interesting that Adam Smith (1776) criticized stock corporations in the *Wealth of Nations* on the basis that both managers and investors may encourage irresponsible corporate activities. In the face of the emergence of stock companies such as the East India Company, the first stock company in history, Smith found ethical problems associated with this corporate structure. According to Smith, the manager of a stock corporation does not sincerely consider the nature of their company as they are merely doing their job by investing money on behalf of others. In the words of Smith, for "The directors of such companies, however, being the managers rather of other people's money than of their own, it cannot well be expected that they should watch over it with the same anxious vigilance with which the partners in a private company frequently watch over their own" (p. 741). Conversely, shareholders do not sincerely participate in corporate management as members, as they simply hold stocks that can always be sold to others in a financial market. Smith's discussion was prophetic if we review the current discussion of corporate governance and its central questions: where the ownership of a company lies and in whose benefit it should act.

Almost one and a half centuries after Smith's prophecy, in the USA of the late 1920s where giant corporate capitalism had developed, Berle and Means (1932) observed the powers of corporate managers grow stronger. According to them, as a result of the development of monopolistic capitalism, giant corporations have become incredibly powerful and their activities strongly influence people's lives, as well as economies and politics. However, in 1929 the largest single shareholders of huge corporations such as the Pennsylvania railroad or US Steel held less than 1 % of the stock on issue. Because the powers of shareholders, as owners of stock corporations, were dispersed and they no longer substantially influenced corporations, Berle and Means concluded that stock corporations are controlled by managers, who undertake actual management process, rather than being controlled by shareholders. Their analysis came to be well known in corporate history for marking a shift from shareholder control to "management control."

After the groundbreaking analysis above, Berle (1955) extended his ideas in *The Twentieth Century Capitalist Revolution*, which can be regarded as the origin of corporate social responsibility. Berle holds that corporations came to have a huge influence on society and people's lives, sometimes exceeding that of government, and that their managers should consider the possible influences of corporate activities on a society and its people and should have a philosophy on which to base their decisions regarding corporate activities. In this sense, a stock corporation ceases to be a form of privately owned organization that serves to increase shareholder profit, but rather is a *social institution* that forms a part of a society and has responsibility to its stakeholders. Nowadays, this idea concerning corporate identification is known as a "stakeholder company," the primary mission of which is to serve its stakeholders, including workers, consumers, business partners, and local communities (see Jensen 2001).

The other contrary position for understanding stock corporations is that of Friedman (1962, 1970), who regards corporate managers solely as agents of investors whose primary mission is to serve investors, as well represented in the title of his paper, "The Social Responsibility of Business Is to Increase Its Profits." In Friedman's view, stock corporations are the private property of shareholders, and their managers are merely agents commissioned by their owners. Thus, the obligations of corporate managers should be to increase shareholder benefit rather than simply to take care of stakeholders. Friedman (1962) states, [in a free economy] "... there is one and only one social responsibility of business—to use its resources and engage in activities designed to increase its profits so long as it stays within the rules of the game, which is to say, engages in open and free competition without deception or fraud" (p. 133). This interpretation of the role of stock corporations as agencies of investors is summarized in the term "shareholder company."

Whether from the position of a "stakeholder company" or a "shareholder company," socially responsible investment proposes a new perspective on the picture of corporate governance. If SRI contributes to the regulation of corporate activities that have negative or positive externalities for stakeholders and boost CSR, it should be promoted from the "stakeholder company" perspective. SRI also can be compatible with the idea of a "shareholder company": if a certain amount of corporate shareholders wish for their corporation to engage in CSR activities or to avoid certain activities that negatively influence society, managers should consider the social values of the company, not only its profits, thus acting as "agents" of investors. In that sense, SRI can use institutional measures to coordinate shareholder and social values. However, whether and how this can be realized should be investigated.

5.3 Experimental Design

To examine whether SRI works as a means to regulate corporate activities that have negative/positive externalities for society, I have designed experiments by modifying the public goods game (see Ledyard 1995; Feher and Gächter 2000). Typical rules of the public goods game require subjects to allocate a certain amount of their private endowments to public goods and to multiply this invested amount and divide it equally among all participants. Any endowments not invested in public goods are kept by subjects and no public contribution is made. The total payoff of all participants is maximized when all participants invest all of their endowments in public goods, that is, at the point of indicating the Pareto optimum (cooperation). However, because subjects always have incentives to seek a free ride (gaining extra benefits from public goods without making an associated public contribution), investing nothing in public goods is a rational choice, and the Nash equilibrium occurs at the point where all participants keep their endowments without making any public contribution, based on the free-riding incentive. Most experimental results for the public goods game show that a certain investment in the public good was observed at the start of the game period, but investments in the public goods game decrease as the game is repeated and approaches the Nash equilibrium.

In my experiments, participant decisions also have externalities to the public, but I designed the game such that interactions occur between subjects with investor roles and those with corporate roles. In the experiments, each subject is assigned the role of either an investor or a corporation. Subjects assigned to the corporation role are required to engage in corporate projects that yield both project profits and public losses/gains. Those assigned to the investor role are required to invest their endowments in a selection of corporations (1–3 corporations), with their 600 point endowments being broken into investment units of 200 points. Endowments invested in a corporation become the "investment fund" of that corporation and enable it to engage in corporate projects. A company that attracts significant investment funds from investors can increase both its corporate profit and public gain/loss yields.

Project profits are designed to be traded off against public gains; that is, public gain decreases (public loss increases) as profit rate increases (see Table 5.1). The rate of public loss or gain is such that $x\%$ of invested funds is divided by the number of participants and each participant is assigned extra negative or positive points. For instance, if company A, which gathered 1000 points in investment funds from investors, allocates all its investment funds entirely to project 6 (return rate

Table 5.1 Return rate and rate of public losses/gains by corporate project

	Project 1	Project 2	Project 3	Project 4	Project 5	Project 6
Rate of return (γ)	10 %	15 %	20 %	30 %	35 %	40 %
Public loss (−) or public gain (+) (P)	+30 %	+20 %	+10 %	−10 %	−20 %	−30 %

40 %; public loss −30 %), the project profit gained through this corporate activity is 400 points, and the company's activities result in a profit deduction of $-300/n$ per participant given n participants. The rates of public losses/gains are designed to be traded off against company return $P_i = 0.5 - 2\gamma_i$ where γ_i designates the return for project i and P_i designates the rate of public gain/loss for project i. If rate of return increases, so too does rate of public loss, whereas if the rate of return decreases, the rate of public gain increases and vice versa, as shown in Table 5.1.

Details of the experimental settings are as follows. Participants are assigned to either the corporation or investor roles and participate in a game that involves seven repetitions. Each period consists of (1) an investment stage, (2) a corporate activity stage, (3) a distribution stage, and (4) an income stage (see Table 5.2). In the investment stage, subjects assigned to the investor role are required to allocate their 600 endowment points, split into units of 200 points, among companies denoted by letters of the alphabet (company A, company B, etc.), where each letter designates an actual participant assigned to the company role. In the following stage, which involves corporate activities, subjects assigned the company role must allocate investment funds they gathered from investors to projects numbered from 1 to 6, each of which yields a certain rate of return and has certain public losses or gains, with the unit of allocation being 100 points (see Table 5.1). After the corporate activity stage, subjects assigned to companies must decide a distribution rate to investors (0–100 %), which designates the proportion of their returns that companies give back to investors. For instance, if a company gains profits of 400 points from its project activities and sets a distribution rate to investors of 60 %, the income of that company will be 160 points, whereas that of its investors will be 240 points. In the final income stage, the final income of each participant, information on each company, total negative/positive externalities, and externalities associated with each participant are displayed on each screen. Investment funds do not count toward the final profit of either investors or companies, which comprises only the profit gained from investments or corporate projects. The information displayed differs by treatment, as explained below.

The experiment involved the following four treatments, with each subject participating in one of them.

- Baseline treatment (hereafter baseline)

  In this treatment, subjects are shown each company's dividend rate (multiples of its return rate and distribution rate) at the end of a period, total public loss or gain of all companies, public loss or gain for each participant, and their own profit for the period.

Table 5.2 Game procedures for one period

Investment Stage [Investors]	Selecting 1-3 companies and invest all of 600 endowment points by 200 points.
Stage of corporate activities [Companies]	Companies allocate investment funds they gathered from investors to corporate activities that yield certain profit and negative/positive externalities by 100 points. A company attracted no investment fund is automatically financed 100 points by a bank.
Distribution Stage [Companies]	Companies decide distribution (0-100%) rate to investors that separate corporate profit with themselves and investors.
Incomestage [Companies and investors]	Information on final income and each companiesis displayed as following by treatment: **[Baseline]:** Dividend rate of each company, total negative/positive externalities **[Information, Punishment, Reward]:** Dividend rate, total negative/positive externalities and negative/positive externality of each company **[Punishment, Reward]:** Whether accident happened or not.

- Treatment with information (hereafter information)

  In the last stage of this treatment, participants are informed of the *public loss/gain yielded by each enterprise* during the period on the screen in addition to each company's dividend rate, the total public loss or gain of all companies, the public loss or gain of each participant, and their own profit for the period.
- Punishment treatment with information (hereafter punishment)

  In this treatment, the return rate of a company that has yielded the largest public loss decreases by half with 50 % probability. For instance, in a case where a company engaged in corporate project 6—with a 40 % return rate and public loss of −30 %—is punished, the return rate becomes 20 %. Other conditions are the same as for the *information* treatment.
- Reward treatment with information (hereafter reward)

  In this treatment, the return rate of a company that has yielded the highest public gain is doubled with 50 % probability. For instance, in a case where a company engaged in corporate project 1—with a 10 % return rate and public gain of +30 %—is rewarded, the return rate becomes 20 %. Other conditions are the same as for the *information* treatment.

By the *baseline* treatment I virtualize a typical financial market, where investors make decisions based on dividend information for each. The *information* treatment virtualizes the situation in a financial market where investors have enough information on corporate activities that are negative/positive to society and can perform SRI based on social preferences. The *punishment* and *reward* treatments virtualize the situation whereby a "good" company (highest public gains) and its investors are financially rewarded, while a "bad" company (causing the highest public losses) and its investors are financially punished. In this treatment, SRI is motivated not only by investor social preferences but also financial incentives.

5.4 Models and Predictions

5.4.1 *Value Function*

Now let me suppose a subject i with the role of an investor has a value function V_i, in a game where the number of participants is n (=2m) and half of participants are allocated the investor role (i=1, 2, ... m), while the remaining half are allocated the corporate role (j=1, 2, ... m). Let me designate λ_{is} as the load factor on the material utility of i (weight on selfishness), λ_{ip} as the load factor on the social preference of i (weight on public), and $0 \leq \lambda_{is}, \lambda_{ip}, \lambda_{is} + \lambda_{ip} = 1$. For simplicity, the distribution rate for investors here is supposed to be a constant $\overline{\phi} = 0.5$. The subject's value function is expressed as follows:

$$\max_{a_{ij}} V_i = \lambda_{is} \sum_{j=1}^{m} a_{ij} \left(\gamma_j \overline{\phi} + \frac{0.5 - 2\gamma_j}{n} \right) + \lambda_{ip} \sum_{j=1}^{m} a_{ij} \left(0.5 - 2\gamma_j \right)$$

where a_{ij} denotes investment fund i invested in company j and γ_j denotes the return rate of company j. Public losses/gains from corporate project activities are designed to be $0.5-2\gamma$; public loss/gain per person resulting from the project activities of company j is designated as $(0.5 - 2\gamma_j)/n$.

Similarly, we can express a company j's value function as follows:

$$\max_{\gamma_j} V_j = \lambda_{js} \sum_{i=1}^{m} a_{ji} \left(\gamma_j \overline{\phi} + \frac{0.5 - 2\gamma_j}{n} \right) + \lambda_{jp} \sum_{i=1}^{m} a_{ji} \left(0.5 - 2\gamma_j \right)$$

where a_{ij} denotes investment funds j gathered from investor i.

If a subject performing the corporate role is completely selfish, meaning his load factors on material utility will be one while those on social preferences will be zero $((\forall i) (\lambda_{is}, \lambda_{ip}) = (1, 0))$, then the optimum response is to engage in the most profitable project with the highest public loss ($\gamma^* = \gamma_{\text{Max}} = 0.4, P^* = P_{\text{Min}} = -0.3$) (see Table 5.1 in Sect. 5.3). Similarly, if a subject performing the investor role is completely selfish, her optimum response is to invest all of her investment funds in a company with the highest profit and highest public loss. If all participants are completely selfish, the total project profit per period is maximized, at $600 \times \text{m} \times 0.4 = 240\text{m}$, but so too is the total public loss, at $600 \times \text{m} \times (-0.3) = -180\text{m}$. Thus, the total final income of all participants becomes the lowest: $(240\text{m} - 180\text{m}) = 60\text{m}$. As the total number of participants is $n = 2\text{m}$, the average final income per participant is 60m/2m = 30 points in this case.

If subjects are completely unselfish—their load factors on material utility are zero and their load factors on social preferences are one $\left((\forall i)\left(\lambda_{is}, \lambda_{ipi}\right) = (0, 1)\right)$— the optimum response of investors to this situation is to invest in companies with the lowest rate of return and highest public gain, while the optimum response of companies is to engage in projects with the lowest rate of return and the highest public gain ($\gamma^* = \gamma_{\text{Min}} = 0.1, \text{P}^* = P_{\text{Max}} = 0.3$) (see Table 5.1 in Sect. 5.3). In this case, total project profit per period is minimized, at $600 \times \text{m} \times 0.1 = 60\text{m}$, while total public gain per period is maximized, at $600 \times \text{m} \times (0.3) = 180\text{m}$. The total profit of all subjects is maximized $(60\text{m} + 180\text{m}) = 240\text{m}$, while in this case the average final income per participant is 240m/2m = 120 points.

As is shown, the experiment is designed such that average income is four times higher if all participants behave unselfishly (120 points) than if all behave selfishly (30 points) (the distribution of the total income of all participants among individuals is ignored here for simplicity). However, every participant is also tempted to be a "free rider" in the former situation, that is, to gain higher returns with higher public loss, receiving the benefit of public gains yielded by other participants. Thus, the institutional settings that enhance cooperative behaviors and consequently increase the total benefit of all participants should be investigated.

5.4.2 Investment Funds and Companies' Performance Information in Past Periods

From the value function of a company as shown above, we have seen that corporate profits depend significantly on *popularity among investors*: a company able to attract significant investment funds can earn huge corporate profits. For instance, suppose a case where company A attracts no investment and thus is funded by a bank to the amount of 100 points, while company B attracts funding of 800 points from investors. In this case, even if company A engages in a corporate project with the highest return rate (40 %) and company B engages in a corporate project with the lowest return rate (10 %), the profit of the former will be only 40 points versus 80 points for the latter. Thus, companies interested in profit maximization should consider investor preference.

Investors decide the allocation of their investment funds (600 points) among companies and in doing so refer to the *performance information of each company in past periods*, as measured by dividends and public gains/losses (in treatments other than the baseline). Because the performance information of all companies is displayed simultaneously in the final stage of the period, investors should compare the performance of each company in their decision-making during the next period. Thus, to attract more investment funds from investors for the following stages, a company should show investors a *relatively* attractive performance compared with other companies.

- Baseline

In the baseline treatment, where information on the public loss of each company is not given to participants, investors should decide the funds they invest in each company by referring to past dividends—determined by multiplying return rate γ by the distribution rate for investors φ. We can express the situation where investment fund A_{jt}^{B}, gathered by company j from investors during period t in the baseline treatment, is a function of all company dividends in the past period $(1, 2, \ldots t-1)$ as follows:

$$A_{jt}^{B} = f\left(\sum_{k=1}^{t-1} \gamma_{1k}\phi_{1k}, \sum_{k=1}^{t-1} \gamma_{2k}\phi_{2k} \ldots \sum_{k=1}^{t-1} \gamma_{jk}\phi_{jk} \ldots \sum_{k=1}^{t-1} \gamma_{mk}\phi_{mk}\right)$$

where γ_{jk} denotes company j's return rate in period k and φ_{jk} denotes company j's distribution rate for investors in period k.

Naturally, the company with the highest aggregate dividend in the past period should attract more investment funds from investors in this treatment. Since companies should be competing to attract investors, they should attempt to set their dividends higher than their rivals. In this case, the highest dividend during a previous period becomes a reference, and companies should set their dividends higher. Even if companies preliminarily have sufficient social preferences and engage in corporate projects with higher public gains, competition would see them shift to a more profitable project with higher public losses as the game proceeds. Companies can also increase their dividend rate by increasing the distribution rate for investors φ, but should refrain from doing so because it directly cuts their final profit by decreasing the distribution rate for themselves. From the above discussion, we can derive the following prediction:

Prediction 1: Companies tend to shift to a higher return rate with higher public losses as the game continues in the baseline treatment; this occurs because investors have no information on the public losses of each company and companies compete to attract investment funds.

- Information treatment

Unlike in the baseline treatment, the public losses/gains yielded by each company are displayed on all participants' screens in the last stage of each period.

Thus, investors, provided they are not completely selfish ($\lambda_{s1} \neq 0$), consider the information on the public losses/gains of each company in their decision-making during the investment stage. Companies can attract investment funds from investors by lowering profit rates—therefore increasing public gains—if there are unselfish investors.

However, selfish investors without social preferences ($\lambda_{s1} = 0$) do not care about the public losses/gains of each company and only consider dividends. In this case, a company engaged in activities with higher returns in past periods can attract investment funds and thus achieve profits. Thus, we can express the situation as the investment funds A^I_{jt} that a company j gathers from investors during period t in the information treatment being a function of the social preferences of all investors ($\lambda_{s1}, \ \lambda_{s2} \ldots \lambda_{sm}$), all companies' public losses/gains in the past period, and the distribution rate for investors in the past period, as follows:

$$A^I_{jt} = f\left(\lambda_{s1}, \ \lambda_{s2\ldots}\lambda_{sm}, \sum_{k=1}^{t-1} P_{1k}, \sum_{k=1}^{t-1} P_{2k} \ldots \sum_{k=1}^{t-1} P_{jk} \ldots \sum_{k=1}^{t-1} P_{mk}, \right.$$
$$\left. \sum_{k=1}^{t-1} \phi_{1k}, \sum_{k=1}^{t-1} \phi_{2k} \ldots \sum_{k=1}^{t-1} \phi_{jk} \ldots \sum_{k=1}^{t-1} \phi_{mk} \right)$$

If one considers public losses/gains automatically, this means also considering return rates, which are functions of public losses/gains.

In this treatment, just as in the baseline treatment, there should be competition among companies to attract investment funds. However, because investors know the public losses/gains of each company, the direction of the competition becomes twofold depending on investor social preference: investors with higher social preference invest in "good" companies with higher public gains, while investors with lower social preference invest in "bad" companies with higher public losses if we assume a constant distribution rate for investors. Thus, in the information treatment the total public loss will be decreased compared with the baseline treatment given the existence of some unselfish investors. Further, given the simultaneous existence of some investors with higher social preferences and some with lower social preferences, both "good" and "bad" companies have chances to attract investment funds from both types of investors. From these discussions, we derive the following predictions:

Prediction 2: Total public losses tend to be greater in the information treatment than the baseline treatment. Because investors are informed of each company's public loss in this treatment, unselfish investors prefer companies with lower public losses. Companies are separated into "good" and "bad" types in this treatment because both have a possibility of attracting investment funds, depending on investor social preferences.

- Punishment/reward treatment

In the punishment and reward treatments, the experimental settings regarding companies' information are the same as in the *information* treatment: the differences lie in whether companies face the 50 % probability of paying a penalty for yielding higher public losses (a punishment that halves their rate of returns) versus the 50 % probability of a reward for yielding the highest public gains (doubling their return rate) in the reward treatment.

In considering expected corporate profit, participants do not need to respond to the possibility of receiving punishment if they are rational and selfish. Suppose a case where a company engages in project 6, which has the highest public loss and maximum return rate ($P_{Min} = -0.3$; $\gamma_{Max} = 0.4$). In this case, the public loss caused by the company is likely to exceed that caused by any other company, although the degree of loss also depends on the amount of investment funds gathered. If we assume for simplicity that the company always causes the highest public loss in this case, the expected corporate profit is $0.4A \times 0.5 \times 0.5 + 0.4A \times 0.5 = 0.3A$, where A denotes the investment funds gathered. In this case, the expected profit equals that in project 4 (0.3A), while projects 1–3 all have a lower expected corporate profit (0.1A; 0.15A; 0.2A). Thus, even given the punishment treatment, companies that are completely selfish and rational should not have any incentive to engage in projects 1, 2, and 3, despite them offering higher public gains; investors also have no such incentive.

Similarly, suppose a case where, under the reward treatment, a company engages in a project with the highest public gains and the lowest return rate ($P_{Max} = 0.3$; $\gamma_{Min} = 0.1$). If we assume the company yields the highest public gains and has a 50 % probability of being rewarded through a doubling of its profit, then the expected corporate profit is $0.1A \times 2 \times 0.5 + 0.1A \times 0.5 = 0.15A$, which is the same as in project 2. Projects 3, 4, 5, and 6 have a higher expected corporate profit (0.2A; 0.3A; 0.35A; 0.4A) in this case. Thus, even in the reward treatment, companies have no incentive to engage in the project with higher public gains if they are completely selfish and rational; this same lack of incentive also exists for investors.

As is discussed, the financial effect of changing expected profit in punishment/reward treatments is theoretically not substantial. Even if we assume that subjects are not completely selfish, these settings give them financial incentives only and thus should not affect their social preferences. However, if subjects are more motivated by these institutional settings than by actual expected profit, the settings may act to reduce public loss. The question thus is whether the institutional settings exert any actual effect in limiting public loss and increasing public gain and whether either punishment or reward is more *effective* for limiting total public loss.

Kahneman and Tversky (1979) have shown that individuals' utility function do not respond to loss and gain at the same rate; that is, the utility decrease that individuals suffer from losses tends to exceed the utility increase they realize from gains: "A salient characteristic of attitudes to changes in welfare is that losses loom larger than gains." This tendency of individuals is widely known as "loss aversion."

If we assume that punishment and reward treatments reduce public losses, we may be able to presume that the former is more effective than the latter because of this tendency and so can derive the following prediction:

- *Prediction 3*: Because individuals tend to evaluate their losses more highly than their gains based on the tendency of "loss aversion," punishment treatment is more effective than reward treatment for limiting total public loss.

5.4.3 Public Gains/Losses, Distribution Rate for Investors, and Company Types

In the above discussions, the distribution rate for investor ϕ was assumed to be constant. However, in the actual game settings, a company can also change the distribution rate for investors. Naturally, if a company sets ϕ lower for a period, this will increase the profit of the company for that period. However, this action may also decrease investment funds from investors from the next period because of the lowered company dividend. Thus, in relation to their long-term profitability, companies must consider both the most appropriate degree of distribution rate for investors and public losses/gains.

As has already been explained, this experiment is designed such that the final income of all participants is minimized when both companies and investors behave selfishly and total public loss is maximized; conversely, income is maximized if all parties act unselfishly and total public gain is maximized. Reflecting on the real situation, if all companies and investors simply pursue their own profit without considering the environment, total profit ultimately is minimized—overfishing leaves the sea depleted of fish; conversely, if all companies and investors care for the environment, they can enjoy natural bounty and resources over the long term. However, even if the latter scenario is preferable, the balance will not be sustainable if either investors or companies gain higher profits.

Thus, an important question involves the institutional settings that are most effective for increasing total income and equally distributing benefits among investors and companies. This question concerns discussion of the stance or philosophy of companies in prioritizing the interests of their shareholders, stakeholders, or society, such as that in Sect. 5.2. An institutional setting that can successfully govern companies' behaviors and balance the benefits of different stakeholders will be preferable from the viewpoint of sustainability.

Degrees of return rate and distribution rate for investors can be used to classify companies into the following four types (see Fig. 5.1):

- Shareholder company

  This type of company engages in corporate activities that are highly profitable but have negative externalities for society. However, shareholders of this company type can gain higher dividends because such companies set higher

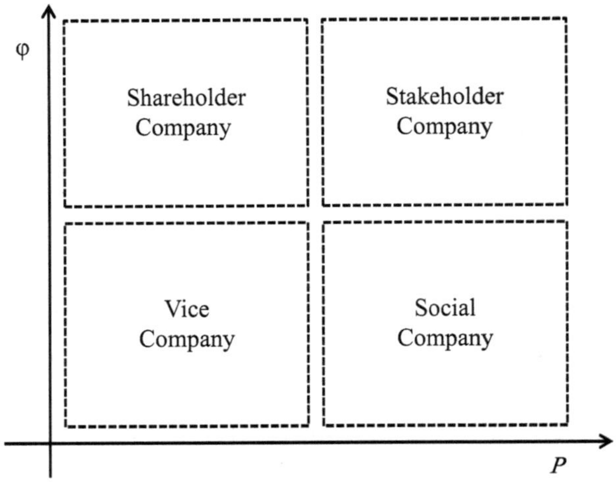

Fig. 5.1 Classifications of company types by public gain/loss (P) and investor

distribution rates for investors. This company type actualizes the philosophy of Friedman (1970) that "the social responsibility of business is to increase its profits" as an agent of its shareholders.

- Stakeholder company

  This type of company engages in corporate activities that are not profitable but have positive externalities for society. This company type also sets higher distribution rates for investors, thus resulting in dividends set at a level that falls around the middle of the range. In this case, the company prioritizes shareholders and stakeholders equally and can be regarded as a "good" company. CSR companies are real-world examples of this situation.

- Vice (money-oriented) company

  This company type engages in corporate activities that yield higher profit and are accompanied by higher negative externalities. Naturally, corporate profit is high, but this company type distributes profit to investors at only a low level, with dividends remaining in the middle of the range despite high profits. Thus, this company type has higher profits than other types. This company type can be regarded as the worst from an ethical perspective because its behavior is oriented to profit maximization and neither society nor shareholders benefit from the profits.

- Social company

  This company type engages in corporate activities that have lower profitability but bring higher public gains. This type of company is oriented to do something "good" for the society, and thus the distribution rate for investors remains lower. Nonprofit organizations would be the typical example in the case considered here.

Naturally, vice companies are clearly harmful, whether to society or shareholders. A shareholder company is much better than a vice company in the sense that it contributes to its shareholders as Friedman expects. However, a shareholder company still results in relatively high negative externalities for the public. A stakeholder company or social company is preferable not only for society but also for companies and investors themselves, because both companies and investors also suffer from negative externalities if all companies are engaged in activities with higher public losses. The difference between a stakeholder company and a social company lies in the distribution rate between investors and companies.

From the viewpoint of corporate governance, we should ask what kinds of institutional settings decrease the number of "vice companies," which do not benefit either investors or stakeholders, and encourage corporations to act as "stakeholder companies" or "social companies." Compared with other treatments, the baseline treatment should approach the "vice company" model because there is a lack of information disclosure on public losses/gains and company yield under the treatment as is discussed in predictions 2 and 3. By analyzing the results of the experiment, in the following section I ask how and to what extent each institutional setting combined with SRI is effective for limiting harmful activities of companies.

5.5 Experimental Results

5.5.1 Overviews

Experiments were performed eight times at the laboratory of Kyoto University from May to June 2015. In total, 109 undergraduate students from all faculties participated in one of the treatments, and the average number of participants per experiment was 13.6. Each experiment took an average of approximately 1 h, including instruction, game, and payment. All participants were given 800 yen ($\cong$6.4 US dollars) as an attendance fee, almost equivalent to 1 h of work for the minimum wage in Japan. This was paid independent of profits gained by the game.

Table 5.3 shows a summary of the final payoff by treatment. Interestingly, the total payoff was higher in the information treatment than the baseline treatment. The payoff was significantly higher in the reward and punishment treatments than the baseline and information treatments. These differences in final payoff mainly stem from degrees of public gains/losses: subjects in the baseline treatments experience larger total public loss, while subjects in the reward/punishment treatment do not. Table 5.3 shows the average public losses/gains in each period by treatment and shows the average public loss to be highest in the baseline treatment and lowest in the punishment treatment. Nine participants suffered deductions for public losses in the information treatment (29 %) as did a further nine in the baseline treatment (33 %). Only one participant suffered a loss in the reward treatment, and no participant suffered a negative payoff involving their final profits in the punishment

Table 5.3 Final payoff[a] by treatment

			Median		
	Max	Min[b]	Investor	Company	Total
Baseline ($N = 27$)	1405	−201	−20	450	117
Information ($N = 31$)	1982	−252	38	412	198
Reward ($N = 28$)	929	−99	560	430	556
Punishment ($N = 23$)	900	271	419	468	441

[a]The unit of measurement is yen. One hundred yen is approximately equal to 1 US dollar.
[b]Participants with negative final payoffs still received their entire attendance fee. That is, their final profit was treated as zero for remuneration purposes. This was done for ethical reasons, namely, to ensure participants received the minimum legal wage per hour

treatment. Notably, in the punishment treatment, where the project profit of a corporation with the highest public loss has a 50 % probability of facing a profit deduction, the total payoff is much higher than in the baseline or information treatments where no financial punishment exists.

The other interesting point is the imparity of final payoff by treatments. In the baseline and information treatments, the gaps are large, whereas in the reward and punishment treatments, the gaps are smaller. In the baseline treatment, the maximum final payoff is 1405 yen and the minimum is −201 yen, for a gap of 1606 yen (≅13.3 US dollars). In contrast, in the punishment treatment, the maximum payoff is 900 yen, and the minimum is 271 yen, for a gap of only 629 yen. Both the baseline and information treatments show large variations in final payoff relative to the punishment and reward treatments. The average absolute deviation from the median value was 346.9 for the baseline, versus 344.7 for the information treatment, 140.7 for the punishment treatment, and 229.4 for the reward treatment.

The relatively higher gaps observed in the baseline and information treatments stem from the "free rider" strategy of some companies. For instance, under the baseline, the company that earned the highest dividend (36 %) in the previous period gathered 2800 yen in the fourth period and engaged in project 6 (with the highest profit and the highest public loss). The public loss made by this company during this period was −840 yen, but the company also gained 1018 yen during this same period, as it set a distribution rate for investors of zero and so retained all project profit. Another subject in the information treatment gathered investment funds of 2200 yen during period 2 and also engaged in project 6, bringing a corporate profit of 880 yen. This subject set a distribution rate of 40 %, but gained profits of 460 yen, yielding a public loss of −660 yen for the period. The higher gap in final payoff between investors and companies was not observed in the reward and punishment treatments, in which companies were motivated to refrain from their free-riding behaviors by punishment or reward for their public losses/gains. Thus, we can summarize these results with the following thesis:

Thesis 1: The imparities of final payoff among participants are relatively high in the baseline and information treatments compared with the reward or punishment treatments.

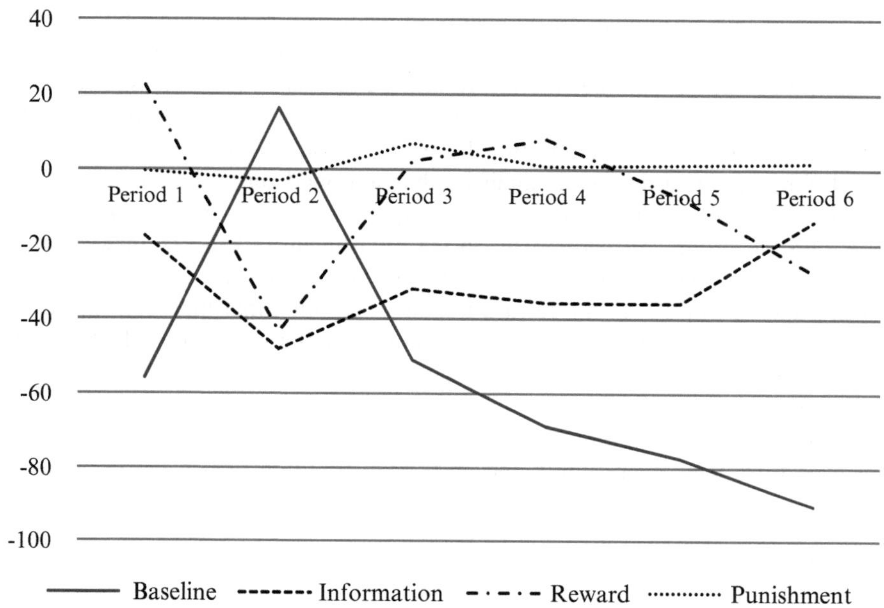

Graph 5.1 Average public gain/loss per person by treatment

5.5.2 *Trends in Public Gain/Loss and Distribution Rate by Treatment*

Graph 5.1 shows the trend of average public gain/loss per person over the game period by treatment. The overall trend for each treatment is quite specific.

In the baseline treatment, the public loss per person increases as the game continues, after a small increase in public gain during period 2. The degree of average loss in the baseline treatment remains highest among all treatments except for period 2. This would explain the lowest average final payoff in the baseline, as shown in Table 5.3. Because most enterprises selected corporate activities with higher profit that yield huge public losses in this treatment, total public losses remains higher throughout the game, with the result that the income levels of each participant are lowered. Actually, in the questionnaire survey conducted after the game, 11 out of 13 participants who performed the company role in the baseline answered that they preferred highly profitable projects—those which bring higher public loss—as a means to gather investment funds.

In the information treatment, the average public loss per person is lower than for the baseline, but remains relatively high compared with the reward and punishment treatments. However, in contrast with the baseline, for the information treatment, the level of public loss does not decrease as the game continues, remaining at around −30. This is reflected in the questionnaire survey for investors in this treatment, in which 5 out of 15 investors (33.3 %) answered that they preferred companies with high public gain.[2] Although the number of investors that prefer higher public gains is not significantly high, we can observe that the rate increases in the information treatment compared with the baseline, resulting in a smaller public loss.

In both the punishment and reward treatments, the average public loss per person remains low compared with the baseline and information treatments. A big difference is that the trend remains stable at around zero throughout the game period in the punishment treatment, whereas in the reward treatment it fluctuates. In line with the results, all participants in the punishment treatments answered that they considered the possibility of punishment in the questionnaire survey. Most participants (10 of 12) in the reward treatment reported that they considered the chance of reward. However, the results show that the punishment had a more significant and stable effect in limiting public loss than rewarding participants in each period.

Graph 5.2 shows the average investor distribution rates decided by companies for each treatment. Interestingly, the level of distribution rate in the information

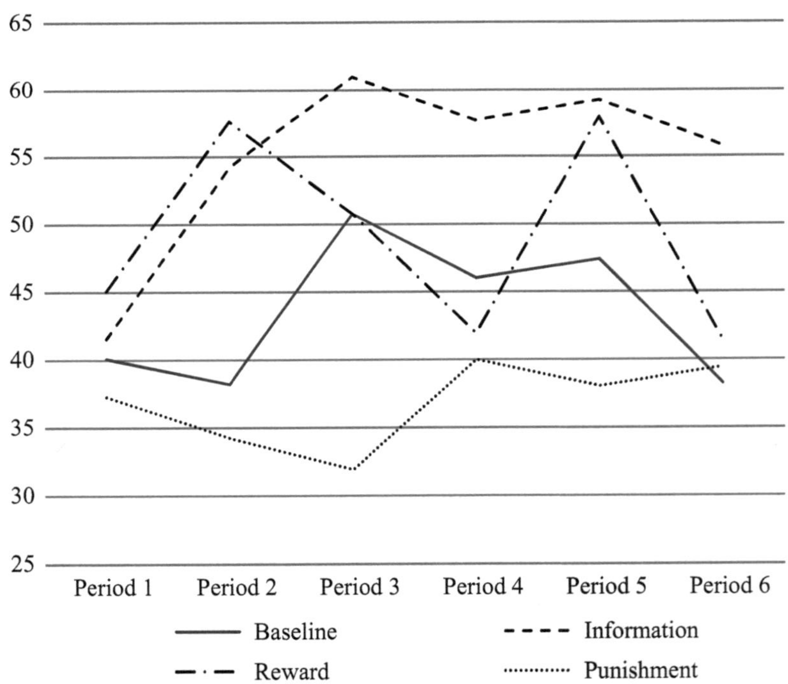

Graph 5.2 Average distribution rate by treatment

[2]The other five (33.3 %) claimed not to evaluate historical records on public losses or gains at all. Three of the five (20 %) preferred companies with high public loss, while two of the five (13.3 %) gave free-form answers. Of this last two, one invested in projects with a positive public gain and relatively high dividend, while the other simply preferred projects with a high dividend.

treatment remains higher over the game period compared with the baseline and punishment treatments. The punishment treatment has the lowest average distribution rate, at less than 40 %. Here the reward treatment also showed a fluctuation across periods in investor distribution rates as public loss/gain, though the levels remained higher than in the punishment treatment. The baseline treatment has an average distribution rate in the middle of the range.

5.5.3 Types of Companies by Treatment

Scatter diagrams of Graph 5.3 show corporate type by treatment in the third, fourth, and fifth periods. Three periods in the middle of the game were selected to avoid the effects of treachery strategies (whereby companies set their distribution rate to zero in the last period) and because of insufficient interactions among participants at the beginning of the game.

We can observe that the number of companies with public gains obviously increased in the information treatment compared with the baseline. Most companies in the baseline treatment (designated by +) were plotted on the left side of the vertical line designating a public loss of zero. Although many companies are plotted on the left side of the vertical line in the information treatment (designated by ∘), interestingly, some companies tend to shift toward the right side of the line compared with the baseline, meaning an increase in their public loss in this treatment. This is in line with the relatively limited average public loss for the information treatment compared with the baseline, as shown in Graph 5.1.

What is interesting in the information treatment is that, although it includes both types of companies, having either public loss or gains, most companies in this treatment set their distribution rate for investors higher compared with the baseline. We can observe that most companies in this treatment were plotted in the upper portions of the diagrams, above the horizontal line denoting the 50 % distribution rate in Graph 5.3. This higher distribution rate relative to other treatments is also evident in the tendency of the average distribution rate in Graph 5.2. According to the classification of company types shown in Fig. 5.1, one could say that a separation occurs between "shareholder companies," which have higher public losses in this treatment, and "stakeholder companies," which have higher public gains, although the former are more dominant. Both types of companies set higher distribution rates for investors, but the former benefit more from free-riding strategies. We can summarize these tendencies as follows:

Thesis 2: Compared with the baseline, the number of companies yielding public loss in the information treatment is limited, but many companies still yield public losses and benefit from a free-riding strategy. A significant tendency of higher distribution rate for investors was observed in the information treatment.

Compared with the baseline and information treatments, the number of companies yielding higher public loss was significantly decreased in the reward and

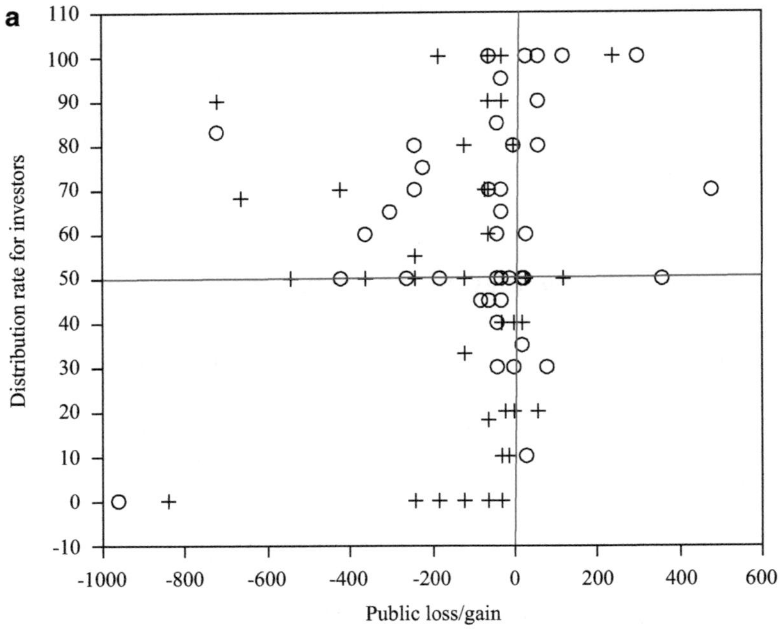

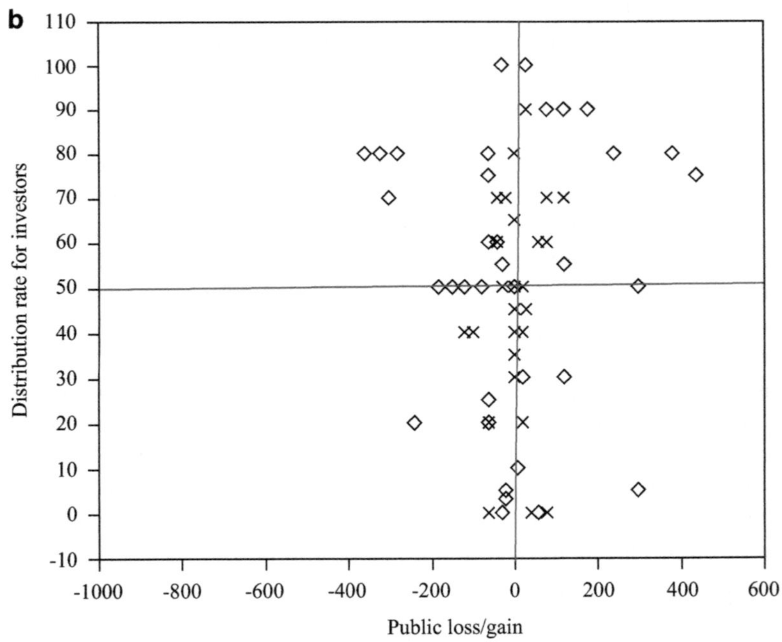

Graph 5.3 Scatter diagram of distribution rate and personal public by treatment in the third, fourth, and fifth periods by treatment. + baseline; ∘ information; ◊ reward; × punishment. A *horizontal line* designates where the distribution rate is 50 %. A *vertical line* designates where the public loss/gain is zero

Although the public loss was decreased in the information treatment relative to the baseline treatment, it remained negative and continued to negatively impact investors and companies with "free-riding" strategies. As is shown in Graph 5.3, there was a separation of "good" companies engaged in activity associated with public gains and "bad" companies engaged in activity associated with public loss in the information treatment. This means that "bad" companies and their investors implemented a free-riding strategy, creating losses for other participants and benefitting from the public gains yielded by "good" companies and investors. The existence of these free-riding strategies led to stable negative public losses and a larger imparity between participants, as is shown in Table 5.3 and Graph 5.1 for this treatment. From these results, we can conclude that information disclosure of bad and good companies works by appealing to investor social preferences; however, the effects are limited because selfish companies and investors can benefit through free-riding strategies.

5.6.2 Punishment Is More Effective than Reward

The results of the experiment also showed that public losses and imparities in payments among subjects were significantly reduced in the reward and punishment treatments relative to the baseline and information treatments. Even taking into consideration the existence of punished companies in which corporate profits are discounted by half in the punishment treatment, the mean of the final payoff in this treatment is almost four times higher than for either the baseline or the two times of information treatment; despite the existence of "rewarded" companies, the mean of final payoff in the reward treatment was almost five times higher than in the baseline and almost three times higher than in the information treatment. These results imply that both institutional settings, reward and punishment, reduced public losses and increased public gains, leading to increased payments for most participants.

However, it is interesting that punishment had a stronger and more stable effect than did reward in limiting public losses during the game period. Most companies in the punishment treatment were plotted around the neutral line of public loss/gains, which stabilized total public loss at a lower level during the period. As is proposed in prediction 3, this results from the fact that subjects evaluate their "loss" in the case of punishment higher than their "gains" in the case of reward and became more sensitive to punishment by producing higher public losses. Consequently, participants in the punishment treatment could have received public gains in almost all periods that led to their relatively higher payments.

It is interesting that companies in the punishment treatment also set the distribution rate for investors to the lowest level and this brought them a type of "social company," in contrast with the distribution rate for investors in the reward treatment, which remains higher; thus, companies in this treatment were classified as "stakeholder companies." This seems to come from companies seeking higher profit by setting a lower distribution rate for investors, as most companies in this treatment engaged in corporate activities with a lower rate of return to minimize their public loss. However, investors in this treatment could be satisfied with a lower distribution rate because their income in each period was not discounted by public loss or they could receive public gains. Consequently, both investors and companies in the punishment treatment could enjoy higher total profits while maintaining a narrower payment gap among participants.

5.6.3 How Can SRI Be an Appropriate Institution?

From these experimental results, we can derive implications regarding socially responsible investments. First, the disclosure of information on corporate social values motivates some investors to invest in "good" companies based on their social preferences. However, such disclosure also showed a vulnerability of the system that only depends on investor "social preference" or "conscience," as free-riding strategies by "bad" companies supported by selfish investors become more beneficial: that is, a "bad" company benefits more from overexploitation of resources in a rich natural environment protected by green enterprises and investors than in a situation where few enterprises or investors care about environmental conservation. Actually, an extreme "vice" company, with a huge profit yielding huge public loss, was observed in the information treatment, and this situation led to high public losses and imparities among participants. Second, the institutional settings that reward the companies most beneficial to the public and punish those most harmful to the public significantly decrease imparity in the final payoff among participants. Third, the experiment showed that a combination of information disclosure and punishment was the most effective way to regularly limit public losses. While rules that reward the "best" company also reduce total public losses, they do not function as a stable and effective punishment for the "worst" company. The results of the experiment imply that recent SRI conducted on a voluntary basis of information disclosure from "good" and "bad" enterprises would be more effective if combined with institutional measures with a compulsory basis, for example, punishment, to reduce harmful enterprise activities and increase total social welfare.

5.7 Concluding Remarks

To examine whether SRI can be an effective institution for governing corporate activities, I have performed experiments comprising investors and companies. I have designed the experiment as a modification of the public goods game and performed four different treatments: baseline, information, punishment, and rewards. The experimental results showed that information disclosure of corporate social values affected investor decision-making and had some effect in limiting harmful corporate treatment, the significant tendency in this treatment was an increased distribution rate for investors. Thus, this treatment is associated with basic corporate tendencies representative of a "shareholder company." In the reward treatment, the number of companies with higher public loss was limited, and they also tend to keep a relatively higher distribution rate for investors. Thus, we can classify this treatment as associated with tendencies representative of a "stakeholder company." A significant tendency toward lower distribution rate for investors and lower public loss was observed in the punishment treatment. Such corporate tendencies can be classified as representative of a "social company." Notably, this classification is based on general tendencies relative with other treatments. However, we can see that the direction of each institutional setting of SRI is effective for governing corporate activities based on these simplified classifications. I shall discuss the interpretations of these results in the next section.

5.6 Discussions

5.6.1 Information Disclosure Works, But Is Not Perfect

As we have seen in the previous section, exposure of information on the public losses/gains of each enterprise reduces total public losses regularly. Despite the lack of any substantial difference between participants in the baseline and information treatment groups, except for the latter having information externalities that each company brought to all participants, total public loss was reduced in the information treatment. Additionally, in the information treatment, total public loss remained stable (around −30), whereas in the baseline treatment, it increased as the game continued. This result derives from the simple thesis that the *social preferences of investors work to some extent* to reduce public losses arising from corporate activities. Whereas investors in the baseline treatment only paid attention to dividends, those in the information treatment considered their public losses/gains, and some refrained from investing in companies with higher public loss.

The other interesting point is that companies have a stronger tendency to increase the distribution rate to investors in the information treatment than the baseline. As shown in Graph 5.2, the distribution rate in the information treatment remains highest during the game period. This result occurs because companies that wish to attract investment funds tend to raise their distribution rate to satisfy both investor's social preferences and selfishness. A completely selfish investor only considers dividend level in his decision-making; conversely, a completely unselfish investor only considers level of public losses/gains. However, because most investors have social and utilitarian preferences, companies can attract investment funds by offering both higher dividends and higher public gains, the latter by increasing the distribution rate to investors. As a result, companies in the information treatment tend to shift toward "shareholder companies" from the "vice companies" typical in the baseline treatment.

punishment treatments, especially the latter. In punishment treatments (designated by ×) most companies maintain lower public losses, sitting around the vertical line of zero. Compared with the punishment treatment, in the reward treatment (designated by ◊), some companies still yielded higher public losses. The spread pattern in the reward treatment closely resembled the pattern of information treatment. Companies in this treatment tend to be separated into "stakeholder companies" and "shareholder companies," although relative to the information treatment they are weighted toward the former. This means that punishments in the punishment treatment have a stable effect on all companies, whereas rewards in the reward treatment do not always limit company public losses.

What was interesting is that companies in the punishment treatment have a significant tendency to have lower distribution rates, as is supported by the average distribution rate shown in Graph 5.3. Interestingly, companies in the punishment treatment tend to converge to a "neutral point", where the public loss is zero and the distribution rate is 50 %. Although the companies in this treatment tend to converge to the zero line of public loss and the 50 % line of distribution rate, they tend to be scattered around the same area as "social companies" compared with other treatments and have lower public losses and lower distribution rates relative to other treatments. This tendency remains throughout the game period, as is also shown in the average public loss in Graph 5.1 and the distribution rate in Graph 5.2. Thus, we could summarize these tendencies in the following thesis:

Thesis 3: The number of companies yielding a public loss was significantly limited in the reward and punishment treatments, compared with the baseline and information treatments. The effect was higher and more stable in the punishment treatment than the reward treatment. A significant tendency for companies to maintain a lower distribution rate for investors was also observed in the punishment treatment.

From the basic tendencies of companies as analyzed above, I could classify each treatment as typically associated with a particular company type, as shown in Table 5.4. The baseline treatment, where public loss remains higher than all the other treatments and the distribution rate for investors remains lower, is associated with corporate tendencies that can be classified as representative of a "vice company" according to the classification criteria from Fig. 5.1. Meanwhile, although the number of companies with higher public loss remains higher in the information

Table 5.4 Typical company types by treatment

		Public losses (P)	
		High	Low
Investor distribution rate (ϕ)	High	Information [shareholder company]	Reward [stakeholder company]
	Low	Baseline [vice company]	Punishment [social company]

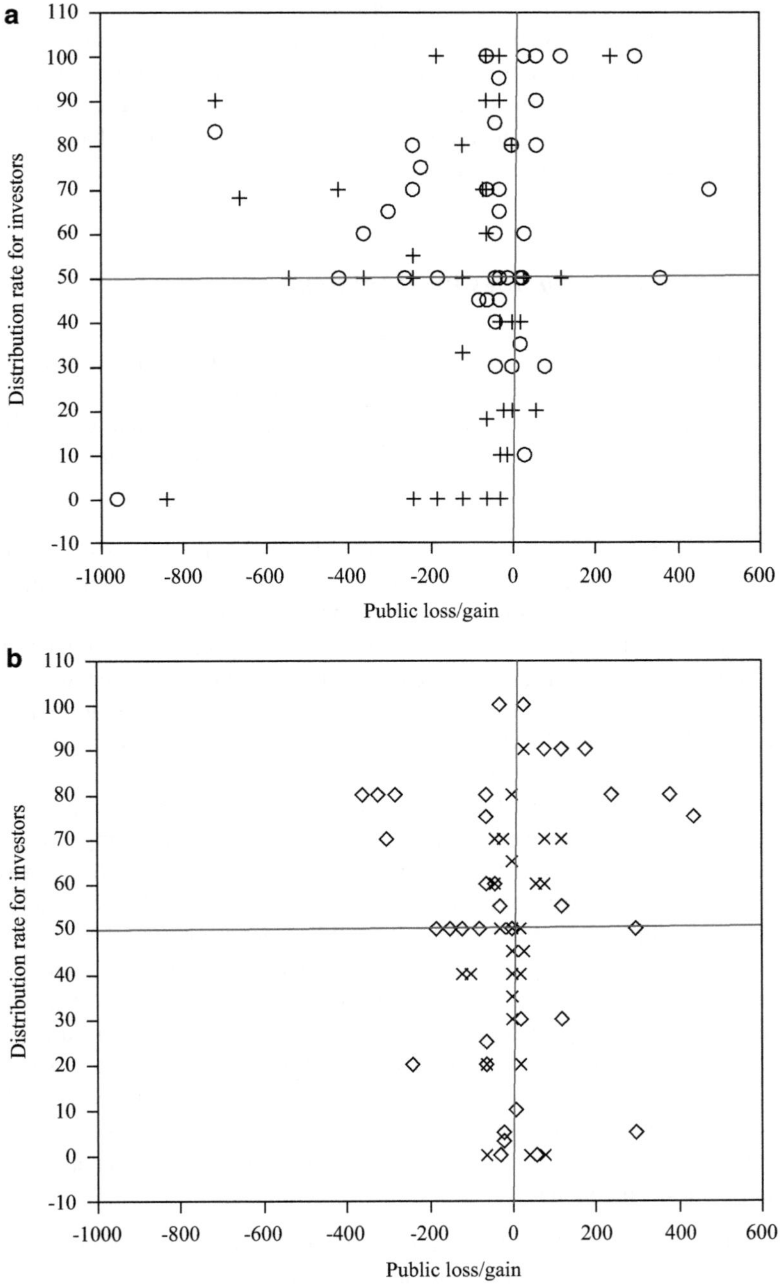

Graph 5.3 Scatter diagram of distribution rate and personal public by treatment in the third, fourth, and fifth periods by treatment. + baseline; ○ information; ◊ reward; × punishment. A *horizontal line* designates where the distribution rate is 50 %. A *vertical line* designates where the public loss/gain is zero

treatment remains higher over the game period compared with the baseline and punishment treatments. The punishment treatment has the lowest average distribution rate, at less than 40 %. Here the reward treatment also showed a fluctuation across periods in investor distribution rates as public loss/gain, though the levels remained higher than in the punishment treatment. The baseline treatment has an average distribution rate in the middle of the range.

5.5.3 Types of Companies by Treatment

Scatter diagrams of Graph 5.3 show corporate type by treatment in the third, fourth, and fifth periods. Three periods in the middle of the game were selected to avoid the effects of treachery strategies (whereby companies set their distribution rate to zero in the last period) and because of insufficient interactions among participants at the beginning of the game.

We can observe that the number of companies with public gains obviously increased in the information treatment compared with the baseline. Most companies in the baseline treatment (designated by +) were plotted on the left side of the vertical line designating a public loss of zero. Although many companies are plotted on the left side of the vertical line in the information treatment (designated by ∘), interestingly, some companies tend to shift toward the right side of the line compared with the baseline, meaning an increase in their public loss in this treatment. This is in line with the relatively limited average public loss for the information treatment compared with the baseline, as shown in Graph 5.1.

What is interesting in the information treatment is that, although it includes both types of companies, having either public loss or gains, most companies in this treatment set their distribution rate for investors higher compared with the baseline. We can observe that most companies in this treatment were plotted in the upper portions of the diagrams, above the horizontal line denoting the 50 % distribution rate in Graph 5.3. This higher distribution rate relative to other treatments is also evident in the tendency of the average distribution rate in Graph 5.2. According to the classification of company types shown in Fig. 5.1, one could say that a separation occurs between "shareholder companies," which have higher public losses in this treatment, and "stakeholder companies," which have higher public gains, although the former are more dominant. Both types of companies set higher distribution rates for investors, but the former benefit more from free-riding strategies. We can summarize these tendencies as follows:

Thesis 2: Compared with the baseline, the number of companies yielding public loss in the information treatment is limited, but many companies still yield public losses and benefit from a free-riding strategy. A significant tendency of higher distribution rate for investors was observed in the information treatment.

Compared with the baseline and information treatments, the number of companies yielding higher public loss was significantly decreased in the reward and activities. However, information disclosure was not satisfactory as it left selfish companies and investors room to pursue free-riding strategies. Institutional settings to reward the company most beneficial to the public, as well as information disclosure, had a significant effect in limiting public losses caused by companies as well as in narrowing gaps in payments among all participants. A rule to punish the company most harmful to the public also had a significant effect but exerted more stable and stronger effects in limiting public losses and narrowing payment gaps. These experimental results imply that SRI can be successful as an institution to govern corporations, provided such investments are not only motivated by investor social preference on a voluntary basis but also contain a rule to punish harmful companies financially. Naturally, these empirical results obtained in a laboratory should be complemented by other empirical studies on real markets or qualitative studies on incentives involving actual investors. However, I believe this research proposes some important hypotheses on how SRI contributes to balancing the values of corporations, investors, and society to maintain sustainable economic development.

Appendix

Economic Experiment: Instruction

Thank you for your participation. We will now introduce the game. Read the material carefully and understand thoroughly. If you have any questions, please raise your hands and inform us.

1. Materials
   Upon taking your seat, please check the instructions and the blank A4 paper on the desk.
2. Participation fees
   When participating in the game, you will each receive a participation fee totaling 800 points (800 yen). On conclusion of the game, each participant will be paid the participation fee plus whatever profit they earned during the game (based on their final score).
3. Investors and companies

   - All participants will be assigned a game role randomly: either investor or company. At the beginning of the game, you will be informed of your assigned role via a message on the screen of your computer. Participants do not know the roles of other participants, including which participants are investors and which are companies, until the end of the game.

- During the game, investors can invest in multiple companies and receive a dividend profit. Companies make decisions on projects and in return receive profit.
- The procedure for one period of the game is "investor's investment → company project selection → profit distribution." The game is repeated seven times.

4. Investors and dividend profit (companies are waiting)

- Investors receive 600 points as their investment fund during each period. When the game starts, the screens of investor participants display the names of the companies (A, B, C, D, etc.) and the input boxes of each company. The names of the companies are distributed to participants according to the company role to which they have been assigned, written in alphabetic script. If no participant is assigned to a given company, this is indicated by the ※ symbol.
- Investors can gain profit by selecting companies and investing in them in units of 200 points, receiving dividend profits accordingly. Investors must invest all 600 points of their investment funds in each period, and these investment funds are not calculated as their income. The dividend information of each company is displayed on the final screen in each period. Also, investors cannot invest in companies without any assigned game participant (companies indicated by the ※ symbol).

  Example: If you invest 200 points in one company (10 % dividend) and 400 points in another company (5 % dividend) in a given period, the investment profit will be calculated as follows: $200 \times 0.1 + 400 \times 0.05 = 20 + 20 = 40$
- Investors should click the OK button after determining their investment distribution. The time limit for performing this task is 2 min. Those investors assigned to the company role should wait while others complete this process.

5. Companies and projects (investors are waiting)

- In this next stage, the screens of participants playing the roles of companies that received capital from investors show the total capital invested by all investors, investment project name (1–6), profit rate, and the rate of public gains/losses for each project. Public gains/losses mean the rate of additional gains/losses that affect all participants. If the investment capital of some companies is 0, they will automatically receive 100 points from the banks. The profit rate and the rate of public gain/loss for each project are shown in Table 5.1.
- Companies invest in projects 1–6 in units of 100 points and can receive the profits from each project accordingly.

  Example: A company collects investment capital of 800 points and then invests 500 points in a project with a 30 % profit rate and 300 points in a project with 10 % profit rate. The final project profit can then be calculated as: $500 \times 0.3 + 300 \times 0.1 = 150 + 30 = 180$

- Corporate projects (1–6) that companies engage in also yield public losses or gains to all participants according to the given rate.

  Example: A company collects investment capital of 800 points and then invests 500 points in a project with a −20 % public loss and 300 points in one with a +30 % public gain. The total public gain and public loss of the company can be calculated as follows: $500\times(-0.2)+300\times(+0.3) = -100+90 = -10$
- The total public gain/loss from each company is divided by the number of participants, and this average value becomes everyone's public gain/loss. The profit of all participants in this period is adjusted (added/deducted) to reflect the public gain/loss.

  Example: Ten participants, company A has a public loss of −40, company B has a public loss of −80, company C has a public gain of +40, company D has a public loss of −50, and company E has a public profit of +20. The average public gain/loss for all participants is then: $[(-80) + (-50) + 30 + (-70) + 20] \div 10 = -15$
- For participants assigned as companies, on finishing the determination of the capital distribution on projects 1–6 with 100 unit points, please click the OK button. The time limit for completing this task is 2 min.

6. The distribution rate of companies and investors (investors are waiting)

- On project completion, the screens of company participants show project profit, public gain/loss, and the input boxes of investors' distribution rate. Participants assigned to the company role can decide the rate for the distribution of project profit to investors. For example, in a case where a company earns project profit of 200 points and sets an investor distribution rate of 60 %, that company's investors will receive 120 points in project profit, while the company receives 80 points.
- The company's dividend rate equals the multiple of the project profit rate of the company (total project profit divided by total investment from companies) and the investor distribution rate. The rate is rounded to the nearest integer.

  Example: If the project profit rate of a company is 28 % and the investor distribution rate is 60 %, then the company dividend rate is:

  $0.28 \times 0.6 = 0.168$ 17%
- For participants assigned to the company role, after entering the investor distribution rate in the input boxes please click the OK button. The time limit for performing this task is 2 min.

7. Accident

   [The reward treatment]

   There is a 50 % probability of an unexpected event occurring in each game period. Should an accident happen, the company that makes the highest public gain (if all companies make a public loss, that with the lowest public loss is selected) sees their project profit doubled. Therefore, the company's dividend rate is also doubled.

For example, company X has the highest public gain. Company X collects 800 points in capital from investors and has a project profit rate of 18 %, investor distribution rate of 60 %, and public gain per participant of 20 points.
The final profit of company X: $800 \times 0.18 \times 2 \times (1 - 0.6) + 20 = 135$
The dividend rate of company X: $0.18 \times 2 \times 0.6 = 0.216$ 22%
[The punishment treatment]
There is a 50 % probability of an unexpected event occurring in each game period. Should an accident happen, the company that makes the highest public loss (if all companies make a public gain, that with the lowest public gain is selected) sees their project profit halved. Therefore, the company's dividend rate is also halved.
For example, company X has the highest public loss. Company X collects 800 points in capital from investors and has a project profit rate of 30 %, investor distribution rate of 60 %, and public gain per participant of 20 points.
The final profit of company X: $800 \times 0.3 \times 1/2 \times (1 - 0.6) + 20 = 68$
The dividend rate of company X: $0.3 \times 1/2 \times 0.6 = 0.09$ 9%

8. Profit

- After companies complete the processes of the investment stage, project stage, and determination of investor distribution rate, both investors and companies can use their screens to view their final profits from the completed period.
  [The baseline treatment]
- The screen displays the dividend rate (the multiple of each company's project profit rate and investor distribution rate) for each company (A, B, C, etc.), the overall public gain/loss for all companies, each participant's public gain/loss (the total public gain/loss of all companies divided by the number of participants), and each participant's final profit for the period. Profits are rounded to the nearest integer.
  [The information treatment]
- The screen displays the dividend rate (the multiple of each company's project profit rate and investor distribution rate) and the public gain/loss for each company (A, B, C, etc.), the overall public gain/loss for all companies, each participant's public gain/loss (the total public gain/loss of all companies divided by the number of participants), and each participant's final profit for the period. Profits are rounded to the nearest integer.
  [The reward and punishment treatment]
- The screen displays whether an unexpected event occurred, as well as the dividend rate (the multiple of each company's project profit rate and investor distribution rate) and the public gain/loss for each company (A, B, C, etc.), the overall public gain/loss for all companies, each participant's public gain/loss (the total public gain/loss of all companies divided by the number of participants), and each participant's final profit for the period. Profits are rounded to the nearest integer.

- An investor's final profit equals the sum of the overall dividend profit from all companies in which they invest, as well as the public gain/loss of each participant. A company's final profit equals the sum of the net project profit, namely, the part of the project profit not distributed to investors, as well as each participant's public gain/loss.
- After profit confirmation, please click the OK button. Please feel free to use the sheet of A4 paper for taking notes. The time limit for completing this task is 2 min.

9. Final score and the point calculation method
   The final score for each participant is calculated as the sum of their profit in all seven periods plus the attendance fee of 800 points. The point scores are converted to money on the basis that 1 point = 1 yen, with the money being distributed when the game concludes. For purposes of distribution, all scores are rounded up to the nearest 10 yen.

※ If you have any questions, please raise your hands.

References

Berle AA Jr (1955) The twentieth century capitalist revolution. Macmillan, London

Berle AA Jr, Means GC (1932) The modern corporation and private property. Macmillan, New York

Baron DP (2001) Private politics, corporate social responsibility, and integrated strategy. J Econ Manag Strateg 10(1):7–45

Bollen N (2007) Mutual fund attributes and investor behavior. J Financ Quant Anal 42:683–708

Borghesi R, Houston JF, Naranjo A (2014) Corporate socially responsible investments: CEO altruism, reputation, and shareholder interests. J Corp Finan 26:164–181

Consolandi C, Innocenti A, Vercelli A (2009) CSR, rationality and the ethical preferences of investors in a laboratory experiment. Res Econ 63:242–252

Feher E, Gächter S (2000) Cooperation and punishment in public goods experiments. Am Econ Rev 90(4):980–994

Friedman M (1962/2002) Capitalism and freedom. The University of Chicago Press, Chicago

Friedman M (1970) The social responsibility of business is to increase its profits. Corporate ethics and corporate governance. Springer, Berlin, pp 173–178

Global Sustainable Investment Alliance (2014) Global sustainable investment review. http://www.gsi-alliance.org/wp-content/uploads/2015/02/GSIA_Review_download.pdf. Accessed 20 Sept 2015

GraffZivin J, Small A (2005) A Modigliani-Miller theory of altruistic corporate social responsibility. Top Econ Anal Policy 5(1):10

Jensen M (2001) Value maximization, stakeholder theory, and the corporate objective function. J Appl Corp Finan 14(3):8–21

Kahneman D, Tversky A (1979) Prospect theory: an analysis of decision under risk. Econometorica 47:263–291

Khanna M, Damon LA (1999) EPA's voluntary 33/50 program: impact on toxic releases and economic performance of firms. J Environ Econ Manag 37:1–25

Ledyard J (1995) Public goods: a survey of experimental research. In: Kagel J, Roth A (eds) Handbook of experimental economics. Princeton University Press, Princeton
Renneboog L, Horst JT, Zhang C (2008) Socially responsible investments: institutional aspects, performance, and investor behavior. J Bank Financ 32:1723–1742
Smith A (1776) An inquiry into the nature and causes of the wealth of nations (1984). Liberty Fund, Indianapolis
Tirol J (2001) Corporate governance. Econometrica 69(1):1–35

Chapter 6
From *Gedankenexperiment* to Social Economics: Wieser's Empiricism and the Social Sciences

Abstract In this research, I have attempted to reformulate Wieser's empiricism based on *gedankenexperiment* as a micro-foundation for his social economics and thus to derive implications for the application of behavioral theories examined by laboratory experiments to social theories. In his attempt to improve Menger's economics, Wieser claims that economics should be an empirical science and develops an original scientific methodology based on experience. By analyzing his method, this research proposes that Wieser's concept of "experience" is divided into four levels: "experience" as stored in language, as obtained via introspection, as derived from *gedankenexperiment*, and as observation of society. According to this research, Wieser's experiences are hierarchical and constitute the empirical basis of each dimension from the micro- to macro-levels in the social sciences. This research discusses that Wieser's method has implications for modern behavioral theories in the sense that it is based on the subjective rationality of humans, which is empirically based. Wieser's method contains situational analysis of social institutions as preconditions of human behaviors, performs empirical tests via *gedankenexperiment* on causal explanations linking human's preferences and social conditions, and involves methodological motivationalism that defines social units as a driving force of social fact. Although his methods had the limitation of being psychological, his method is important as it showed a way to derive social theories from assumptions of behaviors and institutions that are empirically examined.

Keywords Wieser • Empiricism • Gedankenexperiment • Situational logic • Methodological motivationalism

6.1 Introduction

Through the distributive experiments conducted in Chaps. 2, 3, 4, and 5, we could observe that individuals hold not only utilitarian but also social preferences and consider these preferences in their responses to given institutional situations. With

This chapter is a revised version of manuscript: Natsuka Tokumaru, Wieser's Unity of Thought, *Journal of the History of Economic Thought*, vol. 37, no. 4 in December 2015.

N. Tokumaru, *Social Preference, Institution, and Distribution*, Evolutionary Economics and Social Complexity Science 3, DOI 10.1007/978-981-10-0137-6_6

these experiments, I have also examined behavioral assumptions proposed by past theories in the history of economic thought. Additionally, I have discussed implications for social facts that we may derive from the given experimental results. There seems no doubt that past and present behavioral theories are examined and enriched by empirical tests performed under controlled conditions in a laboratory. In that sense, we can say that economic experiments brought new types of "experiences" or "observations" to the social sciences.

However, if economic experiments can enable economists to test and enrich behavioral theories, questions remain regarding their potential application or extension to social theories: How are theories on human behavior at the micro-level, which are empirically examined and enriched in the laboratory, developed into economic theories at the macro-level? What do "observations" or "empirical facts" obtained in a laboratory mean for the whole system of the discipline? How should one derive economic or social theories from these empirical observations in the laboratory? As discussed in Chap. 1, these questions concerning the relationship between experiences and theories, as well as between human behaviors and social facts in the social sciences, have been considered by many authors in the history of economic thought (Menger 1883; Keynes 1891; Weber 1904; Schumpeter 1908; Mises 1933; Hayek 1967). If social facts are explained as an unintended result of intended or unintended human behaviors, it is important to ask how one can extend empirical theories on behaviors to explain social facts in an epistemologically appropriate way.

Friedrich von Wieser, known as one of the originators of modern economics, by systematizing Menger's theories and coining the term "marginal utility" (*Grenznutzen*), also confronted the problems concerning social theories and experiences. In this chapter, I attempted to analyze Wieser's methodology based on empiricism and to link his methods with recent economic theories available for the utilization of experimental method. Actually, Wieser's intention is to establish economics as an "empirical science" by establishing clear and systematic links between experiences (or observations) and theories. Notably, Wieser introduced what he calls *gedankenexperiments* as a micro-level empirical basis for his social theories. While Wieser has been regarded as one of the origins of modern economics, his works, especially *Social Economics* (*Theorie der gesellschaftlichen Wirtschaft*), seem to have heavily influenced institutional economists such as Mitchell and Commons.[1] Further, recent studies (Arena 2010) reevaluate Wieser as a pioneer whose work explains a process of generating rules in institutions that may also impact Hayek's idea of spontaneous order. Thus, one may derive epistemological implications

[1]Mitchell (1917) says of Wieser's theory of social economics that it "... sums up, systematizes and extends the doctrines previously worked out by the author, his master and his fellow disciples. ... it is distinguished by admirable exposition—elegant in proportions, mature in expression and authoritative in source." In chapter 5 of *Institutional Economics*, Commons (1934) critically examines Wieser's value theories.

in relation to how to apply experimental methods to institutional theories, by reexamining the epistemology of Wieser in modern economics.

This chapter is structured as follows. In the next section, I explain the historical background of Wieser's economic theories and propose interpreting them as a reformulation of Menger's empiricism (Sect. 2). After discussing Menger's empiricism (Sect. 3), I propose four possible interpretations of "experience" in Wieser's method (Sect. 4) and particularly the structure of the empiricism (Sect. 5). Finally, I discuss how one can learn Wieser's empirical methods, including *gedankenexperiments*, and apply them to derive economic theories from experimental results (Sect. 6).

6.2 Historical Background: Empiricism from Menger to Wieser

Friedrich von Wieser was a young law student when he first read Carl Menger's *Grundsätze der Volkswirtschaftslehre* (*Principles of Economics*) (Menger 1871), which sparked his interest in economics. In *Grundsätze*, Menger (1871) repeatedly uses the phrase "experience teaches us" (*die Erfahrung lehrt uns*) and makes the following claim in the preface:

> In what follows I have endeavored to reduce the complex phenomena of human economic activity to the simplest elements that can still be subjected to *accurate observation*, to apply to these elements the measure corresponding to their nature, and constantly adhering to this measure, to investigate the manner in which the more complex economic phenomena evolve from their elements according to definite principles. (Menger 1871 Preface, pp. 46–47, emphasis added)

According to Menger (1871), this method—once mistakenly considered a special method only applicable to the natural sciences—is the "empirical method," which is common to all fields of empirical knowledge, including the social sciences (p. 47).

Menger did not doubt that his main epistemological ideas on social sciences were empirical. As has been highlighted, even his concepts of *Grenznutzen* (marginal utility) and equimarginal principle were formulated to enable observation by the introduction of the loss principle (Milford 2010, p. 173). However, postpublication, Menger faced harsh criticism from German historicists, who regarded the *Grundsätze* as an unempirical work. Twelve years later, Menger published a book on the methodology of the social sciences (Menger 1883) that included a critique of the German historical school. This methodological confrontation between Menger and the German historicists eventually developed into what is known as the *Methodenstreit*.

While Menger was engaged in methodological work and discussions in the early 1880s, Wieser obtained his habilitation with the treatise *Über den Ursprung und die Hauptgesetze des wirthschaftlichen Werthes* (*On the Origin and the Main Laws of Economic Value*) (Wieser 1884), in which he extended Menger's theory of value and introduced the term *Grenznutzen* (*marginal utility*). Five years later, he published

Der natürliche Werth (*Natural Value*) (Wieser 1889), which extended Menger's idea of marginality to production theory.[2] His economic research seems to have been completed with his *Theorie der gesellschaftlichen Wirtschaft* (*Social Economics*) (Wieser 1914), about which Hayek (1929) says in glowing terms that it is "... not only the sole consistent treatment of economic theory produced by the modern subjectivist school, but it also constitutes, above all, what may well be the greatest synthesis achieved by economic theory in our time" (p. 20). These works by Wieser partly supported the stance of the Austrian camp in the *Methodenstreit*.

In his attempts to improve Menger's economic theories—the value and production theories—Wieser frequently discussed methodological and epistemological issues. These discussions were characterized as a justification of Menger's empiricism. In the epilogue of *Der natürliche Werth*, he states the following:

> If now, in closing, there is one thing which, more than another, I wish to repeat with special emphasis, it is the intention which has dominated me throughout the whole work, and in every part of it—the intention to be, in the best sense of the word, *empirical*... So far as I can judge of my own work, *I have nowhere pointed to any foreign non-empirical power in the actuality of economic life*. (Wieser 1889, p. 242 emphasis added)

Although Wieser did not leave behind systematic methodological books, he developed his own position,[3] which contributed to the development of the Austrian school. Unfortunately, his extensive writings contain little on his methodological position and economic theories. This partly reflects his peculiar habit of referencing Menger but not other authors and of not specifying the original sources of the ideas he discussed and developed (Streissler 1986, p. 85).

In this chapter, I propose that Wieser's position is the result of his reformulation of the empirical position that Menger develops in his *Grundsätze*.[4] Wieser maintains that economics is an empirical science and supports this claim by discussing marginal utility—the focus of subjective value theory. According to Wieser, the theories of the Austrian school are superior to those of the classical school because they are based on "experience" and provide better explanations of the social world. He states that Menger's value theory is related more to experience than the theories of William Stanley Jevons or Léon Walras, even given that the last introduced a mathematical method to explain the concept of marginality (Wieser 1889, Preface pp. xxiii–xxxiv). However, if the social sciences are justified by "experiences,"

---

[2]Hutchison (1967) highlighted that these two books written by Wieser strongly resemble Menger's *Grundsätze*.

[3]According to Hayek (1929), Wieser was disappointed that Menger did not concentrate on developing his economic theories after *Grundsätze*, but instead engaged in methodological discussions with the historical school (p. 115). However, Wieser (1884) referred to the important role of methodology in his habilitation (p. 3).

[4]Although Menger did not comment on Wieser's works, he was interested in them, especially from a methodological perspective. I found that Menger left exclamation and question marks on many pages of *Der natürliche Werth* and *Theorie der gesellschaftlichen Wirtschaft* (in the collection of the Menger Library, Hitotsubashi University, Tokyo) and highlighted certain portions using underlining in red and green, especially sections discussing methodological issues.

as claimed by Wieser, the following questions arise: What exactly did Wieser mean by "experience" in the social sciences? What are his epistemological and methodological positions? Is his empiricism consistent with that of Menger?

Moreover, this research resolves other problems that perhaps originated because of unique historical circumstances: Why did Wieser change his field of research to sociology and publish *Das Gesetz der Macht* (*The Law of Power*) (Wieser 1926), a book that emphasizes the role of elite leadership, which was regarded as supportive of totalitarianism in that day and, thus, may have led to the downgrading of his work? These research issues are regarded as a riddle in research on the history of economic thought. Streissler (1986) describes this riddle as ". . . .a dichotomy which he [Wieser] was not able to bridge, different strains of thought that he could not blend into a unified whole" (p. 83). Arena (2010) emphasizes Wieser's importance based on his effective integration of economics and economic sociology; moreover, he developed understanding of the emergence of rules. However, the "leap" that he appears to have made from early economics to authoritarian sociology has still not been satisfactorily explained from a methodological perspective.

To address these methodological problems, I first explain the structure of Menger's empiricism, followed by that of Wieser, particularly his distinctive use of the concept of *Erfahrung* (experience) in the social sciences. I propose four possible interpretations of the concept: (i) "experience" stored in language, (ii) "experience" as introspection, (iii) "experience" as a mental experiment, and (iv) "experience" as observation. I then examine the structure of Wieser's empiricism.

6.3 Menger's Empiricism

To understand Wieser's epistemological position as a reformulation of Menger's empiricism, I first explain that empiricism. In Menger's (1883) methodological book *Untersuchungen über die Methode der Sozialwissenschaften, und der politischen Ökonomie insbesondere* (hereafter *Untersuchungen*) (*Investigations into the Method of the Social Sciences with Special Reference to Economics*) he explains his epistemological position, which can be regarded as empiricism.

In *Untersuchungen*, Menger states that the purpose of social sciences is the application of strict general laws (types and typical relationships) to social phenomena. Menger (1883) states that social regularities to some extent can be sought through direct observations of society: "Experience teaches us, rather, that definite phenomena are repeated... in the variation of things" (p. 36). However, he states that one cannot derive strict general laws by directly observing social phenomena in the social sciences because elements interact with each other; thus, direct observation only derives the complex results of such interactions. Menger (1883) states that "There are no strict types in 'empirical reality', i.e., when the phenomena are under consideration in the totality and the whole complexity of their nature" (pp. 56–57). Based on those considerations, Menger (1883) states that prior to observation, social scientists should establish strict general laws using the method he calls "exact orientation of research" and that social phenomena should be understood as special cases of those strict general laws in the process of the "empirical-realistic orientation of research" (p. 45). In that sense, the "exact orientation of research" is a prerequisite of the empirical-realistic orientation of research. Although Menger emphasized that the "exact orientation of research" results in strict general laws based on actual social facts, he presents few concrete methodological explanations of this method, that is, the derivation of such laws. This may occur partly because he intended to raise an objection to the German historicists, who believed that the primary goal of the social sciences is to derive historical laws from direct observation of society.

Without clarifying details, Menger (1883) only states that exact science "...examines, rather, how more complicated phenomena develop from the simplest, in part even unempirical elements of the real world in their (likewise unempirical) isolation from all other influences, with constant consideration of exact (likewise ideal!) measure" (p. 61). *Grundsätze* seems to be an application of what Menger calls the "exact orientation of research," but the book contains little methodological explanation, which leads to the following questions: What exactly is the "exact orientation of research"? How can one derive strict general laws that describe actuality? And how one can justify this method as an empirical one?

6.4 Wieser's Meaning of "Experience"

Following Menger's scientific program, Wieser seems to have intended to give an epistemological justification for the derivation of strict general laws based on experiences. Like Menger, Wieser (1914) states that economics should be characterized as an empirical science: "The method of economic theory is empirical. It is supported by observation and has but one aim, which is to describe actuality" (p. 5). However, *Natürliche Werth*, the fundamental concept of his economic theory, which according to him "... would be recognized by a completely organic and most highly rational community" (Wieser 1889, p. 61), does not seem compatible with our experiences. Some authors (Hutchison 1967; Kauder 1957) regard Wieser's method not as empirical, but rather as essentialist, and as explaining "nature" or the "essence" of things such as value or cost. Ludwig von Mises (1933) considers his concept of "common experience" to belong to the aprioristic and, hence, nonempirical sphere (p. 24). Thus, it is necessary to examine exactly what Wieser meant by "experience" in the social sciences.

To clarify Wieser's use of the term "experience" in his economic theory, I first explain the logical relationship between experience and theory in the empirical sciences by introducing Karl Popper's discussions. According to Popper (1959), statements reporting experience can be logically represented in the form of singular statements such as "at time t and location k, there is a white swan" ($Sa \wedge Wa$). In contrast, theories of empirical sciences are presented in the form of universal statements such as "all swans are white" $(\forall x)(Sx \rightarrow Wx)$. Inductive inferences, such as those suggested by J. S. Mill, derive strictly universal statements from singular statements that describe individual observations, through inferences of truth preservation and content enlargement: "at time t_1 and location k_1, there is a swan and it is white"; "at time t_2 and location k_2, there is a swan and it is white"; therefore, "all swans are white." $(\exists x)(Sx \wedge Wx) \rightarrow (\forall x)(Sx \rightarrow Wx)$. However, these inferences are logically false. Instead of deriving universal statements from singular statements, Popper suggests regarding singular statements reporting experiences as testing empirical theories. Singular statements such as "at time t and location k, there is a swan and it is *not* white" can falsify universal statements, such as "all swans are white," without logical inconsistency. $(\exists x)(Sx \wedge \neg Wx) \iff \neg(\forall x)(Sx \rightarrow Wx)$. In that sense, experiences are regarded as critical standards of these theories, by which the theories may fall short (Popper 1959, pp. 25–30).

Given the notion of experience in empirical sciences, it is necessary to analyze whether "experience" for Wieser was the empirical basis by which he derived strictly universal statements through generalization or the critical standards that provided the basis for universal theories. Because Wieser introduced "experience" in various forms, I propose his concept of experience can be interpreted in four ways:

- "Experience" as stored in language: Wieser argued that people's historical experiences are stored in common, prescientific language and that language analysis is an important source of empirical (social) knowledge. This may have resulted from his intention to justify Menger's method in *Grundsätze*, which seems to have involved language analysis.
- "Experience" as a result of introspection or internal observations of the "motive power" of society: Wieser regards introspection as a special source of empirical knowledge. In his view, introspection provides knowledge on "motive power," which internally motivates social activities.
- "Experience" as a mental experiment: Wieser believed that mental experiments can help examine causal relationships that exist in complex social situations. He proposed the concept of *Grenznutzen* (marginal utility) as a general condition for economic causalities and constructed the theory of *Einfache Wirtschaft* (simple economy), as a result of mental experiments. This view may be considered a result of Wieser's attempt to clarify Menger's concept of causality.
- "Experience" as observation or the result of methodological motivationalism: Wieser was aware that observations of social phenomena form part of the empirical basis of economics. However, according to him, observable social phenomena are the result of interactions of different causalities triggered by different motive powers. In his view, motive powers are triggered not only by humans but also by social organizations or nations. Because he applied the concept of motive power to explain observable social phenomena, I call this position methodological motivationalism. It appears that this particular position can help understand his shift to sociology.

Below, I discuss these possible interpretations in greater detail.

6.4.1 "Experience" as Stored in Common Language

First, I propose that Wieser's concept of "experience" can be interpreted as something stored in common language.

In *Grundsätze*, Menger introduces linguistic analysis, which involves the comparison of an economic concept with a more general concept, and the identification of the strict meanings and properties of the former. At the start of the book, Menger (1871) defines "good" through comparison with the concept of a "thing," which cannot be defined as a "good." According to Menger, a thing can become a good only with the simultaneous presence of four prerequisites: "(1) a human need; (2) such properties that render the thing capable of being brought into a causal connection with the satisfaction of this need; (3) human knowledge of this causal connection and (4) command of the thing sufficient to direct it to the satisfaction" (p. 52). Furthermore, Menger analyzes the identification of "economic goods" through comparison with the concept of a "good," a concept previously identified by himself. The pressing question thus is how can one justify the laws derived from a process that contains conceptual analysis as empirical?

By stating that experience is stored in language, Wieser justifies Menger's method, which comprises linguistic analysis, as empirical. According to Wieser, social sciences, unlike natural sciences, deal with special knowledge of humans, that is, knowledge of "ourselves." This characteristic of social sciences requires a special empirical method. Humans are compelled to provide linguistic explanations to others in their social lives regarding what they are doing or what they want to do and common language evolved through such a communicative process (Wieser 1884 Preface, pp. 3–4). Thus, Wieser maintained that social experiences—the source of knowledge about ourselves—are historically accumulated into the common language that we use daily. He labels such experience stored in language *gemeine Erfahrung* (common experience);

> Much of the store of common experience that is shared by the economic community is deposited in the national language, especially in the basic designations relating to economics and the law of economic relations. ... economic theory, like other practical sciences, has for its subject the content of common experience, long familiar and already named. (Wieser 1914, p. 8)

Based on these considerations, Wieser concluded that the social sciences should not begin with direct observations of the social world, but with people's "common experience" accumulated in language, and that language analysis is important to the derivation of social theories. For Wieser, language analysis is not an unempirical or aprioristic method as usually believed, but an empirical method that is necessary to clarify common experience.

By stating that experience is stored in common prescientific language and that language analysis is an important source of social knowledge, Wieser may have been trying to justify Menger's method itself based on experience.

6.4.2 "Experience" as a Result of Introspection or Inner Observation

I now analyze the second interpretation of "experience" developed by Wieser, possibly to prove that economics is an empirical science; that is, I will analyze his interpretation of "experience" as a result of introspection. Wieser believed that introspection—the inner observations of individuals—functioned as a special source of empirical knowledge in economics.

In *Grundsätze*, "human needs" are central to Menger's explanation of society. As previously stated, Menger's fundamental concept of a "good" is based on human needs, and he seems to have believed that human needs are a general prerequisite for all economic phenomena. According to Menger (1871), "the force that drives them to the surface is the ultimate and general cause of all economic activity, the endeavor of men to satisfy their needs as completely as possible" (p. 192). As Mäki (1990a) observes, the notion of "causal power" is important for Menger's view (p. 299), as Menger seems to have regarded "human needs" as the internal causal power in economics. However, in merely stating that "needs arise from our drives and the drives are imbedded in our nature" (Menger 1871, p. 77), Menger fails to clarify how he reached these conclusions.

By emphasizing the role of introspection as the internal causal power in economics, Wieser justifies Menger's theory, which is based on human needs, as an empirical one. According to Wieser, introspection suggests that individuals consciously evaluate personal situations, such as their preferences, needs, and budgets, and also judge whether certain goods have *Werth* (value), as well as their specific value.[5] Moreover, these subjective estimations by individuals are the fundamental source of all *values* in an economy. He stated that an economy is a system motivated by *values*, which stem from a person's subjective estimation. According to him, value is "the most effective motive of economy" (Wieser 1884, p. 214, translated from the German original), and furthermore an economy is "... is the essence of things in economics. Its laws are to political economy what the law of gravity is to mechanics" (Wieser 1889, Preface, p. 30). In this sense, he called his economics the "philosophy of value" (Wieser 1891). Thus, Wieser regarded introspections as those experiences that lead to knowledge of the fundamental motive power of an economy.

[5]Similar discussions regarding respect for the role of introspection can be found in the works of Mises (Tokumaru 2009). Although Mises himself strongly denied it, he was influenced by Wieser (Streissler 1986, p. 85).

6.4.3 "Experience" as Mental Experiments in the Social Sciences

Because Wieser stated that the social sciences require experiments, his notion of "experience" can be interpreted as equivalent to mental experiments. According to him, "...we Austrians, while we have certainly no wish to be disciples of naturalism, are wholly set on being experimentalists" (Wieser 1891, p. 108). "Like the naturalist performing an experiment, the theoretical economist is bound to isolate, when making observations" (Wieser 1914, p. 5).

In the introduction to *Grundsätze*, Menger stated that the book clarified social causalities invoked by the human desire to attain goods and certain conditions under which causalities occur (Menger 1871 Preface). Like Menger, Wieser believed that economics should provide causal explanations of human economic activity. Wieser believed that mental experiments can help derive causal laws from complex observable social phenomena in social sciences.

To specify the causalities of economics in mental experiments, Wieser proposed *Grenznutzen* (marginal utility) as a general condition, under which economic causalities occur. Wieser believed that humans are by nature already satisfied with being human and are naturally indifferent to things around them; thus, no causal relationship exists between humans and things.

According to Wieser (1889), causal relationships between humans and things occur only if the possession of things contributes to human desires or welfare, that is, if a good provides them with *Nutzen* (utilities) (p. 19). However, the possession of goods also offers "negative utilities" because the owners of goods are originally satisfied with being human. Therefore, the possession of goods simultaneously offers humans contradictory utilities—utilities that are simultaneously negative and positive. Goods simultaneously offer the opposite utilities to humans; therefore, Wieser explained that marginal utility—the utility obtained by one additional unit of a good—gradually decreases until it reaches zero, as indicated in Table 6.1. As the positive utility triggered by possessing goods increases, so too does the negative utility; the total of positive (+) and negative (−) utilities increases if the number of goods is under 5 and then decreases to 0 when the number of goods reaches 11.

When the number of goods is 11, an additional unit of a good brings no utility, and the causal relationship between humans and goods stops at this point (indicated by the underlined numbers in Table 6.1). Thus, in Wieser's view, economic causalities between a human x and goods g occur as long as the marginal utility of x for g is positive (i.e., if $10 \geq g$ in Table 6.1), and such causalities end when the marginal utility reaches zero (i.e., if $g > 11$ in Table 6.1). In this sense, *Grenznutzen* helps distinguish causalities in economics:

> Economic selection of need-values is most accurately made by determining the limit to which the satisfaction of needs may be pushed. Through this delimitation all values are included that are economically required, all improper ones are excluded. ...*The marginal value is strictly adhered to.* (Wieser 1914, p. 125, emphasis added)

Table 6.1 Causal relationships between humans and things

	1	2	3	4	5	6	7	8	9	10	11	Goods
Positive (+)	10	19	27	34	40	45	49	52	54	55	55	Units of value
Negative (-)	0	1	3	6	10	15	21	28	36	45	55	〃
Residual (+)	10	18	24	28	30	30	28	24	18	10	0	〃
Causalities between human an and goods ←								*No causality* →				

Source: Wieser (1889), p. 30. Note: The underline, arrows, and italicization have been added to the original values

Using the concept of *Grenznutzen*, Wieser performs mental experiments: he constructs ideal situations (*Einfache Wirtschaft*) in which economic causalities can be specified. He proposes the concept of *Natürliche Werth*: a value that is decided only by the marginal utilities of individuals. *Natürliche Werth* can be realized only in an ideal society, that is, a "completely organic and most highly rational community" (Wieser 1889, p. 61). Based on the concept of *Natürliche Werth* and other assumptions, he constructed the theory of *Einfache Wirtschaft*, characterized as an ideal economy directed solely by economic causes and free from other social influences. Thus, the theories of *Einfache Wirtschaft*, derived from mental experiments, are causalities that are only specified in economic activities or embedded in society, while the possibility of the effects of other social causalities is ruled out. Wieser (1914) stated that "the theory of the simple economy only explains the condition of the isolated and idealized individual economy that follows its laws of motion without restraint" (p. 151).

Wieser stated that the assumptions of *Der natürliche Werth* and *Einfache Wirtschaft* cannot be observed in the actual social world and might seem to contradict experiences but nevertheless states they are empirical and belong to the social world (Wieser 1889, p. 62). As discussed below, Wieser believed that observable social phenomena are triggered by various types of causalities. Thus, the theory of *Einfache Wirtschaft* that results from mental experiments is a prerequisite for specifying economic causalities in society.

6.4.4 "Experience" as Observation or as the Result of Methodological Motivationalism

It appears that the last possible interpretation of Wieser's "experience" is observation or the result of methodological motivationalism. Unlike Menger and other representatives of the Austrian school, Wieser did not regard observable phenomena as implied by methodological individualism. This results from his ontological position characterized by the concept of "power."

Following Menger's distinction between the "exact orientation of research" and the "empirical and realistic orientation of research," Wieser distinguishes observable social phenomena from pure social theories. Wieser derives economic causalities from mental experiments, but believes that such causalities are not compatible with actual observations of a society. Because observable social facts are always affected by other social, political, and cultural causalities and result from cooperation among these causalities, economic causalities cannot be directly observed in real society: "Complex experiences cannot possibly be interpreted as wholes" (Wieser 1914, p. 5). For instance, Wieser states that the experimental concept of *Natürliche Werth* does not strictly correspond to the actual price observed in the real market, because the market price is not only decided by marginal utility but also by other social factors such as social class, contracts, and customs. He suggests that the price of general goods, such as bread, is decided by the marginal utility of the wealthy buyer (Wieser 1914, pp. 186–187).

In Menger's (1883) view, observable social phenomena are explained theoretically as a result of the interaction of the simplest social elements, as already stated: "...how more complicated phenomena develop from the simplest, in part even unempirical elements of the real world" (p. 61). At the simplest level, Menger presupposes human actions that satisfy human needs, and social facts and processes are in his view the results of these actions. Menger (1871) states, "by economy we understand the precautionary activity of humans directed toward covering their material needs" (p. 63). As Mäki (1990b) explains, this view, which is usually called methodological individualism, also contains the ontological position that can be summarized as follows: "Social entities are unintended consequences of actions by human individuals" (p. 324).

To explain observable phenomena, Wieser seems to have partly developed his position beyond the Austrian theory of methodological individualism by introducing the concept of "power." He states that "power" is the motivating force of society and that social phenomena should be explained as the consequences of such power: "No economic progress is possible unless a force becomes kinetic" (Wieser 1914, p. 19). In *Theorie der gesellschaftlichen Wirtschaft*, he uses the word "power" more than 400 times and states the following: "It seems to me that the highest task of theory was to show in what relations this consciousness and power were in harmony and in opposition in the creation of the social, state, and world economy" (Wieser 1914, p. 17).

For Wieser, individuals are not a fundamental factor in explaining observable society, but importance is ascribed to whether a social unit has "power." Thus, he distinguishes those who possess "power" from those who do not: "Only a strong people can apply the powers of the multitude to social ends with the utmost efficiency and without appreciable waste" (Wieser 1914, p. 19). He regards social organizations, such as the state, not as mere collective entities of individuals, but as important factors that possess the "power" to influence society, saying: "it will be possible to acknowledge social unity only if more effective unifying forces than self-interest are observed, forces that are strong enough to bend even the most powerful" (Wieser 1914, p. 11). In that sense, Wieser does not support methodological individualism. However, if Wieser denies the theoretical structure that methodological individualism employs to describe observable social facts, how can we interpret his position? Because he defines the unit of a social agent from the perspective of whether it has the power to motivate society, I assume his position was one of the methodological motivationalisms. This is both a methodological and an ontological deviation from Menger's position.

Treating Wieser's position as methodological motivationalism can partly explain his shift from economics to sociology. In *Das Gesetz der Macht* (Wieser 1926), published just a year before his death, he inquires about social power, emphasizing the role of leadership. If one interprets his position as methodological motivationalism, the notion of explaining society as a result of power was already found in *Theorie der gesellschaftlichen Wirtschaft* and may represent a natural shift in his subject of study.

6.5 Structure of Wieser's Empiricism

I conclude this paper by clarifying the structure of Wieser's empiricism by relating the following four interpretations of his concept of "experience" that I described earlier.

As Wesley Mitchell highlighted in his review of Wieser's *Theorie der gesellschaftlichen Wirtschaft*, Wieser's economic theory has a hierarchical feature (Mitchell 1917). As indicated by Arena (2010), *Einfache Wirtschaft* (simple economy) is the preliminarily logical step established for "social economy" (p. 111). In *Theorie der gesellschaftlichen Wirtschaft*, one finds that each chapter presupposes what is analyzed in the previous chapter: *Einfache Wirtschaft* is followed by *Volkswirtschaft* (social economy), *Staatswirtschaft* (state economy), and *Weltwirtschaft* (world economy). Wieser seemed consistent in this hierarchical approach to his research, both in this book and in his other works, each of which is grounded in the results obtained from the author's previous works. In his habilitation, Wieser discussed the philosophy of value (Wieser 1884); in *Der natürliche Werth*, he applied his value theory to production and distribution in the economic sphere (Wieser 1889), and he extended it to the economy, including social situations, in *Theorie der gesellschaftlichen Wirtschaft* (Wieser 1914). After completing his economic inquiries, he extended his field of research to sociological or political considerations (Wieser 1926). This hierarchical character of his work parallels the structure of his empiricism; each dimension of empirical knowledge, as described above, constitutes the hierarchy of a complete empirical theory of social sciences. By distinguishing among these different dimensions of experiences, Wieser reformulated and systematized Menger's empiricism. The structure of Wieser's empiricism can be reconstructed from these discussions, as shown in Table 6.2.

Table 6.2 Structure of Wieser's empiricism

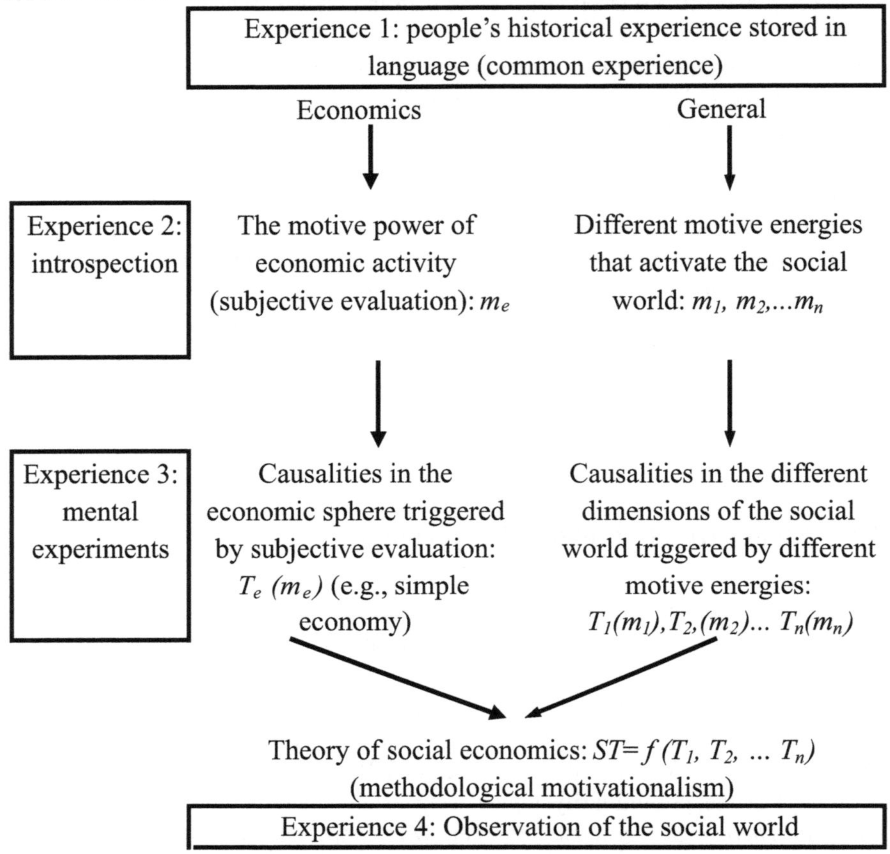

First, the social sciences begin with a common language that constitutes people's historical experiences, which Wieser called "common experiences" (experience as stored in language, Experience 1 in Table 6.2). Introspections then show "motive powers," such as the subjective evaluation of humans, by which economic causalities are triggered (experience as introspection, Experience 2 in Table 6.2). Next, mental experiments are performed to derive causalities triggered by the motive powers in specific areas (such as economy): $T_1(m_1)$, $T_2(m_2)$, $T_3(m_3), \ldots T_n(m_n)$ (experience as mental experiments, Experience 3 in Table 6.2). Finally, social phenomena are observed as a result of the interactions of the different motive powers. This position may be characterized as "methodological motivationalism," which indicates that the social processes are satisfactorily explained as the result of the interactions of different motive energies: $ST = f\ (T_1, T_2, \ldots T_n)$ (experience as observations, Experience 4 in Table 6.2).

As we have seen, Wieser's epistemological stance can be understood as a systematic justification of Menger's economic theory as a form of empiricism. In most ways, Wieser was in line with Menger's scientific program, but diverged from Menger with regard to an ontological view of society, with the latter trying to explain social facts as a consequence of an individual's actions. Wieser's special ontological position, which explains social facts as interactions of motivating powers, leads him to the latest sociological studies, which go beyond mere economics. Wieser believed that social facts could be satisfactorily explained as the result of interactions among different motivations and that social laws could be derived psychologically, that is, by performing mental experiments. For Wieser, statements describing introspection and mental experiments are the source of certain knowledge, from which universal statements are inductively derived. In this sense, he holds a position that can be regarded as *psychological inductivism*, in which experiences are no longer the critical standard of theories, which are justified by psychological inferences alone. Thus, he states, "we, each of us, hear the law pronounced by an *unmistakable inner voice*" (Wieser 1914, p. 8 emphasis added). According to Wieser, contradictions between a social theory and an observation do not falsify a theory, but can lead to other psychological inquiries.

Wieser's particular position of psychological individualism can partly explain his shift to sociological and political studies. In the preface of *Das Gesetz der Macht*, he stated that, after completing his research on economic theories, he confronted World War I and found it to be a subject that could not be explained by an individual's subjective evaluation (such as that in an economy) and was motivated by [political] "power" (Wieser 1926, p. 39). One may therefore say that his later shift to sociological and political research is not a "leap" from economics, but rather an outcome that necessarily emerged from his epistemological position.

6.6 Conclusion: Deriving Implications for Behavioral Theories from Wieser's Empiricism

Here we have seen Wieser's empiricism as a reformulation of Menger's ideas and have analyzed the structure of his empirical economics, as well as his methods, from the perspective of micro-level analysis. The analysis progresses from Wieser's economic theories to his social theories, each with their own coherency and systems, which are closely connected to empirical examinations in each dimension, from lower dimensions to upper dimensions. Although historical constraints prevented Wieser from using experimental methods, it is interesting that he introduced different experimental methods to derive behavioral assumptions: introspections and *gedankenexperiments*. In this section, I discuss implications of Wieser's empiricism potentially applicable to modern economic methodologies. I do this by critically examining his position in four points: (1) subjective rationality, (2) situational analysis of institutions and human behaviors, (3) empirical tests of theories from the micro-level to the macro-level, and (4) methodological motivationalism. Each point is discussed in further detail below.

6.6.1 Subjective Rationality

First, Wieser attempted to understand humans' behavior not from the perspective of objective rationality but based on subjective evaluations of humans under a given set of institutional conditions. This subjective approach to understanding human behavior can be contrasted with the neoclassical assumption of an economic man based on objective rationality, which presupposes that a human mechanically maximizes his utility function knowing all the information of a given situation.

Understanding human behavior as subjective rationality may be important because such behavior brings behavioral assumptions more compatible with the empirical facts of humans. For instance, if one objectively examines the addictive behavior of an alcoholic who continues to drink despite the harmful health effects, their behavior is obviously irrational. However, the behavior can also be interpreted as rational, at least from the perspective of subjective rationality, for example, if the man drinks in an attempt to forget past pain and suffering. This represents an extreme case, but the distinction between objective and subjective rationality is important, although the former seems to conform more closely to logical inferences (e.g., utility maximization under budget constraints).

As I already discussed, Wieser's theory of subjective rationality is somewhat problematic as it is derived from the psychological inductive inference of introspection. Wieser's theory generalizes personal experiences as universal behavioral assumptions by inductive inferences that are logically wrong. How one can claim behavioral assumptions derived from one's personal experience based on these assumptions holding general validity and being applicable to others? One could say certain assumptions of objective rationality in economics were introduced to avoid such generalizations, derived from psychological inductions as Popper (1957, 1994) maintained. One may say social scientists face epistemological problems to be satisfied with both logical coherency and empirical validity at the same time for forming behavioral assumptions.

However, an introduction of the experimental method lets us test the behavioral hypothesis on subjective rationality in objective ways in the laboratory and solve the problem of psychological induction. For instance, experiments by Kahneman and Tversky (1979) showed that individuals tend to be risk averse and dislike situations under uncertainty relative to those under certainty that are supposed to be indifferent according to objective rationality. In their experiment, if one is asked to select from among a set of options with different levels of certainty—whether gaining $100 with a 100 % probability or $200 with a 50 % probability—most people prefer the former, even though both options have the same expected value. The hypothesis of risk aversion is based on the subjective rationality of humans and is more empirically confirmed than objective rationality. The assumption of risk aversion derives not from a psychological basis but from objective tests in the laboratory, which enables us to explain certain social situations that cannot be explained based on objective rationality. Important here is to examine subjective rationality of humans in an objective sense, and experimental methods would contribute to that process in a better manner than that which Wieser attempted.

6.6.2 *Situational Analysis of Institutions and Human Behaviors*

Second, like Menger, Wieser's theory contained situational analysis of social situations that are a necessary prerequisite for activating certain human behaviors.

Wieser introduced language analysis because it describes general social situations and examines the conditions that activate certain human behaviors, as well as the combinations of certain conditions and human behaviors that bring certain social facts. For instance, by analyzing the term "economic goods," both Wieser and Menger clarify human behaviors set under certain social conditions: the term "economic goods" should have two necessary requisites—human's subjective evaluation of the goods on the one hand and scarcity of the goods in a society on the other. Naturally, whether his premise that people's "common experiences" are stored in language may remain open to question, Wieser was engaging in situational analysis of economic facts through observations of common economic experiences. Because we learn most basic economic facts through our daily experiences, Wieser may have thought language analysis can be substituted for observations. What was interesting was that Wieser attempted to describe human behaviors as conditioned given social situations via language analysis.

Wieser recognized that human behaviors are activated in institutional conditions, and both economic and social facts can be explained based on those activated behaviors. Notably, the term "marginal utility," which is now understood in a mathematical system, was first given by Wieser in the context of theoretical relationships that exist between subjective human relationships and institutional conditions. If we use the term marginal utility only in the context of mathematical settings such as budget constraints and supply and demand, empirical contents reflecting the actual society would be lacking, leaving only the invented artificial model. Even if we do not use language analysis as Wieser did, human behaviors should be understood based on analysis of related social conditions to derive empirical causalities in the social sciences.

6.6.3 *Empirical Tests of Theories from Micro-level to Macro-level*

Third, Wieser attempted to test his hypothesis empirically at each level of his hierarchical theoretical system, from the micro-level to the macro-level, as shown in Table 6.2: starting from language analysis as expressing "common experiences" of people and situational analysis of social conditions, introspection as observation of subjective rationality, *gedankenexperiments* as simulations under controlled conditions, and direct observations of society or methodological motivationalism. Although one could question whether empirical sources such as language or introspection hold epistemological validity as discussed here, it is interesting that he attempted to incorporate each level of experience into the whole system of the discipline and so establish economics as an empirical science.

Especially, the *gedankenexperiments* proposed by Wieser involve a similar process to recent economic experiments or simulations except that they are performed in one's mind: after selecting institutional conditions and creating artificial situations, the experiments involve simulation and observation of what occurs under limited conditions. In that sense, Wieser can be called a "pioneer of experimental economics." This method naturally has limitations: it is limited by the personal experience and psychological process of the authors. However, what is important is that via *gedankenexperiments*, Wieser attempted to introduce a simulation process for behaviors and social conditions in the social sciences.

Despite the historical limitations of Wieser, one may find that the necessary prerequisites for explaining social facts from behavioral assumptions are well summarized in his hierarchical system of experiences and theories: human preferences, social conditions, causal analysis between them, and explanation of social facts. First, Weiser describes humans as having subjective preference and rationality and examines this via introspection. Second, he considers that social conditions invoke certain human behaviors and should be analyzed via language analysis. Third, he regards social causalities as explained by a combination of social conditions and human subjective rationality and preferences and as examined by *gedankenexperiments*. Finally, he observes social facts using hypotheses gained through causal analysis of human and social conditions.

Reflecting Wieser's hierarchical system of theories and experiences, I conclude that economic experiments serve as an empirical test of the first three dimensions—subjective rationality or preferences of humans, social conditions, and hypotheses regarding social causalities. By performing experimental tests and analyzing the results, we should examine the kinds of subjective rationality or preference that exist behind individuals' behaviors, as well as the social conditions that invoke certain human behaviors. Then we derive a certain set of behavioral hypothesis, comprising social conditions and human preferences that caused certain behaviors. For instance, behavioral assumptions such as individuals spending an unexpected windfall as soon as they receive it, comprising subjective rationality (satisfying short-term desires) and social conditions (getting extra money), are examined by laboratory experiments and can be extended to explanations of social facts such as public investment increasing demand. From the behavioral hypothesis thus derived, which explains how certain social conditions cause certain behaviors, we can explain social facts at the macro-level.

6.6.4 Methodological Motivationalism

Fourth, in extending his economic theory to social or political theory, Wieser goes beyond the methodological individualism central to the Austrian School of Economics and shifts to a position of *methodological motivationalism.* In this position, minimum social agents are not always individuals, but are defined in terms of whether they have motivational powers that can cause social facts. By observing actual society, Wieser recognized that social facts are not only caused by individuals but also by other social agents such as nations, enterprises, strong leaders, and so on. Instead of changing his position to collectivism that explains social facts holistically like the German historicists, he decided whether a particular agent can be regarded as an economic factor using the critical standard of whether it has a substantial power that causes social facts—whether it motivates a society. His evaluation of strong leadership that may imply supporting totalitarianism should be reexamined, though his idea that society is motivated by power seems to have implications for extending behavioral theories to social theories.

The idea of *methodological motivationalism* is important when we attempt to apply the results of experiments to actual economic phenomena, as it gives us a critical standard that asks whether given certain behavioral patterns can be a "motivating power" in a society. As we have seen in the experiments performed in this book, subjects showed diversified patterns of behaviors in responding to given experimental settings. In applying those methods to actual social phenomena, we should ask whether the given results act as a motivating power in society. For instance, if most subjects involved in a certain production process such as collaboration prefer egalitarian distributive justice to performance-based justice, as is discussed in Chap. 3, this would be regarded as a substantial "trend" in individual preferences that could motivate certain social facts. Thus, one would be able to apply a hypothetical egalitarian payment system that would satisfy people's sense of fairness under similar social conditions. Even in the case where most subjects do not show similar behavioral patterns, a small number of individuals committing certain behaviors such as "free riding" in a given social situation can have motivating power by leading most others to lose their public mindedness. Thus, the idea of *methodological motivationalism* provides us with criteria for applying experimental results to actual social phenomena.

By analyzing Wieser's empiricism, we could have derived some important implications of his methodology for establishing an economics based on experiences. We have seen that his empiricism comprises four different dimensions of experience: language analysis, introspection, *gedankenexperiment*, and observation of the social world or *methodological motivationalism.* Wieser examined theories based on subjective evaluation by introspection or *gedankenexperiments* that yielded problematic results in a theoretical sense; however, the problem can be overcome, especially when more scientific tests are made available for those theories by the introduction to economics of experimental methods. Wieser's methodological position, which I called *methodological motivationalism*, is also important in that it provides criteria for applying experimental results to actual social theory that asks whether something has "motivating power" for a society. His empiricism was limited by the era in which he lived and thus appears to have problems in relation to psychology, but we can still learn from his method of applying theories from micro-behavioral analysis to social economics. From the structure of his empiricism, we can identify his endeavor to develop economics not only as a coherent theoretical system but also as a realistic discipline that should be examined and tested by various kinds of experiences.

References

Arena R (2010) Friedrich von Wieser on institutions and social economics. In: Hagemann H, Nishizawa T, Ikeda Y (eds) Austrian economics in transition: from Carl Menger to Friedrich Hayek. Palgrave Macmillan, Hampshire, pp 109–137

Commons JR (1934) Institutional economics: its place in political economy. Macmillan, New York

Hayek FA (1929/1992) Friedrich von Wieser (1851–1926). In: Klein PG (ed) The fortunes of liberalism: essays on Austrian economics and the ideal of freedom (collected works of F.A. Hayek, vol 4). University of Chicago Press, Chicago, pp 108–125

Hayek FA (1967) Von. studies in philosophy, politics and economics. University of Chicago Press, Chicago

Hutchison TW (1967) A review of economic doctrines 1870–1929. Oxford University Press, Oxford

Kahneman D, Tversky A (1979) Prospect theory: an analysis of decision under risk. Econometrica XLVII:263–291

Kauder E (1957) Intellectual and political roots of the older Austrian school. Z Naturforsch XVII(4):411–425

Keynes JN (1891) The scope and method of political economy. Macmillan, London

Mäki U (1990a) Mengerian economics in realist perspective. In: Caldwell B (ed) Carl Menger and his legacy in economics. Duke University Press, Durham, pp 289–310

Mäki U (1990b) Scientific realism and Austrian explanation. Rev Polit Econ 2(3):310–344

Menger C (1871/2004) Principle of economics (Grundsätze der Volkswirthschaftlehre. Wilhelm Braumüller, Wien). Ludwig von Mises Institute: electronic online edition

Menger C (1883/1985) Untersuchungen über die Methode der Sozialwissenschaften, und der politischen Ökonomie insbesondere. Investigations into the Method of the Social Sciences. (trans: Nock FJ). New York University Press, New York

Milford K (2010) A note on Menger's problem situation and non-essentialist approach to economics. In: Hagemann H, Nishizawa T, Ikeda Y (eds) Austrian economics in transition: from Carl Menger to Friedrich Hayek. Palgrave Macmillan, Hampshire/New York, pp 154–175

Mises Lv (1933/1960) Grundprobleme der Nationalökonomie: Untersuchungen über Verfahren, Aufgaben und Inhalt der Wirtschafts und Gesellschaftslehre. Epistemological Problems of Economics (trans: Reisman G). Van Nostrand, Princeton

Mitchell WC (1917) Wieser's theory of social economics. Polit Sci Q 32(1):95–118

Popper KR (1957) The poverty of historicism. Routledge, London

Popper KR (1959) The logic of scientific discovery. Hutchison & Co. Ltd., London

Popper KR (1994) In search of a better world: lectures and essays from thirty years. Routledge, London

Schumpeter JA (1908) Das Wesen und der Hauptinhalt der theoretischen Nationalökonomie. Duncker & Humblot, Leipzig

Streissler EW (1986) Arma virumque cano: Friedrich von Wieser, the bard as economist. In: Leser N (ed) Die Wiener Schule der Nationalökonomie. Böhlau, Wien, pp 83–106
Tokumaru N (2009) Popper's analysis of the problems of induction and demarcation and Mises' justification of the theoretical social science. In: Cohen RS, Parusnikova Z (eds) Rethinking Popper, Boston studies in the philosophy of science, vol 272. Springer, pp 161–174
Weber M (1904/1922) Die "Objektivität" sozialwissenschaftlicher und sozialpolitischer Erkenntnis. Gesammelte Aufsätze zur Wissenschaftslehre von Max Weber, 1.Aufl., J.C.B.Mohr
Wieser F (1884) Über den Ursprung und die Hauptgesetze des wirtschaftlichen Werthes. Alfred Hölder, Wien
Wieser Fv (1889/1956) Natural Value (trans: Malloch CA). A.M. Kelley, New York
Wieser F (1891) The Austrian school and the theory of value. Econ J 1(1):108–121
Wieser Fv (1914/2003) Social Economics (trans: Hinrichs AF). Routledge, London
Wieser Fv (1926/1983) The Law of Power (trans: Kuhn WE). University of Nebraska-Lincoln, Lincoln

Chapter 7
Conclusion: From Behavioral Theories to Institutional Evolution

Abstract In this chapter, I have attempted to show how empirical behavioral theories given by laboratory experiments contribute to theories of institutional evolution by scrutinizing interactive relationships between humans and institutions. According to this chapter, humans are "institutionalized" and hold a set of behavioral patterns specified by the "going concerns" (organizations) to which they belong. Additionally, humans "institutionalize" working rules of going concerns by coordinating conflicts of interest among individuals. By providing observations of behaviors under a controlled institutional environment, laboratory experiments let us analyze mechanisms and complementarities of existing institutions and also show appropriate directions for institutional reformulations. I discuss that sound institutional evolution should occur through piecemeal social engineering that respects existing social institutions formed through historical processes and that institutional evolution should occur step by step. A goal of institutional evolution is "reasonable value," which can be achieved based on social norms or working rules that stem from people's social preferences.

Keywords Institutional evolution • Behavioral theories • Laboratory experiments • Piecemeal social engineering • Reasonable value

7.1 Introduction

From the laboratory experiments performed in this book, we have seen that individuals have a certain set of social preferences as well as material utility that changes markedly with institutional setting. Additionally, the behavioral assumptions derived from these experimental results can be applied to understanding concrete social situations, such as transaction costs triggered by opportunistic behavior (Chap. 2), effectiveness of performance-based payments given different working styles (Chap. 3), recognition of fairness between workers and investors in functional distribution (Chap. 4), and effectiveness of socially responsible investment as a means of governing corporate activities (Chap. 5). As I have discussed in both the introduction section and the treatment of Wieser's empiricism in Chap. 6, experiments can serve as an empirical test for micro-behavioral theories, from which one can develop macro-level theories of social economy. In other

N. Tokumaru, *Social Preference, Institution, and Distribution*, Evolutionary Economics and Social Complexity Science 3, DOI 10.1007/978-981-10-0137-6_7

words, behavioral theories empirically examined by experiments are necessary to understand economic institutions and the micro-foundations of institutional economics.

However, even if one assumes that human behaviors are necessary foundations for understanding social institutions, one can ask more practical questions—such as how those empirical behavioral assumptions can contribute to theories of institutions. Popper (1994) discusses the way a reconstruction of human behaviors as situational logic should necessarily lead to the theory of institutional evolution and states:

> Institutions do not act; rather, only individuals act, within or on behalf of institutions . . . We might construct a theory of intended and unintended institutional consequences of purposive action. This could also lead to a theory of the creation and the development of institutions. (p. 80)

If human behaviors are not understood solely in a context of situational logic—as they are activated by social institutions but also have a power to change a social situation by their intentions—interactive relations between humans and institutions should be scrutinized. In other words, we should ask both what "institutions" for "humans" are and what "humans" for "institutions" are in order to evolve appropriate institutions for society.

In this chapter, I attempt to show how behavioral theories developed by experimental results can contribute to institutional evolutions and to analyze the interactive relationship between humans and institutions. In the following section, I shall discuss how one should interpret diverse experimental results in institutional contexts. Following Commons, I propose that humans have an internationalized existence and that experimental results can be understood as reflections of behavioral patterns originating from the organizations to which they belong. In the next section, I discuss that humans are not only passive recipients of institutions but can also constitute institutions by setting up working rules of organizations. I then discuss a way to apply those behavioral theories to institutional evolution. Here, I proposed that social reformulations be performed via piecemeal social engineering and that a goal of institutional evolution should be achieving reasonable value, compatible with most individuals' social preferences. In the final section, I give both a summary and conclusions.

7.2 Humans Are "Institutionalized" Existences by "Going Concerns"

Throughout the experimental results presented in this book, we have seen that certain behavioral patterns are triggered by different institutional settings and that the *varieties* of these patterns differ among individuals. However, the criticism that these results are only derived from a limited population—undergraduate students of certain universities in Japan—and should not be generalized to all members of human society seems somewhat convincing. Actually, previous studies show that behavioral patterns differ according to subject attributes: female participants in dictator games tend to prefer more unselfish distributions to male participants; most participants from a particular ethnic group distribute the whole pie to their partners; students who study economics or management theory tend to favor more selfish distributions than students who major in other disciplines (Cf. Camerer 2003, pp. 64–67). If behavioral patterns differ among populations of subjects—such as differences along lines of gender, nationality, or generation—how should one interpret these results as a reflection of actual social facts? Does the diversity of observed behavioral patterns deflate the general validity of experimental results or provide economists with directions with regard to anthropological or biological studies of human behaviors?

Both similar and diverse behavioral patterns observed in experiments may become more theoretically informative based on consideration of Commons' concept of "institutionalized humans," which regards individual ways of thinking or acting as strongly affected by working rules of the "going concerns" (organizations) to which they belong. According to Commons (1934), every individual belongs to various kinds of "going concerns," a comprehensive term for describing human organizations that covers most social groups, such as families, religions, unions, schools, companies, nations, and so on. Commons believed that in the modernized world, where interdependencies among people are strengthened, collective actions become more important for understanding economic activities. Because individuals' social or economic lives are deeply and closely connected with the "going concerns" to which they belong, their decision-making processes cannot be independent of those "going concerns." Commons discusses that every going concern has its own "working rules" that are either accepted informally or authorized as formal regulations, and the activities of each member's activities are conditioned or regulated in the working rules. Through a process by which an individual acts in a going concern or tries to adopt its working rules, that individual comes to develop a certain set of behavioral or thought patterns that eventually become personal "embedded" characteristics. For instance, a child who is born as a member of a nation is raised to adapt to the customs, cultures, or social rules that are dominant in that nation and are treated unfavorably or penalized should they fail to thus adapt. This process of accommodation to one's nation cannot help but affect the child's personality. A similar situation may occur with new employees: they are usually trained or voluntarily try to adopt the working rules in their companies and also develop special business manners or behavioral patterns as members of those companies. Commons identified institutions to include going concerns and working rules, through which humans have an institutionalized existence.

If individuals' behaviors or thoughts are outcomes of institutionalization by going concerns or their working rules, we may regard observed behavioral patterns as reflections of certain institutions. For instance, suppose that an individual x has a set of potential behavioral patterns, which can be expressed as n dimentional vector $B_x = (b_{x1}, b_{x2}, \ldots b_{xn})$, where b_{xa} designates x's behavioral pattern in responding to situation a. Each behavioral pattern originally comes from a certain going concern to which x belongs and thus may be expressed as $b_{x1} \in G_{x1}$. Because an individual belongs to various types of going concerns, as Commons maintained, x has a set of going concerns to which he belongs, which can be expressed as $\cup_{i=1}^{n} G_{xi}$. Naturally, another person y should also have their potential behavioral patterns $B_y = (b_{y1}, b_{y2}, \ldots b_{yn})$ as well as a set of going concerns $\cup_{i=1}^{n} G_{yi}$. If x and y have a common going concern of which both are members, this can be expressed as $\cup_{i=1}^{n} G_{xi} \cap \cup_{i=1}^{n} G_{yi} \neq \phi$, and if there is a going concern to which x belongs but y does not, this can be expressed as $\cup_{i=1}^{n} G_{xi} - \cup_{i=1}^{n} G_{yi} \neq \phi$. Because going concerns institutionalize individual behavioral patterns, one may presuppose that if two behavioral pattern elements of different persons for the same situation belong to a common set of going concerns, the behavioral patterns should be similar: $if\ (b_{xm},\ b_{ym} \in \cup_{i=1}^{n} G_{xi} \cap \cup_{i=1}^{n} G_{yi}) \Rightarrow b_{xm} \sim b_{ym}$. Moreover, if they do not belong to a common set of going concerns, the patterns should be different and vice versa: $if\ (b_{xl},\ b_{yl} \in \overline{\cup_{i=1}^{n} G_{xi} \cap \cup_{i=1}^{n} G_{yi}}) \Rightarrow b_{xl} \neq b_{yl}$.

If one regards experiments as selectively invoking one (or some) behavioral pattern(s) from among others that an individual may have, where those patterns are formed in going concerns, one can analyze diverse or similar behavioral patterns given by experiments from an institutional perspective and derive an institutional hypotheses from them. Let me suppose a linear transformation of one's behavioral pattern vector $f : B^n \rightarrow E^1$, by selectively enhancing one behavioral pattern and ignoring others, expressed as follows:

$f = 0 \times b_{x1} + 0 \times b_{x2} \cdots + a \times b_{xm} \ldots 0 \times b_{x(n-1)} + 0 \times b_{xn} \quad (a > 0)$. The premises described above could be summarized as follows:

1. Each individual has a set of behavioral patterns.
2. Individuals' behavioral patterns originate from a set of going concerns to which they belong.
3. If certain behavioral patterns of different persons originate from the same going concern, those patterns tend to be similar.
4. An experimental setting invokes and enhances one (or some) of the behavioral patterns that individuals (potentially) have.

From these premises, we can analyze the diversity or similarity of the observed behaviors of individuals in an experiment from an institutional perspective. For instance, let me suppose two different experiments (Q, R) involving two participants (x, y) that belong to the same university and have different nationalities, as shown in Fig. 7.1.

The figure shows a situation where the results of experiment Q reveal that the two participants exhibited the same behavioral patterns $(qb_{x1} \sim qb_{y1})$, whereas different behavioral patterns were observed in experiment R ($rb_{x2},\ rb_{y2}$). Instead of judging experiment R as not bringing universal behavioral laws, or trying to explain the results based on different individual characteristics, we could instead discuss institutional comparisons. The similarity of participant behavioral patterns in experiment Q can be explained as follows: the experimental settings invoked a behavioral pattern that is developed in university U (a going concern), and both x and y are students of the same university, meaning the results showed

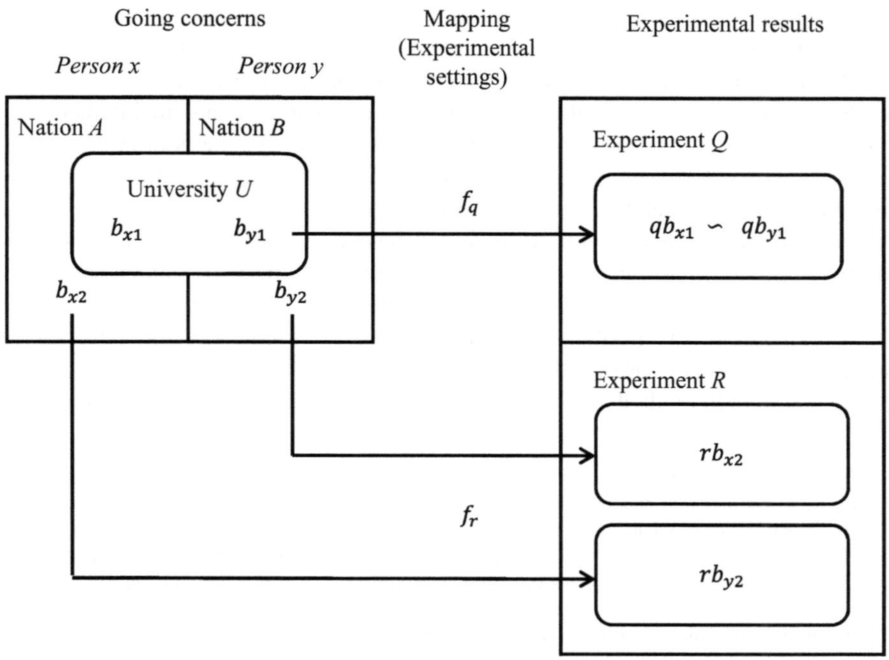

Fig. 7.1 Experimental results as reflections of going concerns

similar behavioral patterns. In contrast with Q, the settings of experiment R may have invoked national behavioral patterns. Because *x* and *y* belong to different nationalities, they may have shown different behavioral patterns in experiment R. These illustrations may be simplified explanations of relationships among going concerns, behavioral patterns, and experimental results, but show a process of deriving an actual institutional hypothesis from a given set of experimental results and how to interpret the diversity or similarity of those results.

7.3 Humans "Institutionalize" Going Concerns and Circular Cumulative Causations

Based on Commons' discussion of humans as institutionalized by going concerns, in the previous section I discussed how one could interpret experimental results from institutional perspectives. However, another question may arise, namely, whether humans are only passive entities, whose attributes depend solely on given going concerns, and who automatically respond to a given set of institutions. Here, I shall propose the other aspect of humans in relation to institutions—that is, humans are also important factors in the formation of institutions—by discussing processes by which humans' behavioral or thought patterns also constitute institutions.

When Commons refers to going concerns, he does not mean a fixed mechanical system that unilaterally controls or regulates its members, but maintained that those going concerns were developed through historical processes of coordinating conflicts of interest among various individuals. According to Commons (1934), individuals have differing interests, and thus conflicts among them are inevitable as part of the social transaction process. However, because individuals exist in a social context and cannot survive without transactions with others, they also have a tendency to accommodate those interests. The coordination process often involves coercion by political authority such as governmental organizations or courts. Common laws are yielded through those processes of resolving conflicts of interest among individuals, as well as through the working rules of going concerns. He states:

> In every economic transaction there is a Conflict of Interests because each participant is trying to get as much and give as little as possible. Yet nobody can live or prosper except by Dependence on what others do in managerial, bargaining, and rationing transactions. Hence, they must come to a working agreement, and, since such agreements are not always possible voluntarily, there always has been some form of collective compulsion to decide disputes. ... To the entire process we give the name, Working Rules of Going Concerns, the purpose of which is to bring Order out of Conflict. (p. 118)

Commons believed that working rules at the informal level of a going concern become formal rules through being formally authorized in that going concern via a common law process. For instance, if a court makes a judgment according to common laws, and if that judgment includes the dominant customs or social norms of the host nation, the judgment becomes a legal precedent and will function as a formal rule of that country. Similarly, many formal transaction rules, business rules, or management rules originally derive from informal rules that are historically and voluntarily formed through the harmonization of interests in each going concern (market, company, and so on) without artificial control or construction.

Therefore, we could find that powers work in two different directions between humans and institutions: one direction is from institutions to humans, by regulating and forming their behaviors, while the other is from humans to institutions, by affecting the process of generating formal or informal rules that form institutions, as shown in Fig. 7.2. Commons believed that via those successive interactive processes between individuals and going concerns, institutions develop or change as they have their own specific systems or characteristics. As we can see from the dotted lines in Fig. 7.2, authorized formal rules derive from informal rules among individuals who regulate individual behavior, and so the informal rules of an organization also affect its formal rules. Institutions develop or enhance their characteristics, via a circulative process that one may regard as institutional evolution, as maintained by Veblen (1899). For instance, Japanese management systems, consisting of a lifetime employment, a seniority-based wage system, and a strong welfare system together called "company socialism," may partly be explained as a formalized version of informal rules, traditions, or customs prevalent among Japanese people.

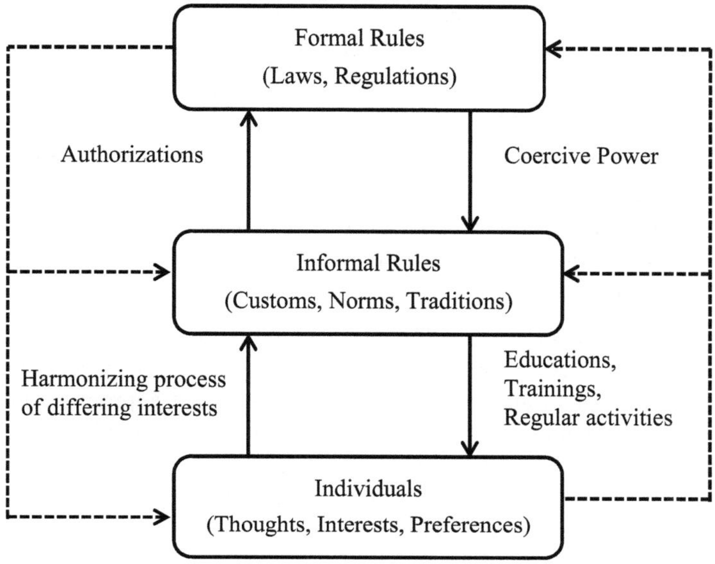

Fig. 7.2 Institutional rules and individuals

Japan has a long tradition of a paternalistic employment style based on a master–servant relationship: the servant devotes and sacrifices themselves to a master and that master's family, while in turn the master takes care of their servant, including not only their work but also their life, marriage, family, welfare, and so on. The seniority-based hierarchy associated with this employment style is a major part of social norms in Japan, a society strongly influenced by Confucianism. Those social norms or traditions developed over the long term in Japanese society through a process of harmonizing people's interests. Those informal rules may have been authorized by modern Japanese enterprises and constitute Japan-specific institutions.

If we recognize the interaction from informal rules comprising individuals' norms, thoughts, behavioral patterns, or social preferences related to formal rules of institutions, we may be able to interpret experimental results as partly showing dominant informal rules among individuals and utilizing them for institutional design. In the experiments performed in Chap. 3, we saw that half of all participants favor an egalitarian distribution when they are required to work in collaboration with individual performance information, which is the closest approximation of the recent workplace. This may imply that recent introductions of performance-based payment systems, which have resulted not through authorization of informal rules but rather under a strong influence of neoliberalistic ideology, are not compatible with informal rules of workers and thus become ineffective. If human beings always consider their self-interest, ignore fairness or social norms, and respond directly to extrinsic incentives, performance-based payments should be effective. In fact though such payments are not effective, as we observed in experiments, thus, we should consider the social preference of individuals for effective institutional designs. From the discussions above, we can derive the following premises:

1. Because individuals have different interests, conflicts of interest are inevitable in human society. However, because humans cannot survive without engaging in transactions with others, individuals also have incentives to coordinate conflicts.
2. In the process of coordinating conflicts, informal rules among individuals emerge. Informal rules become formal rules when authorized by coercive power. Those working rules are the most important factors that constitute going concerns or social institutions.

Economic experiments let us observe a set of norms and individual social preference that are key to the formation of working rules. Thus, economic experiments may have important implications for the design of appropriate institutions that coordinate potential conflicts of interest among individuals. Thus, we can maintain that experiments can have important implications for designing appropriate institutions, specifically by clarifying the social preferences of individuals from which potential social rules originate.

7.4 Beyond Laissez-Faire or Social Constructivism: To Institutional Evolution via Piecemeal Social Engineering

We have seen that individuals and institutions are in a relationship of mutual interaction and that experimental methods can be used for analysis of both. Final questions should be asked with regard to the application of such methods to actual economic policy; that is, how can these analyses contribute to theories of institutional evolutions? Restated, how can an appropriate institution that satisfies more people's interests and preferences be developed from behavioral theories set in an institutional context?

Historically, we have seen two extreme positions regarding economic policies on institution—one is laissez-faire policy and the other is constructivism. The former position stems from excessive trust in market mechanisms, and the latter stems from excessive trust in artificial constructions of institutions. If one understands economic efficiency is best achieved only by market transactions, the role of economic policy is to free the market, with the only norm governing economic agents being "to maximize their profit." This is the path espoused by Friedman (1970). Conversely, if one regards an economy as based on the growth of capital and the exploitation of labor by capitalists who own the means of production, one can agree with Marx that the inevitable political conclusion is the communization of privately owned means of production and their coercive redistribution. The former idea involves minimum controls or interventions on economic policy, while the latter involves more coercive construction of a political system. However, the historical processes have shown that neither direction works perfectly, owing to the market failures that accompany financial crises and the corruption of a socialist economy.

Instead of extreme laissez-faire policies or constructivism, Popper (1957) proposes "piecemeal social engineering" as a means to achieve appropriate institutional evolutions. According to Popper, social facts and processes consist of complex interactions of individual behaviors and other social factors, and thus, accurate predictions of the results that social policies bring to certain societies are impossible. Thus, economic policies should not be performed through utopian social engineering, which attempts to construct and govern comprehensive social process such as planning and controlling production processes by government. Conversely, Popper maintains that reformulations should be performed through piecemeal social engineering via a process of "trial and error," namely, through performing small reformulations and examining the results.

By proposing piecemeal social engineering, Popper attempted to show a way for institutions to evolve based on conservatism and to protect social orders constituted in a historical process. Popper claims that the constructivist approach that performs comprehensive reformulations by coercive power may lead to fatal errors that destroy existing social institutions that are historically formed. Although a social institution may seem unreasonable and outdated, as is the case for feudalism, the system may have an intrinsic reasonability that balances people's interests in satisfying their preferences. One can illustrate this process through conservation work involving a biological environment: one should adopt artificial measurements to protect the environment, on the one hand (e.g., feeding endangered wildlife), but also should carefully monitor whether the measurement triggers unintended results (e.g., disturbing the ecosystem), seeing as the biological system has developed over a very long time has its own way of maintaining a balance. Institutional evolution thus should be performed step by step, via a successive process of trial and error—performing small reformulations, examining the results, and modifying the errors in the reform.

From the discussions above, I wish to discuss how behavioral theories based on experiments can contribute to institutional evolution via piecemeal social engineering. Here, I propose two possibilities regarding the meanings of experimental methods for institutional evolution—providing explanations of present institutions and ideas based on effective institutional reformulations.

First, via analysis and empirical examinations of "institutionalized" humans, behavioral theories given by experiments propose explanations of existing social institutions, systems, mechanisms, and historically formed orders. As is discussed, reasonability, compatibility, intrinsic balance, and harmony may exist within apparently unreasonable or old-fashioned social systems because the systems developed through a long historical process of coordinating people's interests. By analyzing the behavioral patterns of individuals who belong to such social institutions, one can identify the intrinsic logic of the present institutions to which they belong. For instance, societies with an extremely competitive capitalist mind-set may be complemented by traditions of charity and donations to assist the losers in the competitive race. Similarly, the diligent and loyal behaviors exhibited by Japanese employees stem from the tradition of lifelong employment, and hence, the Japanese management style may be a source of corporate competency in the long run. Actually, some macro-level comparative institutional analysis (Hall and Soskice 2001; Amable 2003) showed varieties in capitalism or systems of political economy such as the market-based model or social democratic models, based on analysis of patterns of factors such as the financial market, employment relationships, or welfare system. The means of classifying these diverse capitalist systems differs by author, but it is commonly maintained that each capitalist system has specific institutional complementarities that the institution prioritizes. By examining social institutions comprising a set of specific behavioral patterns, we can judge which institutional factors are requisites and should be conserved for the sake of the uniformity and effectiveness of a given social system and which are not and require reform.

Second, by clarifying individual's social and utilitarian preferences, behavioral theories derived from experiments serve to propose directions for appropriate institutional reformulations that convince and satisfy most members. As discussed, formal rules in an institution basically stem from informal rules that reflect the coordinating process of conflicts of interest among individuals. Thus, appropriate and sustainable institutions should be based on and compatible with members' social preferences and norms. Regarding an appropriate institution, Commons (1934) believed it should be such that "reasonable value" is that obtained via fair competition and transactions under equal opportunity. Not only is economic value gained from market transactions depending on the balance between supply and demand, but "reasonable value" has connotations of procedural fairness in a process of allocation and distribution.[1] By introducing the term of reasonable value, he attempted to show a goal toward which institutions and social policies should be directed—to coordinate people's interests and social norms. He proposes fair competition and equal opportunity as necessary conditions for reasonable value, which may be able to be substituted for other social norms in different societies. If a greedy businessperson earns enormous profits through their political connections, others will not regard the income thus achieved as "reasonable value," because the conditions contradict the socially dominant fair procedures. The society may lose vigor and become unsustainable if such unreasonable corruption prevails. As an institution is basically constituted and affected by its members' social preferences, successful institutional reformulations should be compatible with social norms or member preferences.

[1]For instance, he states, "...the social problem is whether one is giving up a larger share, and the other is therefore receiving a larger share of the social output than is 'reasonable'. If each is obtaining a share justified by his reasonable cost of service and the reasonable value of his service, no matter how much his positive cost or positive income to himself, then the price is persuasive and the value is reasonable" (Commons 1934, p. 333).

7.5 Concluding Remarks

In this research, I have discussed how behavioral theories determined by experiments can contribute to institutional evolution, by scrutinizing two aspects of humans—as "institutionalized" existences and existences that "institutionalize" society. We have seen that the attributes and behavioral patterns of individuals are institutionally conditioned and originate from the "going concerns" to which they belong. By providing a limited and controlled institutional environment, laboratory experiments let us observe certain behavioral patterns that develop in certain institutions. As formal rules forming institutions originate from social norms and individual preferences can be revealed by experiments, laboratory experiments contribute to providing a means of social reformulation. Those social reformulations should be performed via a piecemeal engineering process that attempts to evolve existing institutions through trial and error. "Reasonable value" is a goal at which institutional evolution should be directed and can be achieved via a transaction process based on social norms supported by the social preferences of individuals.

References

Amable B (2003) The diversity of modern capitalism. Oxford University Press, Oxford

Camerer CF (2003) Behavioral game theory: experiments in strategic interaction. Princeton University Press, Princeton

Commons JR (1934) Institutional economics: its place in political economy. Macmillan, New York

Friedman M (1970) The social responsibility of business is to increase its profits. In: Corporate ethics and corporate governance. Springer Berlin Heidelberg, Berlin, pp 173–178

Hall PA, Soskice DW (eds) (2001) Varieties of capitalism: institutional foundation of comparative advantage. Oxford University Press, New York

Popper K (1957) The poverty of historicism. Routledge, London

Popper K (1994) In search of a better world: lectures and essays from thirty years. Routledge, London

Veblen T (1899) The theory of the leisure class: an economic study of institutions. Macmillan, New York